AF344534

A SPECTRUM OF THOUGHT

A SPECTRUM OF THOUGHT

essays in honor of
DENNIS F. KINLAW

edited by Michael L. Peterson

Printed in the United States of America by Parthenon Press, Nashville

Library of Congress Cataloging in Publication Data

A spectrum of thought.
  Bibliography: p.
  1. Theology—Addresses, essays, lectures.
2. Theology, Methodist—History—Addresses, essays, lectures. 3. Bible. O.T.—Criticism, interpretation, etc.—Addresses, essays, lectures. 4. Kinlaw, Dennis F., 1922-   —Addresses, essays, lectures. I. Kinlaw, Dennis F., 1922-   . II. Peterson, Michael L., 1950-
BR50.S66 1982   230'.7   82-16329
ISBN 0-937336-08-4

Francis Asbury Publishing Company, Inc.
Box 7
Wilmore, Kentucky 40390

Francis Asbury Publishing Company, Inc. publishes significant scholarly, educational, and popular books to promote an understanding of the Christian faith.

Dennis F. Kinlaw, B.A., B.D., M.A., Ph.D., LL.D., L.H.D.

CONTENTS

PART THREE: OLD TESTAMENT STUDIES

A SPECTRUM OF THOUGHT

essays in honor of
DENNIS F. KINLAW

INTRODUCTION

The practitioners of Christian scholarship are many compared to the few visionaries who can articulate that ideal and instill it in others. Dennis F. Kinlaw is one of those special few who lives and teaches that the search after truth is a divinely ordained mission, a venture which calls forth the best that is in us. The pursuit of this ideal, displayed so admirably by Dr. Kinlaw, has left powerful impressions on the hearts and minds of his friends, colleagues, and students. Although a gesture far too small, the writers of this volume of essays offer it as a tribute to Dr. Kinlaw on the occasion of his sixtieth birthday.

The Honoré, Dennis F. Kinlaw

A brief look at Dennis Kinlaw's family background, career, and philosophical perspective helps to explain his rare blend of talents and gifts as well as the overall orientation of his life. Born on June 26, 1922, Dr. Kinlaw is the son of a North Carolina lawyer. While a student at Asbury College, he married Elsie Katherine Blake, a college classmate. Dennis Kinlaw received his B.A. degree from Asbury College in 1943 and his B.D. degree from Asbury Theological Seminary in 1946. He did further graduate work at Princeton Theological Seminary, New College, University of Edinburgh, and Duke University. In 1961 he was awarded the M.A. and in 1967 the Ph.D. from Brandeis University. His area of specialization was Mediterranean Studies.

The distinguished career of Dennis Kinlaw is a combination of service to the church and to education. He was ordained in the North Carolina Conference of the United Methodist Church, and has served pastorates in Indiana, North Carolina, and New York. Currently, he is a member of the Kentucky Conference of the United Methodist Church. He is widely known as a fine pulpiteer and an effective expositor of Bible themes.

In 1959, he served for one term as a visiting professor at Seoul Theological Seminary, Seoul, Korea. In 1963, he joined the faculty of Asbury Theological Seminary as professor of Old Testament Languages and Literatures. During his tenure at the Seminary, Dr. Kinlaw also taught Old Testament History and Theology as well as Hebrew and other languages related to the Old and New Testaments. Dr. Kinlaw left the Seminary in 1968 when he was elected to serve as President of Asbury College.

As President of Asbury College for thirteen years, Dennis Kinlaw advanced the institution in every way. The College's endowment was significantly increased, its relation with a broad base of church denominations and missionary organizations was strengthened, and, perhaps most importantly, a dedicated and talented faculty was assembled. While President, Dr. Kinlaw received the honorary degree of Doctor of Laws from Houghton College and the honorary degree of Doctor of Humane Letters from Asbury College. In August of 1981, he resigned from the presidency of Asbury College in order to pursue active preaching and writing and other ministry.

Dr. Kinlaw has contributed to a number of important publications. These include commentaries on Ecclesiastes and the Song of Songs in the *Wesleyan Bible Commentary*, and on Leviticus in the *Beacon Bible Commentary*. He has written articles for a number of magazines, journals, and anthologies which vary from devotional, biblical, and theological, to literary and education in nature.

Dr. Kinlaw serves on a number of Boards of Directors. He is presently Chairman of the Board of Trustees of OMS International, Inc. He serves on the Executive Committee of the Christian Holiness Association. In addition he serves as a member of the board of American Security Life Insurance Company, *Christianity Today*, the Christian Holiness Association, the American Board of Ludhiana Christian Medical College, Toccoa Falls College, Catherine Booth Bible College, and the National Association of Evangelicals.

A student of human culture, Dr. Kinlaw has had a special interest in those ideas—ethical, philosophical, and theological—which shape our thinking and, hence, our destinies. The progressive development of Dr. Kinlaw's distinctive perspective can be detected in his teaching, preaching, lecturing, and writing. In contrast to the modernism, liberalism, and neo-orthodoxy present in his educational experience, he has refused to relinguish orthodox, historical Christianity. Among the key themes which shape his Christian worldview are the absolute existence of a supreme and holy God, the trinitarian nature of the Godhead, God's *ex nihilo* creation of everything that is, the unity and revelatory character of all knowledge, and the responsibility of each individual to serve God with all of his heart and mind. Dr. Kinlaw has shown that the implications of these themes profoundly influence both scholarly study and daily living.

What Dennis Kinlaw has done is to provide a model of a thinking person who rejects the contemporary dichotomy between Christianity and truth. Affirming the perfect harmony between Christian doctrine and genuine knowledge, he has helped many educated Christians avoid this dilemma. He has even pointed out the irony that apparent intellectual problems with Christianity are, when properly analyzed, sources of strength.

This Volume of Essays

The present volume of essays has been in progress for approximately a year and a half. The idea for this *Festschrift* was generated spontaneously out of great affection and regard for the contribution which Dr. Kinlaw has made to the lives of the writers. Naturally, not everyone who feels a special relationship to Dr. Kinlaw could be included. However, the writers in this collection are representative of those in the Asbury community and around the world whose lives and careers have been enhanced by his multi-faceted ministry.

Diversity is perhaps the most prominent feature of this book. The writers of the following essays are persons who have a variety of relationships with Dr. Kinlaw: former teachers, fellow graduate students, former students, colleagues, and friends. The essays themselves cluster around three large categories: Christian scholarship and service, Methodist history and doctrine, and Old Testament studies. And the specific topics display a range of approaches which is both fascinating and refreshing. Yet the greatest degree of diversity is exhibited among the authors themselves. Only a brief inspection of their religious, academic, and professional backgrounds readily suggests that these authors represent a whole spectrum of thought. Hence, we get the justification of the title of this book.

The broad interests, varied associations, and far-reaching influence of Dennis Kinlaw are unmistakably present in this volume. Many *Festschriften* are written within a narrow band of thought or with a monolithic methodology, typifying the relatively limited influence of their honorés. Indeed, the legacy of many religious and educational leaders has been only to produce a succession of followers stamped in their own images. However, the vision and impact of Dr. Kinlaw is not perpetuated here in the sense that the present essays merely mimic or enlarge upon ideas which he has already laid down. Sheerly to parrot Dr. Kinlaw's ideas would be to fall short of his compelling vision. The fuller vision which he has so masterfully communicated entails individuality, creativity, and diversity in the life of intellect.

The Contributors to this Volume

The sense of comradeship among the collaborators on this project, emerging out of a common regard for Dr. Kinlaw, has been great. All participants have felt that the merit of its honoré demands that it be done with great care and attention. They have also graciously committed all royalties from the sale of the book to initiate and endow the Dennis F. Kinlaw Scholarship Fund at Asbury College. In order of their appearance in the *Festschrift*, the contributers are as follows.

Edward L. R. Elson is a well known author, preacher, and lecturer. Dr. Elson took the B.A. from Asbury College in 1928 and the M.Th. from the University of Southern California in 1931. Most know him best as the Chaplain of the United States Senate, a position from which he retired in 1981. During his career, he has been awarded seventeen honorary doctorates from leading colleges and universities, has received eighteen military decorations (including the Legion of Merit, Bronze Star, and French Croix de Guerre), and has been awarded fourteen Freedom Foundation Medals. Among his many books are: *One Moment With God, America's Spiritual Recovery*, and six volumes of Senate prayers.

Harold B. Kuhn has been Professor of Philosophy of Religion at Asbury Theological Seminary for thirty-eight years. Having earned the

S.T.B., S.T.M., and Ph.D. degrees at Harvard University, he remains a member of the Harvard Faculty Club and is as well a member of Theta Phi, Delta Phi Alpha, the Evangelical Theological Society, the American Society of Christian Ethics, the American Philsophical Society, and the Wesleyan Theological Society. Professor Kuhn has contributed chapters to many books, including *Basic Christian Doctrines, Tensions in Contemporary Theology, Baker's Dictionary of the Christian Faith,* and *Contemporary Evangelical Theology.* His numerous articles have appeared in popular periodicals, such as *Christianity Today,* and scholarly journals, such as *Harvard Theological Review.*

James E. Hamilton is Professor of Philosophy, Asbury College. Although Dr. Hamilton obtained the Ph.D. from the State University of New York at Buffalo and has taught at the college level for years, he has pastored for eight years in United Methodist churches and remains an elder in the South Indiana Conference. Dr. Hamilton is a consulting editor to the *Transactions of the Charles S. Peirce Society,* a scholarly journal dealing with American philosophy, and is currently President of the Asa Mahan Society. He is also a member of the American Philosophical Association, Wesleyan Theological Society, Society of Christian Philosophers, Kentucky Philosophical Association, the Society for the Advancement of American Philosophy, and other professional organizations. His professional publications include articles in *The Journal of the History of Philosophy, Wesleyan Theological Journal, Christianity Today,* and *The Herald. Freedom and Grace: The Life of Asa Mahan* is a book which Professor Hamilton recently co-authored with Edward Madden.

Michael L. Peterson is Associate Professor of Philosophy and head of that department at Asbury College. Since receiving the Ph.D. from the State University of New York at Buffalo, Dr. Peterson has published articles in *Christianity Today, Journal of Value Inquiry, Journal of the Evangelical Theological Society, Journal of the American Scientific Affiliation, Sophia,* and *Wesleyan Theological Journal.* His book *Evil and the Christian God* was recently published. Professor Peterson's professional memberships include the American Philosophical Association, the Kentucky Philosophical Association, and the Wesleyan Theological Society. He is currently Managing Editor for the newly formed *Journal of the Society of Christian Philosophers.*

John Chongnahm Cho is President of Seoul Theological Seminary, Seoul, Korea. He obtained the M.Div. from Asbury Theological Seminary and the Ph.D. from Emory University. Dr. Cho presently serves on the Executive Committees of the North East Asia Association of Theological Schools and the International Theological Commission of the World Evangelical Fellowship. He is also a member of the Lausanne Committee for World Evangelization. His visiting teaching posts include Olivet Nazarene College and Azusa Pacific College. A former president of the Korean Bible Society, Dr. Cho has publications including not only articles on John Wesley, but translations of his selected sermons.

Allan Coppedge is Associate Professor of Theology at Asbury Theological Seminary. He was previously Dean and Professor of Old Testament, Biblical Seminary of Colombia in South America. Dr. Coppedge holds the Ph.D. from the University of Cambridge and has done post-doctoral research at The Johns Hopkins University. A member of the Wesleyan Theological Society and the Wesleyan Historical Society, Dr. Coppedge is also an elder of the North Georgia Conference of the United Methodist Church.

Timothy L. Smith is Professor of History at The Johns Hopkins University. Professor Smith received the Ph.D. from Harvard University. His professional memberships include the Society of American Historians, the American Historical Association, the Organization of American Historians, and the American Society of Church History. He has written numerous articles on American religious history. Among his five books are *Revivalism and Social Reform* and *Called Unto Holiness: The Story of the Nazarenes*.

Edward H. Madden is Professor Emeritus of Philosophy, State University of New York at Buffalo. He received the Ph.D. from the University of Iowa. Active in many professional organizations, Dr. Madden has been Senior Visiting Research Fellow, Oxford University, and Research Fellow, Institute for Advanced Study, Princeton University. He has served as Editor of the *Transactions of the C.S. Peirce Society* and as General Editor of the Source Books Series in the History of Science from Harvard University Press. He has written eighty-eight scholarly articles and has authored or co-authored eighteen books, including *Causal Powers, Civil Disobedience and Moral Law in Nineteenth-Century American Philosophy*, and *Causing, Perceiving, and Believing, The Structure of Scientific Thought*, and *The Idea of God: Philosophical Perspectives*.

Cyrus H. Gordon is Professor of Hebraic Studies at New York University. Dr. Gordon earned his Ph.D. degree at the University of Pennsylvania. Formerly Professor of Mediterranean Studies at Brandeis University, he has been a Fellow of the American Academy of Arts and Sciences and the American Academy for Jewish Research. He is a member of the American Oriental Society, the American Institute of Archaeology, the Society of Biblical Literature, the American Philological Association, among other professional organizations. Professor Gordon has written four hundred and fifty articles and twenty books, including *Ugaritic Textbook, The Ancient Near East*, and *The Common Background of Greek and Hebrew Civilizations*.

John N. Oswalt is Professor of Biblical Languages and Literatures, Asbury Theological Seminary. He took the Ph.D. in Mediterranean Studies from Brandeis University. Listed in *Who's Who in Religion*, Dr. Oswalt is active in the Society of Biblical Literature, the Institute for Biblical Research, and the Wesleyan Theological Society. He is a contributor to the *International Standard Bible Encyclopedia* and *What You Should Know About Homosexuality,* and has also penned numerous articles, most of which pertain to cultural and historical setting of ancient Israel.

Victor P. Hamilton is Professor of Religion and Chairman of the Division of Philosophy and Religion at Asbury College. Holding the Ph.D. degree from Brandeis University, he is a member of the Wesleyan Theological Society, the Society of Biblical Literature, and has served as Chairman of the Southeastern Section of the Evangelical Theological Society. Dr. Hamilton has written *Handbook on the Pentateuch* and has contributed to the *Bible Almanac, Christian Ethics*, and *Theological Wordbook of the Old Testament*. He has also translated portions of the *New King James Bible*.

John F. X. Sheehan, S.J., is Professor of Theology, Marquette University. He received the Ph.D. degree from Brandeis University. Dr. Sheehan has taught Hebrew and Ugaritic at Ecole Biblique in Jerusalem; he has been a Fellow of the American Council of Learned Societies, has served on the National Selection Committee for Fulbright awards, and is active in the American Oriental Society, and the Society of Biblical Literature. In addition to his many articles, Father Sheehan's books include *The Threshing Floor* and a translation of Sigmund Mowinckel's *Religion og Kultus*. He has also contributed to *Theology and Discovery: Essays in Honor of Karl Rahner* and *History and Theology: Essays in Honor of J. Coert Rylaarsdam*.

Edwin M. Yamauchi is Professor of History and Director of Graduate Studies in that department at Miami University of Ohio. Professor Yamauchi earned his Ph.D. at Brandeis University. He has been a Research Fellow of the Institute for Advanced Christian Studies, the National Endowment for the Humanities, and the Institute of Holy Land Studies. Professor Yamauchi is not only a member of several scholarly organizations, but also has been President of the Conference on Faith and History as well as Vice-President of the Near East Archaeological Society. The author of over one hundred articles, Dr. Yamauchi has also written *Greece and Babylon, Gnostic Ethics and Mandaean Origins, The Stones and the Scriptures, Pre-Christian Gnosticism, The Archaeology of New Testament Cities*, and other books.

Paul Vincent is Associate Professor of Literature at Asbury College. He earned the Ph.D. degree from Syracuse University. Professor Vincent has done work on the topic of natural law while on a National Endowment for the Humanities Fellowship. Presently, he serves on the Board of *Christian Scholars Review* and is a member of the Modern Language Association.

The preceding entourage of contributors has made what was once an inspired dream develop into a stimulating and helpful volume of essays. On behalf of all who participated in the book, this writer proudly dedicates it to Dennis F. Kinlaw.

Michael L. Peterson
Department of Philosophy
Asbury College

1

LIFE'S SINGLE VOCATION*
Edward L. R. Elson

To Dennis F. Kinlaw whose spirituality, scholarship, and administrative talents in service to Asbury College epitomize the best in my address on the fiftieth anniversary of my graduation. He enhances everything he touches. He has nourished my spiritual and intellectual life as he has thousands of others. May he go from strength to strength.

The Scriptural text:
Jesus said unto him, Thou shalt love the Lord thy God with all thy heart, and with all thy soul, and with all thy mind.
This is the first and great commandment.
And the second is like unto it, Thou shalt love they neighbor as thyself.
(Matthew 22:37-39)

I. Introduction
President Kinlaw, Members of the Board, Members of the faculty, parents, friends and honored members of the Class of 1978. It is to this class we speak today.

Only two barriers remain to your final emancipation from this campus. One is the Baccalaureate sermon, and the second is like unto it, the Commencement Address. Now that we are both sentenced to the first of these requirements, let us make the best of it.

My class, the Class of 1928, has lived and worked elsewhere twelve and a half times as long as we were here. But you will understand the affinity

---

*The following is the text of the Baccalaureate address, Asbury College, June 4, 1978.

we feel for this place by the presence of so many of us on the campus today.

Permit me, then, on behalf of the Class of 1928, to welcome the Class of 1978 to the legion of Asbury Alumni who circle the world. Henceforth, every five years you will return for your reunion in the same cycle with the remnants of our class.

After fifty years we have made our golden pilgrimage to the scenes of yesteryear. We have come just as we are, with our bulges and our baldness, our bridge-work and our bifocals, toting along our pills and vitamins to reinforce the waning vitality. We come, of course, to share the wisdom only acquired by experience. Remember the little doggerel:

> King Solomon and King David
> Lived very merry lives
> With very many lady friends
> And very many wives.
> But when old age came creeping
> With very many qualms
> King Solomon wrote the Proverbs
> And King David wrote the Psalms.

You are so much better looking that we were in 1928. You are taller and tougher. You have been innoculated against diseases which decimated earlier generations. You have been on balanced diets fortified by vitamins from your infancy. Some of us wear athletic scars and several of us battle scars from a war or two. Your athletic equipment has been more protective and repairs to injured bodies more prompt and more complete.

You are better scrubbed and combed and coiffed. Does it surprise you for me to report that some of my classmates took their first shower bath here? When we arrived, water on tap was not a universal home installation. And if middle class homes had running water, frequently it was only cold water brought indoors by gravity from a spring or well. In his memoirs, Dean Jay B. Kenyon wrote that there wasn't a bath tub on the campus when he arrived as a college freshman. In contrast, we lived in relative comfort for our generation. Do you know that you live in a nation which now has 96% of all the bath tubs in the world?

You are the first generation to be devoid of epidemics such as diptheria, smallpox, scarlet fever, mumps, measles, and tuberculosis. A college classmate of mine, beside whom I played a horn in the College band, died as a result of an appendectomy a few days before he was to get his degree. Peritonitis took his life. Had there been penicillin, Howard Keller would probably be living an adult life today. Such a death is almost unheard of today. Such is the improvement in health.

Look at the difference in life expectancy. A young man today can expect to live 50 percent longer than his grandfather. The American Geriatrics Society has predicted that by the end of the century an

American may look forward to a life expectancy of 120 years with Social Security beginning at 105—if you chooose to retire.

Our generation walked as you have walked in the light of a silvery moon down some Kentucky lover's lane with palpatating hearts and wistful longings. Now every Wednesday morning I attend prayer breakfast with a young Senator, Harrison Schmitt, who has been to the moon and back, and is a devout Methodist layman. What a different world! We came on railroad trains drawn by magnificent steam locomotives. Some of us rode three days to get here. Now you come by jet in five hours from any place in the United States.

Tomorrow you will join us as hoiders of a degree from Asbury College. It will be an honorary degree. Every degree is an honorary degree. Some are taken in course and some are achieved in the public domain. But they are all honorary.

The most significant thing about your parchment will be on the college seal with its motto: *ERUDITIO ET RELIGIO*—ERUDITION AND RELIGION—academic excellence and elevated piety. Your most priceless memory, if it is at all like ours, will be the legacy of an undergraduate education in a Christian community at work—and the work has been education.

Asbury College is not a Protestant monastery or convent refining life by rigid discipline which produces automatic responses to every life situation. This College is not a perpetual camp meeting or unbroken religious conference, though life is lived in the Spirit and fresh visitations of the Holy Spirit are expected and welcomed. This is not a professional divinity school. That school is across the street. This institution stakes down its life on precise theological presuppositions; but it is a liberal arts college. The product is an educated Christian person—a person whose life is fulfilled in Jesus Christ and who brings Christ's spirit to bear upon every problem in every crisis of life.

Tomorrow you join the fellowship of two thousand others who have received degrees in the eighty-eight years since J. W. Hughes founded the College. The generations of Alumni list 1576 ministers of the gospel in twenty denominations, 507 missionaries overseas, 185 college presidents, deans, departmental heads, 211 physicians, 75 commissioned Salvation Army officers, 7 bishops, 1 Chaplain of the Senate, the most prolific preacher-author-missionary in half a century, the greatest scholar-author on the Civil War soldier. That is an awesome assembly you will be joining.

The most important thing about the current issue of the *Alumni Ambassador* is not what it says about the Chaplain of the Senate, but what President Kinlaw says is the purpose of this College. On the inside of the cover we find his statement:

The College regards the biblical message of redemption as integral to human wholeness. Students are thus encouraged to accept the transforming grace and presence of Jesus Christ through the cleansing and infilling of the Holy Spirit.

This is a theme carefully reiterated by a layman, Dr. Luce, last night.

That brings me to the theme of this sermon, "Life's Single Vocation." The word "vocation" is derived from *vocare*—a summons or call to a particular course or role.

Jesus had just reduced the Sadducees to speechlessness when the Pharisees accosted him. A religious expert among them asked Jesus "Which is the great commandment in the law?" Promptly, spontaneously, instinctively, Jesus affirmed,

> Thou shalt love the Lord thy God with all thy heart, with all thy soul and with all thy mind.
> This is the first and great commandment.
> And the second is like unto it, Thou shalt love thy neighbor as thyself.
> (Matthew 22:37-39)

This is the total commitment to which we are called. This is life's single vocation. The love which Jesus talks about here is not fleshly, erotic love, nor is it filial affection for family and friends. But Jesus uses the Greek word for love, *agape*, meaning the surrender of the whole being, in its totality, to the living God. The doctrine of the single vocation is the heart and center of the Christian way of life. This was carefully formulated by our spiritual ancestors in the Westminster Assembly of 1643 which among other things produced the Shorter Catechism of my Church. The formula declares that for the Christian there are many ways to make a living but only one way of life—the way of total commitment to God, to the Lordship of Christ.

A man might be a farmer, a blacksmith, a miller, a merchant, a silversmith, a teacher, a preacher, persons of diverse skills and talents but only one vocation. The first question in the catechism is: "What is the chief end of man?" And for over three hundred years anyone schooled in this tradition answers, "The chief end of man is to glorify God and enjoy Him forever." The purpose of life is to serve God, to make known his majesty and rulership, and to know the joy of the Lord in this life and beyond. It is a willing, selfless, total commitment.

There are many honorable ways to make a livelihood but only one way to live—and that is to manifest the splendor of God as revealed in Christ and to do it in all of life. This is the specialty which takes precedence over every other specialty. This is what the past says to the future. And this is the wisdom of God for all time. More important than the degree we carry from this place is the commitment to the single vocation.

If you enter the field of medicine, living the single vocation, then every human being will be regarded as God's child and every effort to prevent suffering, to preserve a vital physical and spiritual existence, will be to manifest God's glory.

Go into law and the person of single vocation will manifest God's glory by seeking to achieve justice under God, the Ruler of a moral universe.

He will acknowledge that all law in civilized society is based upon, derived from, the law first given to Moses on Sinai.

Go into business and the purpose of the person of the single vocation will be the release of economic resources for the common good. Go into architecture or engineering and life's purpose will be to discover the laws of the universe, put there first by the mind of God, and bring them to fulness of expression and service for man who is God's highest creation.

Go into science and manifest God's glory there, and the person of the single vocation will rejoice because beyond the universe is the First Cause—his original premise of the Creative Spirit at the heart of things is big enough for every unfoldment. The scientist will see law and order in the universe. Order witnesses to intelligence, intelligence to a mind, and mind inheres in personality. The Person is God.

While the scientist himself will be working with data derived by scientific methodology, by experimentation, measurement, attestation, he will rejoice as Dr. Werner von Braun pointed out to me one evening at dinner that truth and reality do not always come to men by scientific methodology but also by way of personal experience, by intuition, by spiritual insight, by revelation and in the historical process. The person of the single vocation, whatever his specialty, responds to truth and reality as they reach him over many avenues and by many methods—from the mystic's awareness, the musician's rapture, and the saint's holiness of life as well as from the laboratory and scientific experimentation.

Go into teaching and the person of single vocation will begin on the premise that he is helping God's children come to their birthright as children of the light, that he is teaching not subjects but persons, that his highest endeavor will be to open fresh vistas of insight, discovery and creativity which lead to fullness of life. And if a person enters that higher order which Presbyterians call "teaching elder" or minister of the church, the person of single vocation will regard as the highest role not that of ecclesiastical titan but the personal instrument of God's grace, the transmitter through personality of the Good News of the Living Lord of Life.

If the purpose of life is to make manifest the life of God in the life of man, then the public servant, the Christian statesman, will seek to discover God's will for man. He will seek to find the highest possible moral basis for action, to stake down his position on that platform, to work from that premise. I wish that more Asburians took this spirit into the political arena. I heard of one alumnus who has served in the legislature of Pennsylvania and another in the California legislature. This nation needs people of the single vocation in politics—not to parade their piety, but to bring Christian insights into public affairs. Such a person faces constantly the necessity for making the highest possible moral choice in the *existential situation*. Christian perfection is not flawless political judgment, but the refinement of and growth in moral choice.

We are not perfect. We are not Jesus. There was only one Lord Jesus

Christ. If Jesus were like I am, the sinner that I am, He could not be my Savior. He must be one apart, utterly unique in his person, coming from God, entering our life, becoming part of our life, dying for our salvation. And we are not in the Church because we are flawless in political judgment or pedagogical theory or church administration. We are in the Church because we are sinners redeemed by faith in Christ's finished work. We are not perfect, but we follow a perfect Lord. We are not holy, but we worship a holy God.

In the early days of the Wesleyan movement, in the "class meeting," people were exhorted to "go on to perfection." Such striving was also characteristic of the Keswick movement and later the Oxford Group movement. It appears now in some of the disciplined Christian movements such as Yokefellow International. Yokefellows take the yoke of Christ and say with Paul, "Not as though I had already attained—I press toward the mark of the high calling of God in Christ Jesus." It is holiness of life, perfection in love, fullness of the grace of Christ which mark the way of life's single vocation.

During my growing years as a high school student, my expectation was to attend the United States Military Academy and make the Army a career, and I had been promised an appointment to the Academy. Then in my senior year in high school, during a day alone in a cabin in the woods, I was unmistakably called to the ministry. Not in a huge crowd or in an evangelistic campaign but alone with my Lord that call came to me with a clarity never doubted thereafter and corroborated every day since.

I wrote a letter thanking my congressman for the proferred appointment to the Academy. The government pays cadets to go to the Academy. How could I now be properly educated for the ministry, a seven or eight year program, when there were other Elsons to be put through college? By and by the answer came. An uncle and some friends secured a music scholarship for me on the blowing end of a horn and a job as a janitor in one of the men's dormitories known as Morrison Hall. The college was then only thirty-four years old. For my janitor's job, I received twenty cents an hour, the next year, twenty-five cents an hour. My last year I was the Assistant Pastor of the Presbyterian Church in Wilmore.

So, in the fall of 1927, with some money, with my horn and my job, I began my preparation in this college with the Latin motto ERUDITIO ET RELIGIO—erudition and religion—academic excellence in a Christian community of learners. On this campus the Christian life was the norm. The pagan, the disbeliever, the agnostic was the bizarre or the "odd-ball" person on our campus. Chapel and prayer came as natural as three meals a day. There was a singleness of purpose which produced superior scholars—reflected later in postgraduate schools to which graduates went.

Life's single vocation—glorifying God in the totality of life—was unfolded here in three facets which illuminate the great Commandment:

the dignity of work, the majesty of the mind or the exaltation of the intellect, and the completeness of the Christian commitment.

II. The Dignity of Work

We had the largest organized group of "student volunteers" on any American campus. These "volunteers" were college undergraduates who were preparing to be the foreign missionaries of a dozen different denominations. Student leadership for the national movement came out of this campus.

In our sophomore year we made our class motto "100% for Christ." By Christmas every member of our class was a professing Christian. Rm 36, where for four years we held our Monday night class prayer meeting, was becoming a shrine of deep devotion, a holy of holies. On Thursdays, for two of those years, instead of eating lunch I fasted and met with a small group of disciplined students for prayer and life orientation.

Then, in my senior year, when I was also the Assistant Pastor of the Presbyterian Church there, I began writing prayers, a practice I continued after my ordination until by 1935 I had a book of four-hundred pages of personally composed prayers. Now I know that God was helping me get ready for my present work of Senate Chaplain where I have already prepared one thousand four hundred twenty prayers.

Commencement came in 1925, the end of our freshman year. All the students except the graduating class left for home and summer jobs. However, being on a music scholarship, I had to remain to play in the ceremonies. At first, I resented this stricture. But this obligation threw me, for the first time, into direct association with the greatest living missionary and author of this century, then a missionary to the intellectuals of India, Dr. E. Stanley Jones, an alumnus of Asbury College, who was back on campus to do then what I am dong today. His book, *The Christ of the Indian Road,* had already been translated into more than twenty languages and was selling more than any book since Bunyan's Pilgrim's Progress. Now that book has been translated into over forty languages and has sold more than three million copies. Several of his remaining twenty-eight books have sold over one million copies each. His daughter, Eunice, is the wife of Washington's Methodist Bishop, Dr. James K. Matthews.

On an early morning walk that Commencement season, I watched Dr. Jones, with New Testament in hand, pacing the floor of the front veranda of the home where he was staying as he prepared his address. I will never forget him and his gracious words as he took me into his heart that day more than half a century ago. Later I was to share programs with him in retreats, in services aboard ship, in my pulpit in Washington. Long ago, I repented my resentment at having to play my horn at that Commencement.

If a music scholarship put me in touch with E. Stanley Jones, it was the janitor's job which put me in touch with my greatest teacher, my first professor of theology, Dr. Frank P. Morris. My janitor's work included servicing his lecture room and quarters. He was a great scholar, a superb teacher, and a first rate preacher, a total man in his discipline and dedication. To this day I remember exactly some of his statements. For example,"I have learned that the unconscious presuppositions of my childhood have become the philosophic conclusions of my mature manhood"—a whole philosophy of religious education. He was a man of single vocation, glorifying God in every act, dignifying work, enhancing the intellect, spending himself for Christ. He had cultural depth. He could preach in a cathedral or on a street corner and be equally effective.

If I went to work at 5:00 a.m., the chances were he would be at his desk in his study. If I did my janitor's job late at night, he was refining his lectures for the next day. He also dignified physical work. He had a Model T Ford with shiny brass radiator and beautiful black paint which he carefully serviced one day a week, more as a pet than as a mode of transportation. When I was far enough advanced to take theological courses, I subscribed to every course he taught in systematic theology and learned from him the profound Christian truths about God and man and destiny and duty—truths I will carry with me through this life and beyond. The St. Paul window in the National Presbyterian Church in Washington is a gift from his widow and was dedicated by Dr. Stanger and the Seminary Choir in 1970.

Then there was the inimitable Dr. Henry Clay Morrison, aristocrat in temperament, autocrat in rulership, compassionate and tender in human relations, painless extractor of money from the saints for the College, the last of the silver tongued orators of the American pulpit. A few people here will recall his spending forty minutes to introduce William Jennings Bryan who spoke for an hour and a quarter. And the big debate was which of those two was the greater orator. Bryan was outmatched. But my point regarding Dr. Morrison is how he worked, his prodigious accomplishments: College President, Editor, Evangelist, Chautauqua artist—all at one time.

Dr. Morrison introduced a new word to us. He said, "Lads, don't *foo-doodle.*" "*Foo,*" he explained meant "going about." "*Doodle*" was translated "doing nothing." So foo-doodle meant "going about doing nothing." We were admonished to work, work, work. That was God's order of life, and, therefore, all work may be to the glory of God. Scores of students then had campus jobs, as must be true today. No one made a conscious distinction between those who had to work and those for whom it was not necessary. A student was not degraded by working nor elevated because he didn't. A student might don over-alls or a chef's white cap and apron before breakfast and at nightfall appear at a social gathering in tuxedo or evening dress. All of us were persons, respected when we were respectable, honored when we were honorable. We learned the dignity of all forms of work.

III. The Exaltation of the Intellect

Living out the single vocation means the exaltation of the intellect, the majesty of the mind. You can't go on to Christian perfection without obeying the commandment which says, "Love the Lord thy God with all thy mind." More graduates of two Kentucky Colleges, Asbury College and Berea College, go on to take post-graduate degrees than from all other universities and colleges in the state combined. Why? It is the exaltation of the mind, the honor given by Christian commitment to the intellect. The difference is in the motivation. If one is to serve Christ he can have nothing less than the best intellectual equipment and mental training obtainable.

In a Christian community of learners—in a Christian college—a few things are settled and have ceased to be speculations. Truth is found and forever fixed in the person of Jesus Christ, the one absolute, the fixed point of reference by which everything else is measured. In an academic atmosphere charged with the spirit of the living Christ, and peopled by persons destined to serve Him there is an eagerness of mind for knowledge, an earnestness of spirit for wisdom. Academic excellence in a spiritual community became and has remained a legacy of this place. Life's single vocation is lived out loving the Lord with all the mind He has given us.

IV. The Completeness of Christian Commitment

The single vocation also means completeness of dedication to Christ. As students, many of us were striving week after week, day after day for holiness of heart, for more perfect love, for utter abandon to the will and purpose of life. We would sing—

> I'll go where you want me to go, dear Lord
> Over mountain or plain or sea
> I'll say what you want me to say, dear Lord
> I'll be what you want me to be.

There were fewer than one hundred in my graduating class. One, Bell Irvin Wiley, became the greatest scholar of the American Civil War, the author of twenty-four books, and President of the Civil War Centennial Commission. Another, Sollie McCreless, who had to work his way through school, borrowed a few hundred dollars to start a medical insurance society and now heads one of the great insurance empires of the world. Although he never became a minister, he has been able to endow theological professorships, support missionaries, and give new buildings.

Some who were in my class died young in foreign lands. Dedication was complete and there was a readiness to pay whatever price was necessary for the spread of the gospel. The blood of the martyr was to become the seed of the Church in our generation—in South America, the Philippines, in Africa, in China, in Europe.

What does total commitment mean? It means that nothing is held back: mind, soul, heart, body—all are surrendered to Christ. Jesus commissioned his followers saying, "Ye shall be my witnesses. The word "witness" in English does not really convey what Christ intended his disciples to understand. This is a luminous word, which walks forth from the Greek in a revealing transliteration to declare, "Ye shall be my martyrs." That commission tracks a daring pathway through the apostolic age to our age. The disciples were to shine for Christ and they soon discovered they would burn as they shone. They did go forth. They made martyrdom a proof of Christ's resurrection.

There have been men and women in our age like my colleague, Dr. John D. Hayes. Hayes was born in China. He attended another Christian College, Wooster, where our founder, J. W. Hughes, sent his son Arthur, who became a great Presbyterian Church leader. John Hayes was an honor student, a football and baseball star. He graduated from Princeton Seminary and won a Rhodes scholarship. At Oxford, where he was Captain of the Crew, he met and married Barbara Kelman, daughter of the famous preacher, Dr. John Kelman. Then with his bride he left for China as a missionary-teacher, supported by the congregation I served so long as pastor in Washington.

World War II came; Mrs. Hayes and their children were returned to the United States on the first Gripsholm. John Hayes was imprisoned by the Japanese for four and a half years. When I assumed my pastorate in Washington in 1946, he was one of the assistant ministers while gaining rehabilitation from his war days. He longed to return to China, pleading with the Board of Missions and his doctors to return. He believed he could get along with the Agrarian Reformers who threatened to take over China.

After several years of helpful service on our staff he went back to China without his family. He saw Chiang Kai-Shek's armies retreat and the Communist armies arrive. For a while the Communists paid no attention to the American teacher-evangelist. Then one night he was arrested and at bayonet point taken to a dark, dank prison which in itself was enough to destroy a man.

Subsequently, John Hayes went through the most excruciating experience. They accused him of being an American spy, saying I was his American contact. They tortured him, kept him awake day and night, week after week, brainwashed him. Five times they threatened to cut off his head. But John Hayes was an emissary of Christ, not a spy—a man with a single vocation.

When he came up for trial, the court had all my letters and our Church bulletins which carried the names of Trustees like J. Edgar Hoover and Admiral Sydney Sours, who was President Truman's Security Council Secretary—and the name "*National* Presbyterian Church" consumed their interest.

None of us heard from John Hayes for more than a year and he was presumed to have vanished. Late one night I answered a long distance phone operator who put a man on the phone. It was John Hayes in Seattle and his voice was like a voice from the sepulchre.

In a few days, he was back in Washington. He was bearded and gray, with deep lines but luminous radiant eyes and a countenance which shone with the love of Christ, an incandescence from above, a light refined and made brilliant by suffering. I asked him to celebrate the Lord's Supper with me on Christmas Eve. As John Hayes knelt with me behind the Holy table, a university student near the front of the church, something of an agnostic, exclaimed after the service: "I just could not keep my eyes off that face."

The whole nation became interested in him. *Reader's Digest* carried his witness. A movie, *The Sign of the Hawk*, was based on his life. The Pentagon studied his report and his person to learn more about the effect of brainwashing. One day I asked John Hayes what sustained him in the relentless torture and he said, "Well, Edward, I determined to be true to truth and true to Christ, with or without my head." We too have lived with heroes and martyrs to Christ's glory, as truly as in any age.

We have met and worked with men of the single vocation, and we are called to nothing less. John Hayes completed his career working with students in Indonesia. We had a memorial service in the National Presbyterian Church in Washington attended by diplomats and church officials and hosts of friends. Let no one say John Hayes squandered his life. He gave it at the beginning to Christ, and lived the single vocation in complete commitment to Christ. We join that noble company singing the *Te Deum:*

> The goodly fellowship of the Prophets
> praise thee.
> The noble army of Martyrs praise thee.

And with the hymn writer exclaim:

> They climbed the steep ascent of heaven
> Through peril, toil and pain
> O God, to us, may grace be given
> To follow in their train.

There are many callings and professions, but for the Christian there is only one vocation—to love the Lord with all the heart and mind and soul. This means to reflect the dignity of work, the majesty of the mind, the totality of the Christian's commitment.

God does not promise that we will escape suffering in this vocation. He promises something better. He says, "I will go with you, I will never leave you nor forsake you. Underneath are the everlasting arms even unto the end—of the end—of the end." Amen.

Let us pray in the words of the Convening Prayer in the United States Senate on Tuesday, May 9, 1978, which has been called my Asbury Senate Prayer:

Blessed are the pure in heart: for they shall see God. (Matthew 5:8)

Almighty God, our Creator and Lord, give us pure hearts to see Thee, stout hearts to bear our own burdens, willing hearts to bear the burdens of others and believing hearts to cast our burdens on Thee. Spare us from having cold hearts, indifferent hearts, or careless hearts. Give us hearts that beat in unison with Thee that we may carry forward the divine intention for this Nation and the world.

A heart in every thought renewed,
And full of love divine,
Perfect and right and pure and good,
A copy Lord of Thine.

Charles Wesley
1707-1788

Through Jesus Christ, our Lord. Amen.

2

THE CHRISTIAN SCHOLAR

Harold B. Kuhn

In the preparation of this paper, the person and the gifts and the work of its honoré have been constantly in my thinking. Dr. Dennis F. Kinlaw has shown himself to embody the qualities which characterize the Christian scholar in an impressive measure. These qualities find constant expression in his ministry as educator, writer and pulpiteer. For these as we see them embodied in Dennis Kinlaw, we thank our Lord, Who has taken captive both his mind and his heart.

In his lecture, "The American Scholar," delivered before the Phi Beta Kappa Society at Cambridge, Massachusetts, in 1837, Ralph Waldo Emerson defined the scholar as Man Thinking. This was intended to distinguish the scholar from the merely thinking man, whom he saw in terms of the bookworm. The term "Man Thinking" calls attention, of course, to the possibility of scholarly attainment within "the sound estate of every man."

His ensuing description of Man Thinking is characteristically Emersonian, with its view of the essentially divine in all persons, with its corollary of universal creativity and its dislike of planned mediocrity. As one reads the essay, he/she is challenged to inquire in what respects the Christian Scholar differs from Emerson's model? It is not in the major forms of discipline common to both. It is the task of this current essay to isolate and define the characteristics which mark the Christian scholar from the secularist and merely humanistic model.

It is proposed to deal with the subject under the following rubrics: first, the mind of the Christian scholar; second, the range or scope of the Christian scholar; and finally, the heart of the Christian scholar.

I. The Mind of the Christian Scholar.

This aspect of scholarship is not an easy one to describe, particularly as one seeks to discover the characteristically Christian mode of scholarship. It is interesting that when the quarterly, *The Christian Scholar*, projected an issue describing Christian scholars and Christian scholarship in 1964, many of the promised contributors failed to meet the deadline. This may suggest that the subject has proved to many writers to be a difficult one.

To be sure, the special qualities which accompany true scholarship, whether Christian or not, are common property of the world of scholarly endeavor. Some of these are a reverent regard for the past of mankind and its legacy to us today, a quest for meaning in all phases and aspects of our universe, a sense of awe at the mysteries of what we call nature, and above all, a patient search for truth. These should, each of them, concern vitally the Christian scholar. We would suggest here, that his or her search for truth will include elements frequently lacking in general scholarship, these centering in the major and central realities of Christian faith. Of these, special mention should be made of a God who is high Sovereign of the universe, the incarnation in time of His Son, the Cross-work of Jesus Christ, His resurrection, and His final and ultimate Lordship over all.

To be sure, these elements need not be at all times and in all connections visible. It is necessary, we think, that in the case of Christian scholarship they are *there*, to be implicit and to serve as monitors, guiding and giving shape to the selection of materials, the evaluation of data, and the formation of generalizations.

This being the case, they form the deeper climate of the mind of the Christian scholar. Within this climate of mind, thought and research proceed to assimilate data and to structure them within guidelines which are, as Christians dare to believe, in accordance with the mind of Him who is both life and truth. It is perhaps this which constitutes the reduction of all the processes of thought to "captivity to the obedience of Christ."

It is highly important to note here that the shaping elements of the mind of the Christian scholar are consciously and willingly adopted. If we may judge much of secular thought of our time from appearances, it is precisely the absence of conscious and willingly-adopted principles which makes for the lack of coherence in so much of its scholarship. In other words, it seems evident that many thinkers who by their own admission are non-Christian or anti-Christian are nevertheless powerfully shaped in their methods and their conclusions by principles and paradigms which they have unconsciously accepted, as it were by osmosis, from the conventional wisdom of secularity. It should not be so with the Christian scholar, who by virtue of his/her commitment critically and knowingly selects and adopts principles which are frankly and characteristically Christian.

Among the principles which should serve as guideline for the mind of the Christian scholar, none is more largely determinative than his/her understanding of time, or more precisely, the understanding of the relationship existing between eternity and time. It was Plotinus who, living in the third century of the Christian era, defined time as "the moving image of eternity." Such a conception affords a framework within which events, movements and the career of our world can be brought into focus so as to "make sense."

This suggests as a corollary, that the mind of the Christian engaged in the enterprise of scholarship constantly searches for meaning. While this is not unique to the Christian, the manner in which meaning is sought has distinctively Christian norms and patterns. The alternatives to this are basically two: the view of history as cyclical and the view of history as meaningless. Neither of these can afford any real view of world history. The cyclical view maintains that there is nothing which is either really new or ultimately meaningful. The view of history as chaotic and meaningless affords no basis for regarding the career of either the world or of man to be significant, while it ignores completely the existence and role of God in history.

Any division of history (or of time) which can be meaning-full must take into account that the dimension of the future must be, if it have any significance for the understanding of either the past or the present, informed by the vision of eternity. By this is meant that the real meaning of events must be found within the framework of God's sovereign action—action which is teleological and directed by purposes which find fulfillment only in an eschatological *and* eternal perspective.

This takes the understanding of Christian scholarship far beyond the mere cataloging of data or the chronicling of events. At the heart of the Judeo-Christian world-view is the concept of meaningful duration, with meaning as determined by norms beyond time and belonging to eternity. Eternity thus offers a frame of reference within which temporal (i.e., past and present) sequences can find permanent significance. It is this element which enables the Christian scholar to relate the major "saving" events which Revelation discloses to the broader sweep of history. That is to say, such scholarly activity moves beyond many of the perplexities of the scientific mindset, and finds no stone of stumbling in the proposition that God has intervened crucially in history, in revealing Himself in Holy Writ, and most decisively in the Incarnation of the Eternal Son in time. For it is here that time and eternity intersect most vividly and most crucially—in the entire panorama of the earthly career of Jesus Christ, centering in the master intervention of God in the resurrection of the Son from the dead.

It is from within this perspective that the Christian scholar can view the sweep of history as shaped by, and in the end marshalled to, the service of an eternal and final recapitulation of all things in Christ, "both things in heaven and things on earth, even in Him." Thus, Christian scholarship finds its fulcrum in the confidence that Jesus Christ, as the risen Lord, has the final and ultimate authority over time's sequences, and is thus the ultimate eschatological authority.

The relation of eschatological truth, the truth of eternity as an element to be fulfilled at the end of history, to the proximate truths of history is not always easily discerned. This is due to the fact that we all, including the Christian scholar, now prophesy in part. But this does not rule out for the scholar operating as a committed Christian the possibility of viewing the most contingent qualities of human history as being informed by eternity, as being its "moving image" within which there is frequent and meaningful spin-off in the temporal.

Thus the Christian scholar has for a guiding principle the real and meaningful involvement of eternity with all of mankind's experiences in history, difficult as it may be to perceive this at times. As James Orr saw, now nearly a century ago, the Incarnation of the Eternal Son offers a primary clue to the meaning of our world.

The significance of the holding of the view of time as "the moving image of eternity" as a key to the Christian use of the intellect has been shown to be great. This significance shows itself in a number of ways. We would note, for instance, that it affords protection against what Jacques Barzun calls "The Three Enemies of Intellect."[1] As is well known, the three "enemies" are to Barzun Art, Science and Philanthropy.[2] These are regarded as such insofar as they lead to anti-intellectualism, and/or in their ability to daze the intellect.

Now, the vision of eternity affords an active antidote for the wrong application of these three elements, doing so in ways which are more lateral than frontal. It does, for instance, view art as chiefly valuable for its ability to portray, rather than distort, reality. Referring again to Jacques Barzun, art without wider perspective tends to be, as he says "without learning, and, in a sense, without reason."[3] Against this mindless rejection of the "real" in art, the Christian mind imbued with the feeling for eternity has no taste for the repudiation of common speech, life and knowledge, in favor of the incoherent and the colloquial grasping for "in-words."

The mind of the Christian scholar whose perspective derives from the feeling for the reality of eternity discerns also the atomizing quality of Science, particularly in the diverging and compartmentalizing form which diverse technology assumes. Science tends all too frequently to erect what Barzun calls "citadels throughout the realm of mind" without taking "thought of the means of intellectual interchange among them."[4] Against this fragmentation of thought and of intellectual content, the Christian scholar insists that knowledge must be, because of its common origin in the Divine Mind, a unity. He cannot accept the demand, a view disseminated by many modern forms of technological learning, that Science represents a world apart from the normal "House of Intellect."

Again, the perspective of the Christian scholar causes him to be critical of the "trendy" view, called by Barzun Philanthropy, by which every conceivable form of "learning" is granted the status of "equal opportunity" in the processes of education. This trend is an inchoate blending of study and amusement, with a rejection of the Liberal Arts in favor of doing—of each doing his/her own thing. Christian scholarship cannot do other than view with extreme criticism and misgivings this debasing of the "life of the mind," if for no other reason than that it is grossly earth-bound, tending all too frequently to "cherish the warm confusions of animal existence."[5]

Thus, the Christian scholar is and must be intensely zealous to cherish the "life of the mind," avoiding two extremes. The first is the extreme of supposing that Intellect can speak for the whole man, as rationalism held, and second, that Intellect is the great source and depository for a whole range of deceptions and aggressions, as modernity tends to maintain. Against this, he/she will view with appreciation the firm demands which the right use of the intellect places upon both rigorous discipline and calm deliberation. Such scholarship stands against so many trends in contemporary culture that the persons espousing it come to feel, at times at least, that they are embattled by an invincible host of opponents.

To name but a few: there is a false emphasis upon nonconformity, frequently expressed through slovenliness. There is a lingering belief that the "creative" person is one who not only mounts his/her personal attack upon contemporary culture, but also regards all such attacks as equally valid and virtuous. There is the impatience with normal and connected discourse, and approval for the broken sentence, the studied absence of conversational skill. There is suspicion of any and all forms of coercion, an inveterate dislike for dress codes and for all which is usually indicated by the term "manners."

In all of this, there is antipathy for the long-accepted norms for the employment of Intellect, a substitution of triviality for both form and content of reasoned discourse, particularly for discourse which involves reflection and individual originality. Intellect, on the other hand, demands the use of courtesy, candor, and coherence in discourse, no less than courageous rigor in dealing with facts. Here again, the sentiment for eternity brings seriousness to every aspect of the intellectual enterprise. The quest for Truth is a quest for that which is eternal, and this demands that even matters which might at first thought seem small be treated with the care which belongs to a possible "chip of eternity."

Thus far, the attempt has been to show what elements serve as guidelines for the activity of the mind of the Christian scholar. Noting that the view of time as fleeting vision of eternity, it has been noted also that this quality may and should determine his/her attitude toward "the life of the mind" in general, and toward many of the trends which dominate many of our secular modes of thought. It has emerged that the Christian scholar must in our day swim against many currents of modern thought and expression. This demands a certain independence of the surrounding culture, a certain willingness to be guided by transcendent norms which seem to many sectors of today's culture strangely antique and irrelevant.

II. The Scope of the Christian Scholar

The Christian who seeks to pursue scholarly activity within the Christian orbit must and will work within dimensions of concern which are in some sense characteristically Christian. It is such dimensions which will define and concentrate intellectual effort. Two extremes need to be avoided: the first is that by which specialization rules out comprehensiveness, the second is that of such breadth of operation that work and conclusions become shallow and thus trivialized.

It is important to note that there is a difference between the connoisseur who may profess to possess (or even in reality possess) competence to pass critical judgment upon any and all phases of learning, and the sholar who has discovered early that there are, to him/her at least, boundaries essential to creative thought and exploration. These boundaries are not mere limits set by a desire to be safely encased within intellectual walls, whether by an agoraphobic fear of the panoramic expanse of the larger areas of exploration to which the life of the mind beckons, or whether by a needless and unwarranted feeling of personal inadequacy in the face of the facts.

As John Henry Cardinal Newman points out in his *The Idea of a University*, comprehensiveness in the grasp of truth by the intellect is attained only by the most serious mental effort which will employ "the comparison, the combination, the mutual correction, the continual adaptation, of many partial notions."[6] While this view carries with it the fact that scholarly attainment implies a vast accumulation of intellectual data, it also suggests that "comprehensiveness is necessarily a matter of training,"[7] and thus involves discipline which can only be expressed by the recognition and acceptance of boundaries to the employment of the life of the mind.

The existence of boundaries does not, per se, rule out range and dimensions for the activity of the Christian scholar. It can fairly be said that "the universe is the parish" of the Christian mind. That is to say, no area of investigation is off-limits to the Christian who takes the intellectual enterprise seriously. In reality, the broader the range and scope of Christian scholarly endeavor, the greater the promise for wholeness in the quest for truth. However, with the vast increase in available knowledge in our time, the greater becomes the need for the Christian scholarly mind to focus emphasis upon those areas of learning which offer the greatest promise of relevance for intellectual quest which is characteristically Christian. This would seem to be essential if depth be not sacrificed to extension.

It follows that the Christian scholar is justified in using the greatest of discernment and skill in the matter of selection of the scope of those trails of knowledge which he/she will pursue. This range will thus not be set arbitrarily, and for this reason defined by either expansionist or reductionist moods. Rather, it will be derived from the conviction that all truth is God's truth, and that the Christian will logically pursue those clues which he/she finds in the wider view of knowledge to the footsteps of the Divine. The Christian scholar will, moreover, welcome guidance at this and related points. And if the panorama of time equals "the moving image of eternity," truly Christian scholarship will seek the tutelage of Revelation in the determination of the areas of exploration which offer the prospect of a maximum degree of relevance to the Christian enterprise.

Guidance of this type is promised in the Epistle of James, who assures us that "if any of you lack wisdom, let him ask of God . . . and it shall be given him."[8] The scholar who seeks to be definitely and clearly Christian will find no difficulty in relating this promise to the definition of the scope and range appropriate to Christian scholarship.

The application of this biblical principle implies, further, that the Holy Spirit's role in the total intellectual enterprise is not only a valid one, but one which is indispensable to the Christian scholar. It implies a further willingness for hard conceptual work, and for the application of effort to subjects which merit the best in intellectual activity. After all, there are principles which direct every worthwhile endeavor. This is what education is all about.

Thus the Christian scholar is committed, not only to the exercise of the utmost of his/her ability in the pursuit of truth, but to give the most serious attention to the focus, directions and dimensions of that pursuit. This is a matter which cannot be left to such variables as interest, environmental vogue, or acceptability of motifs in the market place. It is, rather, a matter for the most earnest quest for the guidelines of the Spirit of the God of Truth, the Holy Spirit. It is He who will, if such counsel be sought, not only give directives in the matter of the scope of the intellectual endeavor, but also give enablement to the Christian scholar to pursue such endeavor with genuine excellence.

III. The Heart of the Christian Scholar

It may seem strange at first glance to speak of such a matter as the heart in a discussion of the Christian scholar. Ought not, some will ask, the issue be basically the mental or rational framework within which scholarly pursuits should be made? Such a question stems, in good part at least, from the long-accepted dualism of knowledge, by which it is maintained that there is a vast cleavage between general, or more properly, "rational" knowledge and knowledge which belongs to the inner or subjective life. By this latter is meant, of course, that such knowledge as the religious person professes to have, and which involves the more intimate and subjective aspect of the individual has nothing in common with knowledge gained by means of discursive reason.

Slowly the scholarly world is coming to pay attention to Michael

Polanyi, who for some years prior to his death in 1976 maintained that this is a false and unnecessary dualism. A number of writers, among them Jerry Gill and Bernard Lonergan, are showing the scholarly world in a meaningful and convincing way that all forms of learning and knowing stem from a single basic quality of the human person. A corollary of this is, that the whole person is involved in every and all types of knowledge-situation.

This form of thought falls upon the ears of the supposedly objective scholar with a strange sound. Too frequently scholarship has prided itself upon being detached and objective until it has succeeded in perpetuating the myth of the total detachment of the true scholar. This is dogmatism of the worst sort, and may account, in part at least, for the persistence of secular scholarship in the canonization of unsupported hypotheses as "assured scientific conclusions." Thus, for example, the assumption of the total continuity of the whole of the living structures on our planet has achieved such a degree of acceptance as to render it, to a vast number of scholars, beyond discussion. It is this frame of mind which has produced such a pronounced, sometimes even venomous, opposition to the permitting of any exposure of young minds to the Creation account as an alternative to the conventional view of organic evolution.

The Christian scholar, in finding his/her way through the labyrinth of the "conventional wisdom" of the secular world, will need not only a well-honed mind, but a profound inner commitment to some essential principles derived from a frankly Biblical world-view. This commitment will stem from the deeper levels or springs of the person—from the heart, if you will. At the base of such commitment will lie a relationship to One who came into the stream of our common life, who "spoke as never man spoke" and who could say, in consonance with the total quality of his life, that "I am the way, *the truth*, and the life."

This is to say, that the heart of the Christian scholar will have a supreme attachment to Jesus Christ, "in whom are hid all the treasures of knowledge." This will in turn cause the scholar to examine with an ever-increasing earnestness of purpose the dimensions of the Person of our Lord, and the implications for the realm of knowledge which lie resident in the Incarnation of the Eternal Word, "by whom all things were made that are made." This kind of knowing involves far more than celebration; it implies a prior commitment to obedience to Jesus Christ and to the Book by which He is revealed. Some will term such a position to be mere nebulous mysticism. To this, we would reply, "Mysticism it may be; nebulous it is not."

Highly relevant at this point are the words of our Lord, "if any man's will is to do his will, he shall know. . . ."[9] This suggests that something far more basic to man than the mind holds the ultimate key to knowing the Divine will, and more specifically, to understanding "the teaching." And it is precisely the will which gives expression to the deeper levels of human character—to the "things of the heart."

One of our proverbs expresses this negatively: "A man convinced against his will is of the same opinion still." This suggests, first of all, that the mind is far from being supreme in both doing and knowing, that the intellectual grasp is intimately involved with the ethical and the volitional. The reality of this seems seldom to cross the thinking of much of the world of scholarship, which seems committed to the view that true learning can be severed from true willing. Thus, love of the truth "as it is in Jesus" is no naive expression. Rather, it stands as a key to a whole range of knowledge.

This is a daring thesis! It implies that the person who chooses to ignore the deep, personal claims of Jesus Christ does by this fact close the door to a vast range of knowledge, and becomes open to the acceptance of many propositions and theses which will prove ultimately to be not only false, but tragically misleading. On the other hand, it suggests that the scholar whose heart is set upon knowing and obeying the basics of the Christian Revelation should and can be sensitive to areas and ranges of knowing which may seem trivial and even absurd to the one whose heart is closed to the voice and claims of our Lord. Perhaps even the Christian world lacks a full understanding of the possible creative role of the obedient heart in the enterprise of scholarship.

* * *

The Christian scholar today faces a world in which, as Jacques Barzun says, "sacred illiteracies obtain,"[10] and in which hypotheses incapable of demonstration reign supreme. Vogue determines norms, and the life of the mind is all too frequently subordinated to techniques for the equalization of merit and the normalization of mediocracy. Against these trends, the Christian scholar and Christian scholarship itself must struggle. This struggle must issue, as we have noticed, from a profound love for Truth and for the One Who gave it embodiment in His Person as the Eternal Word manifest in time.

This love for Truth demands personal commitment, consecrated involvement, and unwavering integrity. The scholar who embodies it is above "taking his or her agenda from the world" or capitulating to mere "conventional wisdom." In the Christian scholar, heart and mind unite in the enterprise of bringing all of thought "into captivity to the obedience of Christ." And such an enterprise is, we submit, far from being constricted by intolerable and stifling limits. To the contrary, its dimensions are as wide as the Son of Man Himself.

NOTES

1. Jacques Barzun, *The House of Intellect* (New York: Harper, 1959), pp. 1ff.
2. *Ibid.*, p. 27.
3. *Ibid.*, p. 15.
4. *Ibid.*, p. 19.

5. *Ibid.*, p. 24.
6. John Henry Cardinal Newman, *The Idea of a University* (Westminster, Md.: Christian Classics, 1973), p. 151.
7. *Ibid.*,
8. James 1:15, R.S.V.
9. John 7:17, R.S.V.
10. Barzun, *House*, p. 137.

3

INTELLECTUAL INDEPENDENCE IN THE LIFE OF ASA MAHAN

James E. Hamilton

To Dennis F. Kinlaw I owe an enormous debt of gratitude. His influence in my life intellectually, spiritually, and vocationally has been great. During my seminary years he was my teacher, counsellor, and friend. Since that time, the principles of his life have shaped the direction of my thought and have been the chief model for my highest aspirations.

It is appropriate that the name Asa Mahan should appear in a *Festschrift* to Dennis F. Kinlaw. Both men are alike in important ways. Both have lived lives of intense personal devotion to Christ; both have fulfilled professional roles as evangelist, pastor, teacher, author, and college president; both have risen to places of recognized leadership in the Wesleyan Holiness tradition of American Protestantism; and both have exercised ministries transcending denominational boundaries. It is sometimes forgotten that Dennis Kinlaw, like Asa Mahan, is a philosopher, though not by profession. He majored in philosophy as an undergraduate and pursued his interest piecemeal in graduate school. It was Dr. Kinlaw who taught me how to think philosophically, nurtured my interest in the writings of Mahan, and encouraged me to pursue a doctorate in the field. From these two figures, Kinlaw and Mahan, I learned that Christian commitment and intellectual independence are not mutually exclusive. For these reasons I dedicate to President Dennis Kinlaw this essay.[1]

Asa Mahan, like Dennis Kinlaw, believed that philosophy and religion are inseparable elements within human experience. A false philosophy, said Mahan, is the mother of false religion, while true philosophy is the

41

handmaid of true religion. True philosophy for Mahan grows out of a sense of wonder and curiosity, a love of truth, the recognition of human limitations in the knowing process, and a teachable spirit. Above all, the true philosopher will combine these traits with vigorous and principled independence of mind. In this study we shall note the origin of Mahan's commitment to intellectual independence, examine his understanding of the nature and justification of such independence, and survey the results of this commitment during his career. We shall conclude with a brief summary of the ways in which independence of mind and purity of heart are interrelated.

Asa Mahan grew up in a Calvinistic home with a mother who took her theology seriously. She was, he says, "one of the greatest female thinkers and readers on religious topics that I ever knew."[2] His home was a constant center for discussion of Christian doctrine and young Asa, though only a listener, was the most attentive person present. Within a year after his conversion, he was faced with a choice which greatly determined the character of his entire life and career. Upon what basis would he mold his opinions and make his decisions? Should he be a loyal adherent of a particular group, or should he be an "honest and earnest scholar of truth itself, with my intellect, my conscience, my God, and His Spirit, law, and testimony as my authoritative leaders and guides?"[3] In the former case he would be at home with *his* group and at odds with other groups, while in the latter he would not be fully at home anywhere except with God and his conscience. Deliberately, though "with much inward pain and self-crucifixion" he determined that he would openly and honestly examine all views as he had opportunity, and then "let the weight of evidence, and nothing else, determine my convictions and course of conduct, accepting whatever consequences agreements and disagreements with popular sentiment might bring upon me."[4] Thus at the age of seventeen Asa Mahan made a lifelong commitment to rigorous intellectual independence. We shall examine Mahan's conception of the nature and justification of intellectual independence,[5] and shall note the results of this commitment during his long career.

By intellectual independence Mahan refers to that state of mind in which a person seeks to harmonize all his opinions and convictions with truth alone and to base his decisions exclusively upon the requirements of truth and duty. His aim is not to think with or against the world, but to think truth. He allows no person, group or doctrine to stand between himself and the God of truth as lord over his intellect. He thinks for himself and decides all questions on the basis of available evidence. No other orientation, he argues, so effectively frees the mind from inward biases and prejudices and from outward pressures. Such independence stands in contrast to the mental servitude that comes whenever the mind is swerved from the authority of truth.

Mahan's view of intellectual independence carries several interesting implications which help to explicate the nature of this concept. The first that we shall note is openness to pursuing knowledge in all areas. The free pursuit of truth extends to the full range of potential knowledge. Second, independence of mind does not imply arrogance or self-sufficiency, but intellectual humility and a childlike and teachable spirit. One who seeks to understand as God does, perfectly, will soon become aware of limitations and have good reason to be humble. One whose supreme goal is truth will be ready to receive truth though it come from a child or an enemy. Third, even in the religious arena private rational judgment is the final arbiter of truth whether of revelation itself, of theology, or of preaching. A purported revelation, such as the Bible, must be received according to evidential signs that it is true or that it comes from God. The meaning of its teachings must also, in the final analysis, be determined by one's own intelligence, with the use of the best light available. In difficult areas of theological doctrine an independent thinker will respectfully examine the best writings on opposing sides. When he finds brilliant and saintly theologians to differ, he will neither become indifferent, inferring that one doctrine must be as good as another, nor despair, concluding that the truth is past finding out. Nor will he arbitrarily select one view over another. Rather, he will seek to extract what is good and true from them all. Similarly, church congregations should not passively accept as authoritative the messages of their pastors. The preacher is not a judge but an advocate speaking in the presence of those who must judge for themselves the character of his expositions. A final implication is that intellectual independence opens the door to civil disobedience. We must not allow civil authorities to do our thinking for us. To be sure we are to obey those who have the rule over us. However, such obedience is expressly prohibited where it would imply a violation of fidelity to God and of our convictions of duty.

Mahan justifies his concept of intellectual freedom in two ways, as fundamental to human dignity and as a corollary of Christian commitment. Essential to human dignity is the capacity to know and understand, and to *grow* in knowledge and understanding. Moreover the mind, like the body, grows strongest only when it is *exercised* in appropriate ways. It must tax its energies in solving "the varied problems of truth and duty, which the universe of matter and mind, which the word, works, and providence of God, present to its consideration." People whose lives are characterized by "continued indulgence of an idle unreflective curiosity in sightseeing," exercising chiefly the senses and overburdening the memory with the weight of unexplained facts are, says Mahan, "melancholy specimens of mental imbecility." Similarly, mere passive reception of the thoughts of others weighs the mind down and palsies its energies. Human dignity requires probing for causes and reasons, pondering also questions of human duty and destiny. Only the labor, or rather the luxury, of independent thought can strengthen and develop the intrinsic capabilities of our rational nature.

Intellectual independence, however, is not only a fundamental requirement of human dignity, but a corollary of Christianity. It is ironic that Karl Marx and Asa Mahan both came to London in late 1849. Marx held that religion, especially Christianity, is inherently hostile to liberty of thought and human creativity. While he pursued his studies in the British Museum, Mahan was proclaiming by spoken and written word that no conceivable influence is better suited to encouraging freedom of thought than that of genuine Christianity. His reasoning is this. According to Christianity, God is infinite and perfect, a being of complete justice, goodness, and truth. Hence, God will be satisfied with nothing less than truth and uprightness in his creatures. A Christian therefore is one who seeks to harmonize all his opinions and judgments with God's view of things, and all of his activities with God's will. In other words, Christianity intrinsically influences its adherents to face fully in the direction of objectivity and righteousness. This goal of objectivity in the pursuit of truth is, as we have seen, the hallmark of intellectual independence. Moreover, by thinking independently we shall follow the footsteps of our fathers in the faith. Speaking particularly to fellow Protestants, Mahan points out that Wesley and Calvin were not slavish adherents to tradition but free inquirers after truth. He remarks:

> I have sometimes thought that were such men as Calvin and Wesley here they would demand an apology of many of their modern followers . . . for having implicitly copied their sentiments, instead of imitating their God-like examples as honest and humble disciples of truth, and yet daring to appear before the world as their representatives.

The consequences of Asa Mahan's commitment to intellectual independence can be seen in his long and colorful career. We shall take note first of the area of methodology and then turn to the substantive realm of his opinions themselves. Mahan always insisted upon the method of open discussion as a social corollary of intellectual independence in the pursuit of truth. He writes:

> Truth has its foundation in reason and fact. The grand characteristic that distinguishes it from error . . . is that the former alone will stand the test of rigid investigation. Truth seeks light. Error shuns it . . . Hence, while the friends of truth should in no case allow themselves in bitter altercations, they should never fear or shun the collision of truth with error. They should everywhere court with the public an open and fundamental investigaion of the foundation of every article of their faith, together with a most rigid scrutiny of its validity, as contrasted with the opposite sentiments. The moment they betray fear or hesitation, in respect to meeting such a crisis, they give to their opinions the appearance of error; and to the opposite dogmas that of truth.[6]

In the classroom at Oberlin the student was taught to "receive nothing upon trust . . . and to exercise the most perfect freedom of discussion and inquiry before all his teachers."[7] Mahan personally encouraged students of all persuasions to give the strongest reasons for their beliefs and to question any position which he might assume. This procedure, he believed, opened the students' minds to rational conviction in the presence of valid evidence.

As college president Mahan introduced the public practice at Oberlin of hearing all sides of an issue. Thus he brought William Lloyd Garrison and Stephen and Abby Foster to Oberlin and met them in debate before the gathered community. Early in his tenure, Mahan debated classics professor Seth Waldo on the relative merits of studying the heathen and Hebrew classics. Some students, feeling that the new president had scored a signal victory, built a bonfire and for a lark tossed their worn out Virgils into it, carefully preserving their good copies for the next day's recitation. When the press reported a serious burning of the classics, Mahan was mortified. However, his sense of humor did not desert him and he remarked that never before had the classics given off so much light. Unfortunately, Professor Waldo became needlessly frightened about the future of the classics at Oberlin and resigned, much to President Mahan's regret. Even his disagreement with colleagues in the sensitive area of moral theory received attention in public debate. In 1839 a debate of several days continuance began in the college chapel between Mahan and Professor J. P. Cowles, with Professor Charles G. Finney presiding. It was this debate that seems to have crystallized the difference between Mahan's views and those of Finney.

The above cases exemplify Mahan's use of discussion and debate in the service of free inquiry. It is very important for our purposes to realize that for Asa Mahan the purpose of debate is eliciting truth, not achieving victory. Thus he writes:

> A Christian minister must never strive for mastery in arguments. Consequently he must avoid everything which has the appearance of unfairness. . . . No advantage should be taken of the weakness of an opponent. In general the object should be not merely to answer the arguments and objections of an opponent, but to elucidate the subject. . . . Isolate the real question at issue. State it just as it is, and then join issue upon that.[8]

But these restrictions in no way diminished Mahan's relish for debates. When he appeared in Cleveland in 1855 for a public debate on the subject of spiritualism (a debate that continued for ten successive evenings, except Sunday), the *Plain Dealer* reported that "President Mahan, eager for the contest, was on hand, cool, self-possessed, and resolute as Sampson when about to tear down the gates of Gaza."

Mahan had early anticipated that because of his commitment to truth his views would often be such that he would differ from those close to him. We shall now indicate briefly a number of instances which illustrate that he had anticipated correctly. First, although cradled in high Calvinism, he embraced the free will position soon after his conversion and thus found himself in what was known as the New School. Second, in Cincinnati he stood alone among the pastorate for the immediate abolition of slavery. Third, at Lane Theological Seminary he supported the students against his fellow trustees in their vote to restrict the students not only from participating in antislavery activities but from discussing slavery in private as well. Fourth, at Oberlin he took the lead in departing from the theological orthodoxy of the Congregational Church by propagating Wesleyan holiness doctrine. Fifth, as president of Oberlin and Adrian Colleges he opposed the rigid hierarchial and detailed discipline structures then common at similar institutions. In his mind the chief regulative principle of a college should be Christian thought and influence, its government should be "in the strictest sense, *parental*" and its community bonds should be those of a family. Sixth, both at Oberlin and Adrian Mahan advocated reform of the prevailing classical model of education in the direction of a broader curriculum with alternative possibilities available to students. His proposals, however, were outvoted at Oberlin and were only marginally successful at Adrian.

Seventh, although Mahan had previously opposed coeducation, he found it already in existence at Oberlin and soon became its most ardent defender and the chief faculty advocate of its extension. There were numerous restrictions upon women at Oberlin. Some of these Mahan unsuccessfully attempted to remove. For example, when he pressed for Lucy Stone to read her own essay at commencement, he was overruled by a majority of the faculty. Eighth, when abolition societies or women's rights conventions showed signs of yielding to the anti-religious sentiments of people like William Lloyd Garrison, Mahan's voice was frequently heard contending for Holy Scripture as the greatest friend of human dignity and human rights in history. Ninth, in the political realm Mahan threw his influence successively into the founding of the Liberty, Free Soil and Republican Parties. Later, when President Grant seemed to shelter corruption in his administration and to support Radical Reconstruction policies which perpetuated hostility between North and South, Mahan joined the shortlived Liberal Republican Party and ran for Congress on the Greeley ticket of 1872.

Finally, Mahan even disagreed with his beloved associate at Oberlin, Charles G. Finney, in a matter close to them both, the theory of moral obligation. Mahan is a deontologist, holding that rightness is a basic concept in ethics, while Finney is a teleologist, contending that rightness is a derivatve concept, based upon some consequential good which is pursued. Each devotes considerable written space to refuting the other's position. Interestingly, in *The Baptism of the Holy Ghost*, Mahan refers to the disagreement in order to illustrate that intellectual independence and consequent difference of opinion are not inconsistent with purity of heart:

> On a very few questions in moral philosophy and theology, Brother Finney and myself have arrived at opposite conclusions. Yet each has the same assurance as

before, that the other is "full of faith and of the Holy Ghost," and never were our mutual love and esteem stronger than now. We differ just where minds under the influence of the purest integrity and the highest form of Divine illumination are liable to differ.[9]

A study of this sort would be incomplete without some indication of the relationship between intellectual independence and that twin preoccupation of Mahan's life, purity of heart. Already some indications of the ways in which each affects the other have been noted. I will now briefly summarize Mahan's position, beginning with the influence of purity of heart. For Mahan we must remember, a necessary feature of purity of heart is devotion to truth. Intellectual independence in turn is by definition that state of mind which necessarily accompanies devotion to truth. It is a state in which the mind has liberty to range over the entire field of knowledge and to develop opinions on the basis of available evidence. Impurity of heart, by way of contrast, would involve subjection to non-rational impulse, desire and emotion, and would be accompanied by a state of mind in which the intellect would find much hindrance in the effort to be objective.

According to Mahan, purity of heart also affects intellectual independence by liberating the energies of the mind. Singleness of intention in itself concentrates and invigorates intellectual activity. When the heart is purified in the Christian experience of sanctification, the mind should normally be enabled to think with greater intensity and energy, yet in a way that manifests balance and discipline.

Strong and yet perfectly balanced and regulated action is the highest form of activity of which we can possibly conceive. This is the form which the gospel is pre-eminently adapted to secure.[10]

In turn, intellectual independence also affects purity of heart, primarily by opening the mind to rational conviction in the presence of valid evidence. Mahan holds that truth has a sanctifying influence upon the heart, but only when it is perceived to be in fact truth. If we hold an opinion on some grounds other than original inquiry even though it might happen to be true, it "can never act as a vitalising power in our own hearts."[11] It is possible to cling to and zealously propagate some truth as a prejudice, never caring that is in fact true. For example, one may be attracted to a true opinion by a desire for fame, wealth, peer approval or the like. Opinions, thus embraced and maintained, only harden and corrupt the heart. On the other hand, rational convictions of truth based upon a candid personal investigation of available evidence have beneficial influence in molding the heart and character. Accordingly, Mahan asserts, the verdict at the final judgment "will not turn upon what his opinions were, but what was the spirit under the influence of which they were acquired and held."[12]

In a beautiful rhetorical way Mahan relates intellectual independence

to his vision of human potential and destiny. He has been speaking of the
wonder which the mysteries of life inspire in young children. He writes:

> Oh, that feeling of wonder in man! It is the source of all true greatness, if it is
> only rightly directed. Now let this child possess and preserve a pure heart, and
> by the grace of God he may do it without fail; let him become a pupil of
> universal truth, and preserve in all his researches a manly, sanctified
> independence, and what a thinker will he become! . . . And when this mind has
> done with the thinking of time, and takes his place amid the great thinkers of
> eternity, there
> > 'sage he stands,
> > With Atlantean shoulders fit to bear
> > The weight of mightiest monarchies.'

Yes, 'sage he stands,' with thought, the disclosure of which will instruct heaven
itself. . . . Say not, hearer, I can never ascend to such heights as these. You
may do it, in the heaven-directed progress of your future being, and by a proper
development of your mental powers, you may be their associates.[13]

NOTES

1. Portions of this paper have been drawn from Edward H. Madden and James E.
Hamilton, *Freedom and Grace: The Life of Asa Mahan* (Metuchen, N.J.: Scarecrow Press,
1982).

2. Asa Mahan, *Autobiography: Intellectual, Moral and Spiritual* (London: J. Woolmer,
1882), p. 2.

3. Asa Mahan, *Out of Darkness Into Light* (New York: Willard Tract Repository, 1876),
p. 81.

4. *Ibid.*, p. 80.

5. Much of what follows on these two topics is based upon Asa Mahan, "The Relation of
Christianity to the Freedom of Thought and Action," Asa Mahan Archives, Morrison-
Kenyon Library, Asbury College.

6. Asa Mahan, "Certain Fundamental Principles, Together With Their Applications,"
Oberlin Quarterly Review, II (November, 1846), p. 237.

7. *Autobiography*, p. 271.

8. Asa Mahan, "Manuscript Writings, Miscellaneous," Archives, Shipman Library,
Adrian College.

9. Asa Mahan, *The Baptism of the Holy Ghost* (Noblesville, Ind.: J. Edwin Newby, 1966),
p. 21.

10. Asa Mahan, "Spiritual Writings of Prof. Thomas C. Upham," *Oberlin Quarterly
Review*, IV (January, 1849), p. 124.

11. *Out of Darkness,* p. 85.

12. Asa Mahan, *Science of Moral Philosophy*, p. 309.

13. "Freedom of Thought and Action," pp. 151-153.

4

THE LORD OF TRUTH*

Michael L. Peterson

To Dennis Kinlaw, whose vision for education that is Christian changed my life, I am indeed a debtor.

I. Introduction

Seventeen centuries ago, the church father Tertullian asked the question: "What indeed, has Athens to do with Jerusalem? What concord is there between the Academy and The Church?"[1] Of course, what Tertullian was asking is: What is the relationship between reason and the pursuit of worldly knowledge, on the one hand, and faith and the revelation of God, on the other. Tertullian's own answer is implied in a rhetorical way in the question itself. He held not only that Christian revelation is self-sufficient, but that there is tension or conflict between the spiritual mission of the Church and the role of the Academy.

The position of Tertullian is clearly in the minority in the history of Christian thought. The majority of Christian thinkers have declared an important and intimate relationship between the life of the intellect and the life of faith.[2] If the collective reasoning of these thinkers could be summed up, it would be that the Academy and the Church—education and Christian commitment—are essentially related because they are both after truth. To put it more strongly, God is the Lord of Truth,[3] not simply the Lord of biblical truth, but of all truth wherever it may be found.[4] This is the more dominant, more positive tradition within Christian orthodoxy.

---

*The following is the text of an address to Faculty Retreat, Asbury College, September 3, 1981.

49

Asbury College and the ideals for which it stands are located firmly within this "majority" position. However, our official commitment to God as the Lord of Truth can become a mere shibboleth unless we faithfully review its meaning and continually renew our understanding. Now, in discussing the topic of truth, I first want to put my audience at ease: rest assured that I do not intend to stand here and recite every truth which I know or think I know. Nobody seems to have time these busy days for that! What I do want to do is to analyze in a general way what is entailed in stating that our God is the Lord of Truth; and from this analysis I will construct a sort of ideal conceptualization of what we ought to be about. Although the subject is large and complex, I organize what I have to say around three main points: the Source of Truth; the Nature of Truth; and the Knowledge of Truth. Along the way, I hope to offer new insights and perhaps fresh inspiration for those of us at Asbury who seek to make education the extension and fulfillment of Christian commitment.

II. The Source of Truth

A. The Creator of Reality

For orthodox Christianity, God is the source of all truth. There are two ways in which we can speak of God as the source and fountainhead of truth. First, as Aquinas has told us, truth is based on reality, on what exists. There are two broad categories of existence, or being, which Christians recognize: (1) God and (2) His creation. Beyond these two realities there is nothing else. The eternal and sovereign God freely chose to create everything that is out of absolute nothing. No other cosmology, ancient or modern, has attained this grand conception.[5] Whether we speak of the Egyptian belief that the god Ptah formed the world from primordial mud, or of Plato's account (in the *Timaeus*) of the Demiurge fashioning the world out of pre-existent matter and universal form, or even of the modern evolutionary naturalist's doctrine that matter is eternal through all its transmutations, we still speak of visions of reality which are remarkably inferior to that of the Judeo-Christian tradition. In the Judeo-Christian conception of creation, there are no alien factors or co-existing realities which conditioned God or influenced His creative activity. Hence, all truths—truths about God Himself and truths about His created order—are rooted in God alone. When we recite the Apostles' Creed ("I believe in God the Father Almighty, Maker of heaven and earth . . ."), we tacitly affirm this unique insight.

B. The Locus of All Truth

The second way in which God is the source of all truth pertains to His perfect and universal knowledge. Put simply, the Divine Mind knows the truth about all things; God perceives the interrelations of all truths and knows them as a unified, coherent whole. God is, then, the *locus of truth*. The idea that there is rationality behind the universe takes on distinctively Christian significance in the concept of the *logos*. The Greeks associated the *logos* with a rational principle or power at work in the world, but Christian thinkers (for example, the gospel writer John, the early church father Tatian, and the medieval philosopher Augustine) go a step further and identify the *logos* with Jesus Christ. Jesus is the *logos* of God, and biblical passages stating that Jesus is "the wisdom of God," "the one through whom all worlds were created," and "the one in whom all things consist" must be interpreted from this perspective.

C. The *Imago Dei* and Education

Now the God of truth is not content simply to contemplate His own perfect knowledge throughout eternity. Instead He has created finite minds which are like His infinite mind in important respects. Man is made in God's image and is thus *rational spirit*. At the very least, this means that man can explore and discover a great many truths about God and His creation.

Although God has formed in man a nature which seeks truth and understanding, man's knowledge of truth cannot be exhaustive or infallible. This fallibility is more due to *finitude* than to *sin*. Obviously, a very complicated and fascinating debate regarding the relation of moral and spiritual error to intellectual error arises here, but it is a debate which we cannot pursue. Suffice it to say that we must be very careful not to suggest that the Fall and the subsequent reign of sin in human life has totally obliterated man's capacity for knowing truth. Such a thesis not only would be self-defeating, since then we could not reliably claim to know that *it* is true, but also would run afoul of certain broad and consistent teachings of the Scripture.

The innate human tendency to seek knowledge finds sophisticated corporate expression in *formal education*. Formal education represents a sustained effort to record, systematize, and transmit the knowledge and culture which we have attained. In principle, the school can be interpreted as being a *divinely ordained human institution*. From a biblical point of view, the school is more than the outgrowth of a natural tendency in humankind: it is verbally mandated in Genesis when God tells Adam to "take dominion" over the created order. "Taking dominion" ultimately implies rational supervision and control, and education is obviously the logical extension of this idea.

Interestingly, many theologies of education—and particularly Protestant ones, I might add—have failed to see education in this light. Instead they have proclaimed that the divinely ordained human institutions are exactly three in number: the family, the church, and the state. Depending on which theology of education you read, then, education becomes a derivitive of one or the other of the three fundamental institutions. Authors who attempt to make education derivitive in this way typically commit one or both of two fallacies: either they have an overly literalistic reading of Genesis and other relevant parts of the Bible, and thus do not see some of its slightly more subtle but perfectly valid implications for education, or they have an inadequate concept of education in the first place, and thus never develop their scriptural interpretations in the direction of a full-blown endorsement of education.

As far as I can see, in terms of the direct statements of the Creator and in terms of man's innate tendency toward truth, no good argument is possible for accepting the family, church, and state, but rejecting the school, as divinely ordained institutions. Of course, the other three institutions are committed to various kinds of education and training.[6] But if I am correct, then there is a status and dignity for formal schooling which we must incorporate into our theology of education.

D. The Collapse of the Sacred-Secular Distinction

It would be wrong at this point to assume that the proper domain of the school is "secular" or "worldly" knowledge, whereas the proper domain of the church is "sacred" or "spiritual" knowledge. The primary reason why this would be erroneous is that the sacred-secular distinction does not apply at all. In view of what we have already affirmed about God's being the source of truth, we have grounds for collapsing the misleading distinction altogether. God is one. He is a unity; all truth stems from Him and is known as a whole by Him. When we see that all truth is God's truth wherever it may be found, then we have no basis for insisting that only "religious knowledge" has *eternal* value or *spiritual* significance. Furthermore, we have no basis for saying that a religious vocation or calling is of *more* value than any other. When done for the glory of God, the most mundane tasks—such as political involvement, business undertaking, and disciplined study—have eternal value. All of creation is God's and *all* truths about creation are God's. In a very real sense, therefore, legitimate involvement in creation, conducted in light of the truth we know, is *sacred*.

The repudiation of the sacred-secular distinction is, of course, a major theme of the Protestant Reformation. And this theme is one root of the promise of a Christian liberal arts college to educate the whole person. In *The Idea of a Christian College*, Arthur Holmes tells us that "Liberal education is an opportunity to become more fully a human person in the image of God, to see life whole rather than fragmented, to transcend the provincialism of our place in history, our geographic location or our job."[7] This lofty talk sounds very fine in theory. Certainly, in our thoughtful moments, most of us know full well that we are to reject the spurious sacred-secular distinction. However, there seem to be times when vestiges of the distinction can be detected in our activities.

To cite an example close to home, whenever we too sharply distinguish between exercises which are exclusively religious and those which are distinctively academic, we run the risk of falling into the sacred-secular dichotomy and, hence, of losing the holistic conception which we officially endorse. In order to reduce the risk, we must actively expose those false assurances that we have escaped the seductive bifurcation of sacred and secular. It will not do, for example, to comfort ourselves by saying that we have *both* chapel *and* instructional classes at Asbury College, or that we have *both* prayer *and* a lecture within each class period, and so forth. All this represents is that we have put the religious and the academic in close proximity to one another, that we have *juxtaposed* faith and learning. But for us to settle for this relationship alone is to fall tragically short of our declared goal of *integrating* faith and learning. A student (or a professor, for that matter) could participate in the mere juxtaposition of faith and learning by attending a large secular university and getting involved in a Christian fellowship group at the same time. It takes constant vigilance on our part to keep from being satisfied in just giving an education within an atmosphere of piety. Our instrinsic character as a Christian liberal arts college is at *least* that, but it is also *far more* than that.

The ideal of all truth being founded and unified in God demands that there be lively *integration* of the content of the Christian faith with the content of the various academic disciplines. Having this ideal means that academic classes should be more than taking potshots at variant points of view and more than superficial moralizing about the values and actions of those who are not like us. Our classes should contain thorough attempts to analyze and evaluate fundamental issues according to a Christian frame of reference. By the same token, having the holistic ideal also means that chapel and other religious activities should maintain the intellectual credibility appropriate to an institution of higher learning, and must never denigrate the academic as less important than the religious. What we want to produce are not Christians who are also scholars, but Christian scholars. What we need is not Christianity alongside education, but Christian education.

III. The Nature of Truth

A. What is Truth?

One of the classic and enduring questions of humankind is: What is truth? The question is difficult, but we can make some inroads into it. *Truth,* in the sense that I have been using it, is a *property of propositions.*[8] When a proposition corresponds to reality, it possesses the property "truth"; when it fails to correspond, it is "false." It will be helpful as we proceed to use propositions and their capacity to exhibit truth as a key idea. Let us now unpack this idea.

Obviously, there are different kinds of reality, different sectors of being, we might say. The physical, the psychological, the historical, the mathematical, the aesthetic, and the social are just a few of the many kinds of reality we face. Likewise, we can speak of different types of propositions about these realities, that is, different types of truth. Quite clearly, the kind of truth expressed by the statement "The sum of the angles of a right triangle is equal to 180 degrees" is different from the kind of truth expressed by the statement "Columbus discovered America in

1492." And the statement "God is a Trinity" is still another kind of truth. Examples could be readily multiplied to demonstrate an amazing plurity of truths based on the manifold reality which confronts man.

From the position of Christian theism, we know that the multifarious character of reality reflects the richness and plenitude of a creative and loving God. And we affirm that all truths about reality are unified in Him. Furthermore we know that He has created man as a rational agent located within reality and has given him the ability to learn many truths about it. This implies that "knowledge of truth" has both *intrinsic* and *utility* value. On the one hand, truth is to be valued in itself because it is God's and because it gives understanding for its own sake. On the other hand, truth is to be valued for its practical significance: it can help lead one to God or it can help one get around in God's creation.

B. The Architecture of Truth

When we contemplate the vast number of truths about God's created order, we should not think of them coming in monotonous array, with no special order or arrangement. Given the *rational reality* which God has created, we may legitimately speak of the truths about it having a *rational structure*. We can imagine there being an edifice of truth, if you will. Although I would not press the metaphor too far, we might think of the various truths about reality as forming the foundations, the building blocks, and so forth. The most basic and universal truths about reality form the foundations; propositions that oneself exists, that the external world exists, and that sensory perception is generally reliable would qualify here. The distinct kinds of truths and methodologies for seeking them can be grouped into disciplines and used to make up parts of the superstructure.

Within the structure of truth, then, man as a rational agent is free to explore and discover in any and all areas. There are highly specific truths for him to learn as well as broad and pervasive principles; there are truths about the physical world, about mathematics, and about the social and psychological aspects of human life. Additionally, there seem to be "truths about truths," if you will allow me to speak that way to make a point; that is, there are truths about how the truths of the various disciplines and the truths about life in general fit into a meaningful, systematic whole. These second-level truths are what define worldviews, and they are of paramount concern to the serious rational agent.

For a person to articulate precisely which general and important propositions he considers to be true, and then how they are supposed to fit together, is for him to manifest his *worldview*. The worldview is the architectural design, so to speak, for the edifice of truths. A worldview "puts it all together," so to speak. Peter Berger indicates that a worldview donates to the individual thinker, or even to a whole cognitive community, a picture of reality and how humanity is related to it. Unfortunately, educated and well-intentioned people do not always agree on how the architecture should be designed; they simply disagree on worldviews—they diverge on the question of how things fit together. Should the existence of God be a foundational truth? Which values deserve man's undying allegiance? Should one kind of truth have some sort of priority over other kinds? Such questions are answered differently by different thinkers and schools of thought. No one is completely a Christian educator, and no one has received a thoroughly Christian education, until the issue of worldview has been faced and the distinctiveness of the Christian worldview has been grasped. The Christian worldview provides the blueprint for the architecture of all other truths which we and our students will seek and come to know. It is logical to expect the curriculum structure at a Christian institution of higher learning to mirror its perception of how truth fits together into a meaningful, systematic whole.

C. Curriculum Design and the Structure of Truth

For us, the immediate ramifications of the idea of the architecture of truth are in the area of curricular design. The course offerings and sequences at an institution of higher learning should reflect the various constellations of truth which have been and are being discovered, and should place them in proper perspective. The curriculum should include those areas of knowledge which are considered so basic that the student is required to study them as well as those areas which the student may elect to study.

I am not sure whether we have faced the issue in precisely these terms. There are a number of issues here which are very pertinent. We might consider, for example, whether mathematics is given its proper due in our core curriculum. Or, we might ponder whether our emphasis on breadth in a liberal arts curriculum does not sacrifice healthy and legitimate specialization. After all, the Latin word for "liberal" (*libere*) means "to free," and we must not disparage the freeing or liberating power of working out an idea to a very fine point or of researching a topic with a great degree of thoroughness. Does our emphasis on a large number of core courses taken over a wide spectrum of disciplines detract from this other meaning of "liberal"? Remember, the original liberal arts were relatively few in number.[10] Please realize that I am not raising any objections here, or making any proposals. I am simply trying to show that the statement that all truth is God's truth can face us with some potent curricular matters.

IV. The Knowledge of Truth
A. Product and Process

We must now move from talking about truth and the Creator of Truth to the *knowledge* of it. Perhaps I should not speak in static terms of the *knowledge* of truth, but of the *search* after truth, to borrow Descartes' phrase. To speak of the *search* after truth is to emphasize the dynamic activity in which the mind is engaged rather than a static achievement. The distinction which I am laboring here is that between knowledge as a *product* and knowledge as a *process*. Of course, truth or knowledge is something in itself, and we often believe that we have actually secured a measure of it for ourselves. I am not denying this at all. What I am urging is that we see what is probably the more important side to the knowledge of truth—the *active, processive* side in which the mind is stretching and exploring and evaluating. As educators, we must also be intensely concerned with this dimension of knowledge.

Let us now extend the implications of the idea of "knowledge as process." First, it implies that the sheer *attainment of truth* is not the whole story. The *impact of the search after truth upon the mind* is also important. It is the role of one who provides education in the truth to stimulate and to sharpen the minds of students, to try to make their minds flexible and free. Students should be exposed to great ideas in order to avoid pettiness and triviality. They must be shown real models of persons forming responsible judgments, and must be encouraged to emulate them. Students ought to become acquainted with a wide variety of concepts and differing positions, so that they may learn to sort out truth from error and may begin to develop the intellectual virtue of tolerance. This indeed is a grandiose program; but if each of us does his part, the results may have lasting value.

To be sure, this program dictates that we educators must refrain from dispensing prepackaged answers, and must never be content with students' merely getting our lecture notes efficiently copied and dutifully memorized. Robert Persig makes this kind of point in a rather unusual way in his best-selling novel, *Zen and the Art of Motorcycle Maintenance*.[9] The book is neither about Zen Buddhism nor about motorcycles; it is about man's inner search for responsible selfhood and mental independence. Two motorcyclists travel through the Pacific Northwest. One of them has gradually educated himself to fix his own cycle when it breaks down; the other has formed the habit of taking his bike to the hometown mechanic. It is fascinating to see how the two bikers behave when mechanical difficulties come their way on the open road. The message for us is clear: we can guide students, we can present our best judgments on pressing issues, and we can tell them where we think error lies. But we must ultimately try to get them to seek the truth *for themselves*. Our students will hit the open road eventually, and then how will they respond?

When the effort and the risk of genuine education seem too great, we may unconsciously slip into intellectual dogmatism, even of the most religiously approvable and socially acceptable kind. Frequently, our students will reinforce this activity; but we must resist their wanting the end *product* without going through the right *process*. Arthur Holmes writes:

> I suspect that a considerable amount of student cynicism and skepticism can be traced to attempts to dogmatically impose a faith rather than presenting it

graciously and reasonably, and to the practice of pontificating "answers" rather than assisting students in grappling with issues for themselves in the light of their heritage of Christian faith and thought. We can get so busy taking the motes of immaturity out of students' eyes that we forget the beams of finiteness, fallibility and inflexibility in our own eyes.[10]

We can see, then, that the process of searching for truth is a fragile thing which must be protected and cultivated with the greatest care.

A second and related implication of the notion of the knowledge process is that there is "no royal road to truth."[11] As Christian educators, we should not entertain romantic fantasies about the search. The process of seeking truth, in whatever area we work, is a struggle and always susceptible to error. Not even the Christian who believes that all truth is God's can claim an "easier" time of it. We can have the confidence that God's created reality is intelligible, and we can put truths about it in a clearer and more helpful perspective than those who lack this confidence. However, Christians must find out truths about the world through the same hazardous intellectual process that all persons must employ. Although we Christians have God's *special revelation* in Scripture, we must come to know God's *general revelation* in the world on its own terms, and those terms are simply the intellectual processes that God has established.

The *intellect* is the *divinely given faculty* for knowing truths about the world. Mental activity is part of the *creational order* of things; it is God's plan for us as finite creatures in His image. Having identified ourselves as Christians with the *redemptional order* does not alter or cancel the creational plan. Allow me to illustrate the point. I am sometimes taken aback when a student, full of well-meaning religious zeal, says, "Prof., God has given me the gift of wisdom," and what he seems to be intimating is that God has "zapped" him rather instantaneously with some sort of extraordinary insight into things. Now the student is not to be berated for this impetuous conclusion. Yet, all things considered, it does not square with the general biblical teaching regarding the attainment of wisdom. Indeed God is the Giver of Wisdom, but His process for doing so involves a long and thoughtful life lived in His presence. Perhaps cleverness or a happy solution to an immediate problem, or particular divine guidance in a troublesome situation, might be gained in a relatively short time (or even on the spur of the moment), but not *wisdom* in the full sense.

B. The Ethics of the Intellectual Process

The integrity of the intellectual process is so important that many thinkers have spoken of an *ethical responsibility* which attaches to it. It is not just *that* one seeks truth, but *how* one seeks it, that is of extreme significance. Teachers and learners would do well to heed this advice. Ethically speaking, we do not have the right to believe anything whatever. Our belief in the truth of some proposition must come only after careful investigation into the relevant evidence. To explain this ethical requirement, W. K. Clifford, a nineteenth century philosopher, tells the following story:

> A shipowner was about to send to sea an emigrant-ship. He knew that she was old, and not over-well built at the first; that she had seen many seas and climes, and often had needed repairs. Doubts had been suggested to him that possibly she was not seaworthy. These doubts preyed upon his mind, and made him unhappy; he thought that perhaps he ought to have her thoroughly overhauled and refitted, even though this should put him to great expense. Before the ship sailed, however, he succeeded in overcoming these melancholy reflections. He said to himself that she had gone safely through so many voyages and weathered many storms and that it was idle to suppose she would not come safely home from this trip also. He would put his trust in Providence, which could hardly fail to protect all these unhappy families that were leaving their fatherland to seek for better times elsewhere. He would dismiss from his mind all ungenerous suspicions about the honesty of builders and contractors. In such ways he acquired a sincere and comfortable conviction that his vessel was thoroughly safe and seaworthy; he watched her departure with a light heart, and benevolent wishes for the success of the exiles in their strange new home that was to be; and he got his insurance-money when she went down in mid-ocean and told no tales.[12]

Clifford asks rhetorically about what we shall say of the shipowner. Clearly, we shall say that he is guilty for the death of those people.

Granted, the shipowner "sincerely" believed in the soundness of the ship, or so we are told in the hypothetical story. However, he believed in a manner which violates the ethics of the intellectual life. Actually, he "had no right to believe on such evidence as was before him." He had acquired his belief by stifling doubts and avoiding close scrutiny of the facts. Clifford correctly indicates that even if we alter the story a bit and suppose that the ship was not unsound after all, the shipowner is still as guilty as before. The question of right or wrong here does not have to do with the actual truth or falsity of the belief, but with *the way in which the belief is attained and held.* John Stuart Mill makes this same point in his classic essay *On Liberty.* Mill states that the truth may reside in the mind as a prejudice, as a superstition, and that this is beneath the dignity of a rational being.[13] A belief—even a true belief—may be acquired in the *wrong way* and not because it is responsibly evaluated and seen *as true.*

This whole issue takes on additional significance for us when we realize that many thinkers, such as Clifford, accuse *religious believers* of violating the ethics of belief. Unfortunately, some believers too frequently give critics the occasion to attack on these grounds. Some believers have simply succeeded in making themselves credulous persons, defending themselves by saying that their religious belief is a purely private matter without any rational or ethical constraints. It is no wonder that thoughtful nonbelievers sometimes characterize believers as persons who believe on fancy, push away doubts, and direct their minds toward the comfortable and the familiar.

Christian educators cannot allow themselves or their students to acquiesce in the comfortable and the familiar, and thereby foster a kind of provinciality which detracts from a greater understanding of Christianity and of the world at large. Suppose, for instance, that a college student learns of some new and different ideas, particularly relating to religion; and let us say that he runs in to *doubt* about his own religious commitment. We cannot completely help him by advising him to pray those doubts away or to will them away with Christian assurance. The advice to draw close to God is only a preliminary step. Eventually, the student must be encouraged and helped to work through those doubts in an *intellectual process.* If he acquired the doubts by *thinking,* then he must ultimately get rid of them by *thinking.* No amount of spiritual devotion, firm resolve, or sheer will power can eliminate them. The student must come to see his Christian commitment, or whatever point of his Christian commitment he is wondering about, to be valid in a way appropriate to his intellectual understanding. This, as we have said, is God's way: "Come, let us reason together," saith the Lord.

The present discussion can be pressed to a more fundamental level. This has to do with the manner in which we understand Christian conversion. So frequently we hear people called to Christian commitment as though it is solely a matter of *choice,* or an act of the will—and this is identified with *faith.* But we have just recognized that the *mind* must be involved in appropriate ways when forming a belief in something. Although making a willful choice to become reconciled to God is certainly part of conversion, it is not ideally the initial part of it. The *will* is suited to *follow* the *intellect* in what the intellect judges to be *true.* In a Christian institution of higher learning, we must be especially careful not to take this fact too lightly. A person must be called to conversion, or to sanctification for that matter, *only when* his mind sufficiently grasps the truth about God and His initiative toward man. Think how ludicrous it is to ask someone just to choose to believe something before his mind is prepared. If Dr. Vincent, say, were to ask me to believe that there are only twelve people sitting in this room right at the moment, I simply could not direct my will to believe it. My intellect contains all sorts of evidence to the contrary. The will must follow the intellect; the intellect is the compass for truth. And that is God's way. Of course, if the Dean arose and told me to believe it, my will would do so immediately! The moral here, quite straightforwardly, is that in educational environment we must be sensitive not to *coerce belief* in any way—in conformity of opinion, or doctrinal purity, or homogeneity of life-style. Belief ought to be captured only by *good reasons.* The process of giving and taking reasons means that the risk of doubt, error, and insecurity is present. But risk is the necessary corollary of a truly free and responsible community in which the mind's quest for truth is taken seriously.

C. The Christological Center of Truth

One of the reassuring things for a Christian engaged in the search after truth is seeing that knowledge has a center, a focus—and that this is Jesus

Christ. In Him is hidden all the wisdom and treasures of God. And we are admonished to "bring all thoughts into captivity to Him." In keeping with our theme of intellectual ethics, however, we must say that there is a proper way of bringing thoughts into captivity, and there are many improper ways: peer pressure, propaganda, hypnotism, and drug therapy only begin the list of unacceptable ways. To inculcate belief by claiming that such-and-such is what evangelicalism believes, or that thus-and-so is a comforting doctrine, or that good Wesleyans always affirm X is to stop gravely short of the divinely given process for apprehending truth.

A children's story by Madeleine L'Engle provides a gripping illustration of this point. In *A Wrinkle in Time,* Mrs. L'Engle describes the situation of several children who find a way of traveling through space and time.[14] What has happened is that Charles Wallace (who is about six years old) and Meg (who is about ten or so) have lost their father. He is a scientist who has strangely disappeared from his laboratory at home. Precocious Charles Wallace finds reason to believe that his father is being held captive by some sinister force in the universe. He also is able to figure out the method which his father developed for traveling bodily through the galaxy: it is called "wrinkling," but you will have to read the book to find out more about it. At any rate, Charles Wallace, Meg, and her boyfriend Calvin (and I promise that no theological message is implied in my mention of this last name!) start on an expedition through space and time to rescue the beleaguered scientist. They soon find out that the whole universe is under attack by a dark and malignant force, and that some planets have wholly succumbed to it. After some exciting exploration and detective work, they find that their father-scientist is being held on one particular planet which has capitulated to the evil influence. The emissary of cosmic evil on that planet is known as the "man with red eyes," and they know that they must confront him.

The adventuresome triad arrives on the planet just outside its capital city, in a suburb filled with neatly organized homes and well-behaved children at play. In fact, at the very time the three earthlings land, all of the tots who were bouncing their balls in unison up and down on the sidewalks are simultaneously called to come for supper: all of the mothers up and down the street pop their heads out of the front doors and gather them in. Not taking time to ponder this curiously uniform behavior, the rescue party makes its way toward the large metallic skyscraper in the center of the city where they were sure to face the man with red eyes. Consider the account:

> As they approached the end of the room their steps slowed. Before them was a platform. On the platform was a chair, and on the chair was a man.
>
> What was there about him that seemed to contain all the coldness and darkness they had felt as they plunged through the Black Thing on their way to this planet?
>
> "I have been waiting for you, my dears," the man said. His voice was kind and gentle, not at all the cold and frightening voice Meg had expected. It took

her a moment to realize that though the voice came from the man, he had not opened his mouth or moved his lips at all, that no real words had been spoken to fall upon her ears, that he had somehow communicated directly into their brains.

"But how does it happen that there are three of you?" the man asked.

Charles Wallace spoke with harsh boldness, but Meg could feel him trembling. "Oh, Calvin just came along for the ride."

"Oh, he did, did he?" For a moment there was a sharpness to the voice that spoke inside their minds. Then it relaxed and became soothing again. "I hope that it has been a pleasant one so far."

"Very educational," Charles Wallace said.

"Let Calvin speak for himself," the man ordered.

Calvin growled, his lips tight, his body rigid. "I have nothing to say."

Meg stared at the man in horrified fascination. His eyes were bright and had a reddish glow. Above his head was a light, and it glowed in the same manner as the eyes, pulsing, throbbing, in steady rhythm.

Charles Wallace shut his eyes tightly. "Close your eyes," he said to Meg and Calvin. "Don't look at the light. Don't look at his eyes. He'll hypnotize you."

"Clever, aren't you? Focusing your eyes would, of course, help," the soothing voice went on, "but there are other ways, my little man. Oh, yes, there are other ways."

"If you try it on me I shall kick you!" Charles Wallace said. It was the first time Meg had ever heard Charles Wallace suggesting violence.

"Oh, will you, indeed, my little man?" The thought was tolerant, amused, but four men in dark smocks appeared and flanked the children.

"Now, my dears," the words continued, "I shall of course have no need of recourse to violence, but I thought perhaps it would *save you pain* if I showed you at once that it would do you no good to try to oppose me. You see, what you will soon realize is that there is no need to fight me. Not only is there no need, but you will not have the slightest *desire* to do so. For why should you wish to fight someone who is here only to *save you pain and trouble?* For you, as well as for the rest of all the *happy, useful people* on this planet, I, in my own strength, am willing to assume all the pain, all the responsibility, all the burdens of thought and decision."

"We will make our own decisions, thank you," Charles Wallace said.

"But of course. And our decisions will be one, yours and mine. Don't you see how much better, how much *easier* for you that is? Let me show you. Let us say the multiplication table together."

"No," Charles Wallace said.

"Once one is one. Once two is two. Once three is three."

"Mary had a little lamb!" Charles Wallace shouted. "Its fleece was white as snow!"[14]

Charles Wallace breaks into a nursery rhyme to block out the hypnotic signals.

Now I suppose that my interpretation of this encounter is fairly obvious. I take this "man with red eyes" to be a type of *false Christ*. His call was for the children to relinquish the burden of thought and decision to him, to let him think for them. After all, he promised to make them "happy" and "useful" people, just like all of the others on that planet.

However, as we have already seen, no one should believe anything because doing so will make him happy, useful, spiritual, or anything else—but only because he sees it as true. The *real Christ* does not offer an end to intellectual hard work; He calls us right back to it.

Another scenario comes to mind regarding this same basic issue. In *The Screwtape Letters,* C. S. Lewis has old uncle Screwtape, who is sort of a general of demons in hell, writing to his nephew Wormwood, who is an apprentice demon trying to lead a young man astray. The very first letter in this highly unusual correspondence contains advice for Wormwood to discontinue the attempt to *reason* his victim to hell, to stop leading him to literature which contains arguments to the effect that Christianity is *false.* Here is what shrewd old Screwtape writes:

> The trouble with argument is that it moves the whole struggle onto the Enemy's own ground. [And here "Enemy" refers to God.] He [the Enemy] can argue too; whereas in really practical propaganda of the kind I am suggesting He has been shown for centuries to be greatly the inferior of Our Father Below. By the very act of arguing, you awake the patient's reason; and once it is awake, who can foresee the result? Even if a particular train of thought can be twisted so as to end in our favor, you will find that you have been strengthening in your patient the fatal habit of attending to universal issues and withdrawing his attention from the stream of immediate sense experiences. Teach him to call it "real life" and don't let him ask what he means by "real."[15]

The rest of this horrifying letter needs to be read in context. The message, however, is abundantly clear. God is the Lord of truth and argument, the Master of giving reasons—and we should not fear the intellectul process. Intellect is an ally of genuine religion, not a nemesis.

Interestingly, this point finds corroboration in the way II Corinthians 10:5 is translated in the Revised Standard Version: "We destroy *arguments* and every proud obstacle to knowledge of God, and take every thought captive to obey Christ."[16] *Arguments,* of course, are simply *reasons for beliefs,* premises for conclusions. Anytime we accept a belief as true on the basis of reasons, we are embracing an argument—whether or not we know that this is what we are doing. Argument in this sense is *the only legitimate way to take a thought captive.* As the vignette from Madeleine L'Engle and the excerpts from C. S. Lewis intimate, we must give reasons for our beliefs. There is no way to destroy an argument but on its own grounds; one must come up with better reasons and superior logic. One cannot have faith enough to go around an adverse argument, or close one's eyes to it. Then it will have won, it will have destroyed him, so to say.

There is absolutely no inconsistency at all between Christian commitment and seeking the truth. In fact, it could be argued that one draws life from the other, that they are inseparably bound together. Commitment to Christ gives us a focus for truth; and concern for truth keeps us from accepting false substitutes for Christ. In his book, *The*

Drama of Atheist Humanism, Henri de Lubac suggests that one great fallacy of the modern age is not simply that it has rejected Christ, but that it has abandoned Socrates.[17] In so far as *Socrates* represents the *love of truth,* de Lubac is saying that, when regard for objective, rational truth declined in our age, the possibility of maintaining Christianity as a *true* religion was undermined. Commitment to Christ is then caricatured as purely emotional or subjective. Until our age recovers the high regard for real truth, calls to genuine religious commitment may continue to fall on deaf ears.

It is part of our role as Christian educators, therefore, to help restore the love of truth and the earnest search after it. And we must not breathe even the slightest hint that there is a dichotomy between the intellectual life properly understood and the religious life. Indeed, because of our devotion to Christ, we should not merely endeavor to *know* and *teach* the truth in whatever area it may be found, but to *love* the truth and to inspire others to love it too. After all, people are impelled not so much by what they *know,* but by what they *love.* And to love truth is to love something of Christ.

V. Conclusion

I suppose that the preceding comments may seem hopelessly idealistic. While I agree that they are idealistic, I do not think that they are hopeless. Every community must have ideals on which to set its sites and by which to unify its activities. We may not always live up to our ideal, but the existence of the ideal is of supreme importance. I personally cannot think of any vision more exhilarating or more worthwhile. It deserves the best stewardship of our intellectual talents, demands the best efforts in our performances, and elicits some of the deepest longings of our hearts. We need the ideal—we need periodically to reflect on what it means for our God to be *the Lord of all truth.* For in this there is great hope!

NOTES

1. Tertullian, *On the Prescription against Heretics,* ch. 7.

2. See E. G. Bewkes, *et al.*, and J. C. Keene, *The Western Heritage of Faith and Reason,* 2nd ed. (New York: Harper and Row, 1963).

3. Biblical passages which suggest this title include: Dt 32:4; Ps 31:5; Ps 36:15; Isa 65:16.

4. This phrase is Arthur Holmes'; see *All Truth is God's Truth* (Grand Rapids: Eerdmans, 1977).

5. See Henri Frankfort, *et al.*, *The Intellectual Adventure of Ancient Man* (Chicago: University of Chicago Press, 1946).

6. See Jacques Maritain, *Education at the Crossroads* (New Haven: Yale University Press, 1943), p. 24.

7. Arthur Holmes, *The Idea of a Christian College* (Grand Rapids: Eerdmans, 1975), p. 44.

8. A proposition is understood here as an abstract cognitive entity, the conceptual content of a sentence.

9. Robert Pirsig, *Zen and the Art of Motorcycle Maintenance* (New York: Bantam Books, 1974).

10. Holmes, *Christian College,* pp. 78-79.

11. Holmes' phrase in *All Truth*, ch. 5.

12. W. K. Clifford, *Lectures and Essays* (1879), reprinted in Brody, ed., *Readings in the Philosophy of Religion* (Englewood Cliffs: Prentice-Hall, 1974), pp. 241-242.

13. John Stuart Mill, *On Liberty*, ch. 2.

14. Madeleine L'Engle, *A Wrinkle in Time* (New York: Dell Pub. Co., 1962), pp. 120-22; some italics mine.

15. C. S. Lewis, *The Screwtape Letters* (New York: Macmillan, 1961), p. 8.

16. Italics mine.

17. Henri de Lubac, S. J., *The Drama of Atheist Humanism* (New York: New American Library, 1963).

Methodist History and Doctrine

5

JOHN WESLEY'S VIEW OF FALLEN MAN
John Chongnahm Cho

It was 1959 that I came to know and love Dr. Dennis F. Kinlaw, when he ministered as a visiting professor in Seoul Theological Seminary. It was my high privilege to work as his interpreter. It is Dr. Kinlaw through whom my interest was first drawn to the theology of Wesley, and who inspired and supported my further theological training in America. The friendship with him and his family has been a source of encouragement and blessing for my ministry for which I am ever grateful to God.

I. Introduction

Dr. William Hordern, a Lutheran scholar, once said, "I was raised on the assertion that Wesley had no theology and that he taught a religion of experience alone, but it is now evident that Wesley was a powerful theologian."[1] He further observed that in recent years many Methodists have returned to Wesley and have rediscovered John Wesley as a great theologian.

At this point, *The Rediscovery of John Wesley* by George C. Cell, which was published in 1935, made a recognizable contribution toward the rediscovery of Wesley as a theologian. Cell points out that Wesley was misunderstood as though he were of Liberal Arminianism, being far from the theology of the Reformers, and he made so little contribution to the history of Christian thought. But through his study Cell asserted that Wesley was rather reaffirming the main principles of the Reformer's theology and has overcome the decline of Christianity which came under the influence of the Enlightenment.[2] The theme of Cell has been well accepted and developed further by later Wesleyan scholars.[3]

Skevington Wood writes, "*sola gratia* and *sola fide* were the twin watchwords of the Reformation, and they found an echo in Wesley's preaching."[4] That is to say, Wesley regards the problem of original sin very seriously. For Wesley "the starting point of the Gospel is the total inability of the sinner to make the tiniest contribution toward his own salvation."[5] It is the interest of this paper to see how Wesley theologized the doctrine of *original sin*. What is the result of Adam's sin upon his descendants? What is the condition of fallen man in his relationship to the gospel?

For Wesley to preach the whole council of God as it is revealed in the Bible, "There must be a clear association of God's sovereignty and man's responsibility."[6] This was Wesley's position. Then on what ground does Wesley maintain such a position concerning fallen man? What are the methodology and dynamics of his theologizing?

II. Adam's Sin and its Effects Upon the Human Race

Wesley believed that Adam was created in the image of God. God's image consisted of a threefold character: the natural, the political, and the moral image.[7] Therefore, according to Wesley, the nature of man is spirit or soul, which includes endowment with the faculties of reason, will, and liberty. Man has dominion over the lower creatures. Furthermore, man, in his original condition, lived in righteousness and true holiness. Man was full of love which was the sole principle of his tempers, thoughts, words, and actions.[8] From the right use of all his faculties, man maintained a continued relationship of love and obedience to God.[9]

But Wesley believed that when Adam disobeyed God, he fell from the original state in which God created him. Wesley believed that this disobedience or rebellion of Adam was the result of the misuse of liberty and that the responsibility rests with Adam, not with God.[10]

In consequence of his rebellion, he lost the life of God. He was separated from Him in union with whom his spiritual life consisted.[11] Man's faculties of reason, will and liberty were then corrupted and man's love and obedience to God were replaced by self-love and self-will.[12]

Adam was primogenitor and the federal head of mankind, according to Wesley.[13] Therefore, when Adam sinned, the effect was upon all human kind, for "Adam's first sin was the sin of a public person" representing all his descendants.[14]

Wesley believed that all men are therefore totally corrupt and children of wrath. Prior to any act of his own, each descendant of Adam shares in the depravity and guilt of the original sin. Wesley writes:

> This is undoubtedly true; therefore God does not look upon infants as innocent, but as involved in the guilt of Adam's sin; otherwise death, the punishment denounced against that sin, could not be inflicted upon them.[15]

This view of John Wesley was made more clear when he was confronted with the opposition of John Taylor. In 1740 John Taylor published a treatise, *The Scripture Doctrine of Original Sin Proposed to Free and Candid Examination*. Taylor was a learned Presbyterian minister. He was the pastor of a church in Norwich. He was the first president of the Presbyterian Theological College at Warrington until his death in 1761. Taylor was leaning toward Socinianism and denied original sin.[16] Wesley was very upset and said, if Taylor is right, "I cannot see that we have much need of Christianity." There would then be no room to talk about salvation.[17] In 1757 Wesley wrote a long treatise, *The Doctrine of Original Sin According to Scripture, Reason and Experience.*[18] A part of this treatise was written in a sermonic form again in 1759 under the title, "Original Sin."[19] In this treatise, Wesley refuted Taylor's position and maintained strongly both the corruption of human nature and the original guilt. Wesley writes:

> "We are children of wrath by nature; we were born fallen creatures; we came into the world sinners, and as such, liable to wrath in consequence of the fall of our first father."[20]

"Children of wrath" here means that they are liable to some degree of wrath and punishment. Therefore, it involves the guilt of original sin. Wesley says, "It is undeniable that guilt is imputed to all for the sin of Adam."[21] Wesley argues that the fact that all mankind in all ages have died, including infants themselves, proves this, for "none is liable to death, but for sin."[22] He further argues, if infants are not sinners how is Christ the Savior of all men? If you deny that original sin of infants, it would mean that God punishes innocent, guiltless creatures.[23] "Then it follows that infants are sinners; that they are lost, and without Christ, are undone forever."[24]

We notice that Wesley makes a pastoral distinction between original sin, imputed guilt and inherent depravity. Wesley writes:

> We have a clear evidence both of what Divines term, original sin imputed, and of original sin inherent. The former is the sin of Adam, so far reckoned ours as to constitute us in some degree guilty; the later, a want of original righteousness and a corruption of nature.[25]

Wesley also makes a distinction between the guilt of Adam and the original guilt of his descendants.

> In one sense, indeed Adam's sin was not ours. It was not our personal fault, our actual transgression. But in another sense it was ours; it was the sin of our common representative: And, as such, St. Paul shows it is imputed to us and all his descendants.[26]

But to be sure, such a distinction should not be taken as though Wesley takes lightly the imputed guilt in mankind. Wesley believes that such a view which he expressed in his treatise is not only a truth agreeable to Scripture and reason, but a truth of the utmost importance.[27] This is a truth, according to Wesley, known only to "grace healed eyes,"[28] and the truth which heathens and blind natural men do not discern. Wesley thinks, "none of them [heathens] knew of his total corruption."[29] "But as soon as God opens the eyes of their understanding, they see the state they were in before."[30] He says, "This, therefore, is the first grand distinguishing point between Heathenism and Christianity."[31] This is Wesley's position.

How does Wesley then differ from the Calvinism of his day? Has he come to "the very edge of Calvinism?"[32] Another question is whether he maintains consistency in his teaching on original sin. Some interpreters of Wesley think that Wesley did not hold the guilt of original sin but only corruption of the nature. To answer these questions, more extended consideration must be given in the following pages.

III. The Present Condition of Fallen Man: Man in the State of Grace

Wesley usually begins his preaching of salvation with the condition of man. When he preached of "the justification by faith," Wesley stated:

> Thus by one man sin entered into the world, and death by sin. And so death passed upon all man, as being contained in him who was the common father and representative of us all. For as by one man's disobedience all were made sinners, so by that offence of one, judgment came upon all men to condemnation. In this state, we were, even all mankind, when God so loved the world, and He gave His only begotten Son.[33]

Again when he preached on the New Birth, Wesley stated:

> And in Adam all die, all humankind, all the children of men who were then in Adam's loins. The natural consequence of this is, that every descendant from him comes into the world spiritually dead, dead to God, wholly dead in sin; entirely void of the life of God; void of the image of God, of all that righteousness and holiness wherein Adam was created. Instead of this, every man born into the world now bears the image of the devil, in pride and self-will; the image of the beast, in sensual appetites and desires . . . the entire corruption of our nature.[34]

Wesley concluded this first section of his sermon with this. This, then, is the foundation of new birth.[35]

Hillman observes that it is "Wesley's normal procedure in evangelistic preaching to establish the sinfulness of the hearers and on this basis to offer then the grace of God."[36] Therefore, in Wesley, if the spiritual man finds favour with God, it is only by the Grace of God, but he believes that "the process of salvation begins when he becomes conscious of his sinfulness with conviction of sin.[37] Therefore Wesley in his sermon, "The Way to the Kingdom," preached that to enter into the Kingdom, first, repent, that is, know oneself.

> Know thyself to be a sinner . . . . . .
> Know that corruption of thy inmost nature, ...
> Know that thou art corrupted in every power,

> in every faculty of thy soul, that thou art
> totally corrupted in every one of these . . . .
> Such is the inbred corruption of the heart,
> of thy very inmost nature.[38]

We observe here that Wesley is, as Hillman points out, concerned to describe the present condition of the sinner rather than original sin.[39] The question of the guilt of original sin and the idea of our original guilt imputed to man is not mentioned in his preaching.[40] This brings some questions to the mind of interpreters of Wesley. Would it mean, then, that Wesley had an inconsistency in his teaching on the original sin? Some of Wesley's interpreters thought that Wesley did not believe in original guilt, but only the corruption of the nature. They thought Wesley maintained the guilt of personal sin only. They thought that Wesley held the doctrine of partial depravity rather than total depravity by the fall. For Wesley mentioned elsewhere that part of the image of God (natural image) remained even after the fall.[41]

However, this writer thinks that such an interpretation is not just to Wesley. Wesley, I think, did not have inconsistency in his mind. To support this view, we must bear this in our mind that his treatise on original sin, in which he strongly maintains the original guilt as well as total corruption of human kind by the fall, was written in a later year (1757) than those sermons. Moreover, we note that Wesley preached these sermons repeatedly in the 1750's.[42] Wesley re-edited those sermons in his latter years, for example in 1771 and again in 1787-8, rearranging the order of sermons. But Wesley made no remarks anywhere on any change he made in his teaching. This seems to prove that in the mind of Wesley there was no change or inconsistency concerning the doctrine of original sin. Cox believes "it has not been proved that Wesley changed his mind."[43] How should we then correlate these words which appear to be different?

"At this point," Furhman says, "it is necessary to point out that there is another view of man in Wesley's writings. Alongside his view of fallen man as totally corrupt and guilty of Adam's sin, he lays out his view of fallen man as seen in the state of grace."[44] That is to say that Wesley presents the condition of man in a much milder way, saying some of the image of God even now is to be found in the worst of man.[45] No man, however primitive, ever existed without a measure of free will; man is morally responsible for his actions.[46] Wesley presupposes that he is already in a state of grace, namely, under the operation of the prevenient grace. As Cox says, "Wesley saw fallen man as living, not now under a covenant of works, but under a covenant of grace,"[47] because of the grace of God whence our salvation is free in all and free for all.[48] Therefore, Furhman points out, as opposed as these viewpoints seem to be, Wesley correlates them with his idea of prevenient grace. Wesley would not see opposition between the two, but on the contrary, the closest connection.[49]

Wesley must have presupposed when he preached, that the fallen man is already the recipient of God's grace—prevenient grace. For Wesley believes that "by preventing grace the guilt of original sin is cancelled." "By the righteousness of Christ the original guilt is cancelled as soon as men are sent into the world.[50] "There is a measure of free-will supernaturally restored to every man."[51]

It seems important therefore for us to observe, as Robert E. Cushman points out, that Wesley makes no sharp divorcement between nature and grace in his description of the fallen man because man's whole existence is enveloped by the wooing activity of God. Nevertheless the distinction between nature and grace in fallen man is not dissolved.[52] To state this in another way, in Wesley, as Rogers says, "While nature and grace are thus distinct Wesley conceives them to be in an intimate and complementary relationship in a vital and functional unity."[53] This approach appears to be a characteristic of Wesley's theologizing. Chiles says that in Wesley's view of original sin, the "irreconcilable tension" between sin and grace forms the bedrock of his theology. This is the dynamic of Wesley's theologizing. And if this is neglected, interpretation of Wesley's position inevitably becomes ambiguous or compromising, being unjust to Wesley.[54]

We mentioned earlier that at the close of the nineteenth century, some Wesleyan students rejected the original guilt. It appears to be that they came to reject original guilt because they tended to view man's responsive freedom in anthropological rather than soteriological setting. They departed from Wesley in their theological methodology, so as to derive another conclusion.[55]

IV. Conclusion: Dynamics of Wesley's Theologizing and its Significance
We have observed that Wesley's main thrust of his preaching is to declare the saving grace of God, the whole counsel of God, and anthropology is the existential reference. Therefore, Wesley's doctrine of the fallen man, as Lindström notes, is necessarily linked up with the essential purpose of the Gospel, which is from God's grace instead of from man's free-will."[56] As Starkey points out, "soteriology is prior to anthropology in Wesley."[57] Wesley develops the doctrine of the fallen man in the soteriological setting. At this point, his idea of prevenient grace takes a very important role, but it is not the interest of this paper to discuss his doctrine of prevenient grace.

We have also observed that in his view of the fallen man, Wesley maintains the total depravity of human nature and the original guilt by the fall of Adam. He is with Paul and Augustine on this. At this point there is widespread agreement among interpreters of Wesley's theology.[58] But this collective approach is combined in Wesley with the individual approach in which he maintains that each individual is also responsible, with his idea of prevenient grace. In this approach, Wesley makes no sharp divorcement between nature and grace in the fallen man, but he keeps the tension between the assertion of sin and the promptings of grace. Wesley finds the dynamics of his theologizing in the irreconcilable tension which he maintains between the assertion of sin and the promptings of grace of God, with his idea of preventing grace. Therefore, Wesley interprets in a uniquely significant way the man *coram deo,* because he views the fallen man as a sinner because of Adam, at the same time as a recipient of grace because of Christ.

Such an approach by Wesley reveals its significance when it is applied to the relationship between God's grace and man's responsibility for salvation. At this point, I think Wesley makes a significant contribution to theology. Wesley in his sermon, "On Working Out Our Own Salvation," based on the text, Phil. 2:12-13, maintains the idea of *sola gratia* and total depravity of the fallen man. He says that without God it is not possible for man to do anything well. But Wesley, at the same time, maintains that man is able to work and man must be responsible since God worketh in man:

> Yea, it is impossible for any man, for any that is born of a woman, unless God worketh in him.
> Seeing all men are by nature, not only sick, but dead in trespasses and in sins, it is not possible for them to do anything well till God raises them from the dead. . . . Yet this is no excuse for those who continue in sin. . . . For allowing that all the souls of men are dead in sin by nature, this excuses none. Seeing there is no man that is in a state of mere nature; there is no man, unless he has quenched the Spirit, that is wholly void of the grace of God. . . . You can do something, through Christ strengthening you.[59]

Thus Wesley is able to maintain man's responsibility for his own salvation, without falling into Pelagianism. At the same time, Wesley does not fall into the difficulty which Augustianism and Calvinism enter. The working relationship between God's grace and man, in Wesley, is also distinguished from the synergism of the Roman Catholic, semi-pelagianism. For in Wesley, "First God works; therefore you can work."[60] Cox calls Wesley's view synergism in the framework of monergism.[61] L. Starkey calls it "evangelical synergism."[62] Wesley is able to hold such a view because of the dynamics of his theologizing which we observed. Wesley is able to solve the difficulty of the theologians of grace, like the Reformers, Augustine and Barth, even emphasizing the *sola gratia.*

Moreover, it would not be difficult for us to apprehend that it was this methodology and position which made Wesley safeguard the doctrine of the fallen man from the teaching of "stillness" of the Moravianism of his day, on the one hand, and from the teaching of "good works" of the Roman Catholic church on the other.

It seems also true that when this approach is applied to the doctrine of Christian life, it makes a constructive contribution. We note that Wesley is able to safeguard the doctrine of Christian life from both a shallow view of sin and pessimism of nature. For in Wesley Christian life is not understood as a smooth movement, like a train moving on the tracks, not taking seriously the sin problem. Wesley was conscious of even the grave result of the unconscious sin occasioned by the infirmities in the sanctified.[63] Therefore, in Wesley, repentance of believers is fully necessary. On the other hand, he was not pessimistic because of the gravity of sin, but he was optimistic about Christian life because of the promptings of God's grace, the blood of atonement of Christ "continually applied" for His children who depend on "His intercession for us."[64] This theological approach is well reflected in his sermon, "The Repentance of Believers," which was written in 1767. We could easily observe that an underlying presupposition of Wesley's theology here is the emphasis on the grace—"where sin increased, grace abounded all the more,"[65] and this is taken in the dialectical tension between the assertion of sin and the promptings of grace. This is the dynamic of his theologizing. Therefore, in Wesley, salvation of man begins by the grace of God and is maintained by grace, and will be completed by the grace of God. Man, however, is responsible only "if the time and opportunity is given."[66] For the rest it is God who does the work for man, so long as man is in the faith relationship with Christ, the High Priest. Wesley preaches:

> Thus it is, that in the children of God, repentance and faith exactly answer each other. By repentance we feel the sin remaining in our hearts and cleaving to our words and actions. By faith, we receive the power of God in Christ, purifying our hearts, cleansing our hands. By repentance we are still sensible that we deserve punishment for all our tempers, and words, and actions; by faith, we are conscious that our Advocate with the Father is continually turning aside all condemnation and punishment from us. Repentance says, "without Him I can do nothing." Faith says, "I can do all things through Christ strengthening me."[67]

Thus, in Wesley, "the repentance (i.e. the assertion of his sin) and faith (i.e. the assertion of grace) are full as necessary, in order for our continuance and growth in grace . . . to our entering into the Kingdom."[68] But to be sure, Wesley keeps this tension with much more emphasis on the grace, for "where sin increased, grace abounded all the more (Rom 5:20)." Here is the optimism about grace in Wesley which supercedes the pessimism about the sin nature,[69] wherein Wesley is to be distinguished from Luther and the neo-reformation theologians. Their doctrine of the fallen man often tends to view the Christian life as a constant struggle between sin and grace, *simul justus et peccator* or as "impossible possibility."

Furthermore, we would note some significant contributions that Wesley could make in the contemporary theological enterprises when his approach and position are applied. For example, Wesley's position on the fallen man would offer a constructive help toward the theology of missions.

First of all, Wesley's theology would insist on the one hand upon the universal need of salvation by God's grace because of his assertion of the depth and universality of man's sin, and on the other hand, emphasize the possibility and hope of salvation for all men, because of his assertion of the free grace of God in all and for all. But, in doing so, Wesley's theology would safeguard the doctrine of salvation by grace alone from the danger of both Universalism and divine determinism, because it is Wesley's position that maintains the responsibility in the fallen man who is already in the state of grace. Thus, in Wesley, the hope of salvation for all men is emphasized and yet the responsibility of man and the Church's mission is equally stressed. In this way, Wesley's theology would bring a welcome relief, soundly biblical deliverance from the dilemma which resides in the house of Lutheran and Barthian theology.

Secondly, Wesley's position would bring another welcome contribution in the search for a solution from the dilemma at the issue of the point of contact: continuity or discontinuity between God (the Gospel) and man (culture) in missions. It appears that there is a dilemma in the theology of missions because if one maintains the continuity between God and man, it often tends to identify nature and grace as do Romanticists, Pantheists, Deists and modern liberal Humanists; on the other hand, when one maintains the discontinuity between the two, as do the Reformers, Barthians and Kraemer, it leads to the impasse in his finding the point of contact, dialogue and the ground for apologetic approach in missions. This is a perennial issue in the cross cultural missions. But, when we are true to Wesley's position and approach, a healthy solution will be found from this dilemma. For Wesley's approach is not "either/or" in its abstract inference, but, "both/and," a correlation of the two into a creative synthesis, keeping a dialectical tension between grace and nature.

So keeping the tension (discontinuity) between God and man, Wesley finds the point of contact in terms of the work of grace which is initiated by God and already operative in the fallen man. By doing so, Wesley, without identifying nature with grace, provides the point of contact in missions and, moreover his theology gives hope and encouragement in missions because it finds the ground of missions in the operation of God's grace in the world. Thus, Wesley's position, when true to its own dynamics of theologizing, will provide a respectable, relevant solution to the contemporary theology of missions.

It may be reasonably assumed that Wesley's approach and position will also provide constructive contributions in other contemporary theological frontiers. This represents a challenge to, and a responsibility for, the students of Wesley today and in the future.

NOTES

1. William Hordern, "Recent Trends in Systematic Theology" in *Canadian Journal of Theology,* vol. 3 (1961), p. 87.

2. George G. Cell, *The Rediscovery of John Wesley* (Nashville: Abingdon, 1946), pp. 5-9

3. William Cannon, *The Theology of John Wesley* (Nashville, Abingdon, 1946); H. Lindström, *Wesley and Sanctification* (London: The Epworth Press, 1946).

4. Skevington Wood, *John Wesley: the Burning Heart* (Grand Rapids: Eerdman, 1967), p. 220.

5. *Ibid.*, p. 230.

6. *Ibid.*, p. 150; see also "Thoughts Concerning Gospel Ministers" in *The Works of John Wesley,* ed. by Jackson, X, p. 456. (Hereafter the abbreviation WORKS will be used.)

7. *Standard Sermons of John Wesley,* ed. by Sugden, II, p. 228. (Hereafter the abbreviation STS will be used.) See WORKS, IX, pp. 293, 355, in which it appears that Wesley accepted Isaac Watts' view in *The Ruin and Recovery of Mankind.*

8. STS II, p. 228.

9. WORKS, VI, p. 243 (sermon, "The General Deliverance").

10. STS, II, p. 229; cf. WORKS, X, p. 468.

11. STS, II, p. 229, STS, I, p. 117.

12. STS, II, pp. 229-230.

13. For Adam as the primogenitor, STS, II, p. 230; also WORKS, V, pp. 224, 247. For Adam as the federal head, WORKS, IX, pp. 332, 427, 240.

14. WORKS, IX, p. 418.

15. WORKS, IX, p. 316.

16. STS, II, p. 207.

17. WORKS, IX, p. 194.

18. It is the long 269 page treatise contained in the WORKS, IX.

19. See STS, II, p. 207ff.

20. WORKS, IX, p. 419.

21. WORKS, IX, p. 426.

22. *Ibid.*

23. WORKS, IX, p. 428.

24. *Ibid.*

25. WORKS, IX, p. 420.

26. WORKS, IX, p. 418.

27. WORKS, IX, p. 429.

28. Colin Williams, *John Wesley's Theology Today* (New York: Abingdon, 1960), p. 52.

29. STS, II, p. 222.

30. STS, II, p. 215.

31. STS, II, p. 222.

32. WORKS, VIII, p. 285.

33. STS, I, pp. 117-18, sermon, "Justification by Faith" (1739); cf. STS, I, pp. 37-38, "Salvation by Faith" (1738).

34. STS, II, pp. 230-31, "New Birth" (1740); see also STS, I, p. 268, "The Circumcision of the Heart" (1733), and STS II, p. 223, "Original Sin," (1759).

35. *Ibid.*

36. Robert John Hillman, "Grace in the Preaching of Calvin and Wesley," unpublished Ph.D. dissertation at Fuller Theological Seminary, 1978, p. 63.

37. Lindström, *Wesley,* p. 33.

38. STS, I, pp. 155-156, "The Way to the Kingdom" (1742).

39. Hillman, dissertation, p. 69.

40. Charles A. Rogers, "The Concept of Prevenient Grace in the Theology of John Wesley," unpublished Ph.D. dissertation at Duke University, 1967, pp. 111-112.

41. WORKS, VI, p. 223, sermon, "On the Fall of Man."

42. See STS, II, p. 208f; II, p. 226.

43. Leo Cox, *John Wesley's Concept of Perfection* (Kansas City: Beacon Hill Press, 1964), p. 29. Wesley often made some remarks when he changed his view in his life. For example, see STS, I, p. 269 (The Circumcision of the Heart, on Faith); sermon on "Faith" I:11 (Of the Faith of the Servant); *Letters* V, pp. 358-59 (March 1768 On the Assurance of Faith). Note also that Wesley published these sermons (New Birth, Original Sin) in 1760 in the 4th volume.

44. Eldon R. Furhman, "The Wesleyan Doctrine of Grace in the Theology of John Wesley," unpublished Ph.D. dissertation at State University of Iowa, 1963, p. 105.

45. WORKS, VI, p. 223, "On the Fall of Man."

46. WORKS, X, pp. 457-459 "Thoughts Upon Necessity."

47. Cox, *Perfection*, p. 31.

48. WORKS, VII, p. 373, "Free Grace."

49. Wesley's argument is also well revealed in his sermon "On Working Out Our Own Salvation," in WORKS, VI, pp. 506-13.

50. *Letters,* VI, p. 240, cf. WORKS, VIII, 277, IX, 303.

51. WORKS, X, p. 240. Also see, WORKS, X, p. 392, "Some Remarks on Mr. Hill's Review of All the Doctrines Taught by John Wesley."

52. Robert Cushman, "Salvation for all: Wesley and Calvinism," in *Methodism*, ed. by W. K. Anderson (Nashville, The Methodist Publishing House, 1947), p. 110.

53. Rogers, dissertation p. 164.

54. Chiles, *Theological Transition in American Methodism: 1790-1935* (Nashville: Abingdon, 1965), pp. 120-21.

55. Some examples of this departure among Wesleyan students such as Watson, Miley and Knudson are shown in Chiles' book, *Transition*, p. 124ff.

56. Lindström, *Wesley*, p. 32.

57. L. Starkey Jr., "The Work of the Holy Spirit in the Theology of John Wesley," unpublished Ph.D. dissertation at Columbia University, 1953, p. 200.

58. See Cannon, *Theology*, p. 200ff. Robert E. Cushman, "Salvation for All" in *Methodism* ed. by Anderson, pp. 106-08. Lindström, *Wesley*, p. 12. L. Starkey Jr., dissertation, p. 124 ff. Cell, *Rediscovery*, pp. 25, 272. Chiles, *Transition*, p. 119. Furhman, dissertation, p. 105. Cox, *Perfection*, pp. 29, 47.

59. WORKS, VI. pp. 512-13.

60. WORKS, VI. p. 511.

61. Cox, *Perfection*, p. 43.

62. Starkey, dissertation, p. 116.

63. STS, II. 389; also see *A Plain Account of Christian Perfection* by Wesley, p. 52.

64. STS, II, p. 393.

65. Romans 5:20; see WORKS IX, p. 303.

66. STS, II, p. 456, "Scripture Way of Salvation." Here Wesley says, "Fruits (of repentance) . . . are only necessary conditionally, if there be time and opportunity for them; otherwise a man may be sanctified without them."

67. STS II, p. 394.

68. STS II, p. 380; the words in parenthesis are mine.

69. Williams, *Wesley's Theology*, p. 190.

6

JOHN WESLEY AND THE ISSUE OF AUTHORITY IN THEOLOGICAL PLURALISM

Allan Coppedge

In deepest appreciation to Dr. Dennis Kinlaw for modelling that Wesleyan ideal of disciplined mind and warm heart; for challenging me to be a part of the training of spiritual leadership in the Wesleyan tradition through teaching; for showing me how to think with a largeness of vision; and for personally investing in me through counsel and fellowship to assist me in being all God wants me to be.

The 1972 *Discipline of the United Methodist Church* contains the new theological position of Methodism adopted at the General Conference of the Church for that year. It is basically a statement of theological pluralism designed to acknowledge the existing theological climate of the Church. A major part of this doctrinal pluralism has to do with the question of the criteria for truth in Christian theology, and one aspect of being pluralistic is described in terms of a commitment to multiple authorities in religious matters. The "four norms for doctrinal formulations" that are laid down by the *Discipline* are Scripture, tradition, experience and reason. The use of these sources and guidelines for Christian theology is defined for us:

These four are interdependent; none can be defined unambiguously. They allow for, indeed they positively encourage, variety in United Methodist theologizing. Jointly, they have provided a broad and stable context for reflection and formulation. Interpreted with appropriate flexibility and self-discipline, they may instruct us as we carry forward our never-ending tasks of theologizing in The United Methodist Church.[1]

Although described somewhat ambiguously, the relationship of these several criteria to each other is pictured as that of four equally valid and authoritative standards. "These four norms for doctrinal formulation are not simply parallel and none can be subsumed by any other."[2] There is a reference to "a primacy that goes with Scripture," but the word "primacy" may mean various things to different people. Clearly in this context "primacy" is not used to mean final authority. The *Discipline* continues, "In practice, however, theological reflection may find its point of departure in tradition, 'experience,' or rational analysis. What matters most is that all four guidelines be brought to bear upon every doctrinal consideration."[3] While even traditional Protestant orthodoxy may bring to bear all four of the listed criteria in consideration of a doctrinal issue, the difference is that the United Methodist statement does not ever identify any one of the norms as the final authority for truth, and by not so doing clearly implies that there is no such ultimate criteria in religious matters. This has certainly not been the position of evangelical Protestantism, which from the time of the Reformation has clearly declared its faith in the final authority of the Scripture.

When multiple criteria for truth are used, even when referred to by the more imprecise term of "guidelines," certain problems inevitably arise when one of the adopted authorities comes into conflict with another. Which of the several "guidelines" then becomes the final authority in matters of truth? If one of the criteria is not designated as the ultimate authority by which the others must be judged right or wrong, then in practice the individual is left to decide, in each situation demanding a decision, which one of the criteria he chooses to make the authority for that particular choice. In reality, however, not one of the criteria actually becomes authoritative in any situation, because the final choice is always left to the individual. Each man becomes his own final authority in matters of truth.

The question that immediately faces many United Methodists in the twentieth century is, "Where does John Wesley fit into this discussion?" The frequent reference of those who are promoting theological pluralism to a "Wesleyan quadrilateral" would seem to indicate that Wesley himself used these four criteria in a similar manner. Yet, Wesley borrowed from the Church of England an Article of Religion on the sufficiency of the Holy Scriptures that was written during the Reformation age and included in the Articles for the Methodist Church of America which appears to align him with the Classical Protestant position regarding the final authority of the Scripture. Which is correct? Did Wesley view the four norms as co-ordinate authorities of equal value, or did he believe that the Scripture was the final authority in matters of truth? If the first is true, then it will be quite right to classify him as a strong supporter of at least this aspect of theological pluralism. If the second option is correct, then it will be very difficult to claim Wesley as the forerunner of contemporary theological pluralism. In fact, he might even be found to be a vocal opponent of the current doctrinal stance of Methodism.

Because the basic question is so intimately bound up with Wesley's attitude toward the Scripture, our study begins with the development of his views about the Word of God. Wesley's understanding of the role of the Bible was first shaped in the Epworth rectory under the influence of his father. Samuel Wesley had a deep personal commitment to the Scripture as the Word of God, and his own scholarly writings reflect his passion for the Bible.[4] An indication of its importance can be seen in his counsel that John not enter into Holy Orders unprepared, and the most significant part of this preparation was personal familiarity with the Bible, based on a knowledge of the text in the original languages. John later paid tribute to his father in a review of his early years:

> From a child I was taught to love and reverence the Scripure, the oracles of God; and next to these, to esteem the primitive Fathers, the writers of the three first centuries. Next after the primitive church I esteem our own, the Church of England, as the most scriptural national church in the world.[5]

If what John was taught was an accurate reflection of his father's conviction about the order of religious authority, then it is clear that for Samuel Wesley Scripture was to be given priority over tradition.

This crucial importance of the Bible was reinforced for John during the Oxford years by his reading of Jeremy Taylor's *The Rule and Exercises of Holy Living*. Taylor repeatedly returns for his base authority to the Word of God, which he confines to the Bible. All commandments and revelations, promises and threatenings, stories and sermons in the Bible belong to the Word of God, and even the best books of devotion or sermons cannot be compared with it. As Martin Schmidt rightly observes, "It was certainly of significance for John Wesley's development that in this book he was so strongly directed to the Bible."[6]

The relation of Scripture to authority was probably more specifically raised for Wesley at the time of his ordination. Receiving Holy Orders in the Church of England required subscription to the Thirty-nine Articles of Religion, and one of these Articles dealt with the role of Scripture in the Church. Wesley's correspondence with his parents during this time clearly indicates he was giving the Articles very careful attention. In particular Article XVII on Predestination raised enough problems for him to question whether or not he could in good conscience subscribe to the Articles without reservation.[7] After much consideration and a careful study of John Ellis' *A Defense of the Thirty-Nine Articles of the Church of England*.[8] Wesley was able to commit himself to the Articles, and later was to reaffirm that allegiance:

> In saying, 'I teach the doctrines of the Church of England', I do, and always did, mean . . . I teach the doctrines which are comprised in those Articles and

Homilies to which all the clergy of the Church of England solemnly profess to assert, and that in their plain, unforced, grammatical meaning.[9]

It was Article VI on the Holy Scriptures that specifically spelled out the Anglican position on religious authority:

Holy Scripture containeth all things necessary to Salvation: so that whatsoever is not read therein, nor may be proved thereby, is not to be required of any man, that it should be believed as an Article of faith, or to be thought requisite or necessary to Salvation.[10]

The Article then makes a distinction between the canonical books "of whose authority was never any doubt in the Church," and the apocryphal books. The latter are read by the Church "for example of life and instruction of manners; but it doth not apply them to establish any Doctrine." By this the Church of England aligned itself with Classical Protestantism's commitment to *sola scriptura*. In addition to the declaration that the Scriptures contain all things necessary for salvation, the Article makes it clear that no doctrine is to "be believed as an article of faith" unless it may be read in the Bible or proved thereby. So by this declaration of faith the Holy Scriptures were definitely established as final authority in the Church, and clearly distinguished from tradition.

A standard interpretation of the Articles in Wesley's day was Bishop Gilbert Burnet. In discussing this Article Burnet points out that the important point to be established is "the rule of this faith." He then shows how the Church of England differs from the Roman Church:

We . . . affirm, that the scriptures are a complete rule of faith, and that the whole Christian religion is contained in them, and no where else; and although we make great use of tradition, especially that which is most ancient and nearest the source, to help us to a clear understanding of the scriptures; yet as to matters of faith we reject all oral tradition . . . and we refuse to receive any doctrine, that is not either expressly contained in scripture, or clearly proved from it.[11]

The fact that the Scripture was recognized in the Church of England as the final authority in all matters of doctrine and practice was certainly not lost upon the conscientious young Wesley as he poured over the Articles of Religion in preparation for his ordination. Further, the very action of subscribing to the Articles at that time is a very strong indicator that Wesley was beginning to make the Bible his "complete rule" in matters of religious authority.

In looking back over early Methodism Wesley pinpointed 1729 as the year in which he "began not only to read but to study the Bible, as the one, the only standard of truth, and the only model of pure religion."[12] This was the year he began to meet with the Oxford Methodists for the serious study of certain key books, including the Greek Testament.

Although Heitzenrater has pointed out that the Oxford circle did not begin their more concentrated study of the Bible until 1734-35,[13] still 1729 is a significant point at which a fresh appreciation of the Scriptures is realized by Wesley. Yet, when Wesley wrote in 1766 that it was the year 1729 in which he began to study the Bible as "the only standard of truth," even he may be placing the date too early. That certainly was his position in 1766, but in 1729 he still had not finished working through two thorny issues related to authority, viz., the relation of Scripture to experience, which was to pertain to his struggle with the mystics in the mid-1730's, and the relation of Scripture to tradition, which was to relate to his evaluation of the Early Church during his sojourn in Georgia.

The first of these questions to be answered, i.e., the relationship of experience to Scripture, is wrapped up with Wesley's involvement with the mystics. Robert Tuttle has pointed out that between 1732-1735 Wesley became heavily influenced by the speculative mysticism of William Law. During this time Wesley traveled several times to London for personal interviews with Law. Wesley had been attracted to Law by his books *A Serious Call to a Devout and Holy Life* and *Christian Perfection,* but by the time Law had become Wesley's spiritual director in the mid-thirties he had become a convert to the German mysticism of Tauler and Boehme. Under this influence Wesley began to search after salvation and assurance by means of contemplation. Here the emphasis was upon personal experience of God according to the mystical scheme of inner penance.[14] Wesley summarized the views of the mystics in a letter to his brother Samuel in November, 1736, in which he pointed out his chief objection was that they rejected the means of grace as God's scripturally ordained instruments for communicating His favor to men. Wesley synthesized the mystics' approach:

> All means are not necessary for all men; therefore each person must use such means, and such only, as he finds necessary for him. But since we can never attain our end by being wedded to the same means; therefore we must not obstinately cleave unto anything, lest it become an hindrance, not an help. Observe, farther, when the end is attained, the means cease.[15]

One of the chief means was the Scripture, which the mystics bypassed: "The Scripture they need not read; for it is only His letter with whom they converse face to face." It was this view of the means of grace, and the Scriptures in particular, that Wesley came to see in Georgia as the rock which nearly shipwrecked all his faith. On his return voyage to England he penned his evaluation of those who placed experience above Scripture:

> All other enemies of Christianity are triflers; the Mystics are the most dangerous of its enemies. They stab it in the vitals; and its most serious professors are most likely to fall by them. May I praise Him who hath snatched me out of this fire.[16]

It is important to realize that Wesley was rejecting the mystics' emphasis upon experience, because they set aside the means of grace. Just as important, however, is the underlying reason that Wesley placed such a high premium on the means of grace. They were crucial in his eyes because they were the "scripturally ordained" means of grace:

> According to this, according to the decision of holy writ, all who desire the grace of God are to wait for it in the means which He hath ordained; in using, not in laying them aside.[17]

The authority for evaluating their importance was the Bible, rather than experience or tradition. So that by the time he returned from Georgia, the Scriptures had become the touchstone by which he tried all opinions.

This same question arose again when Wesley had to confront a mystical quietism in the early years of the revival. The debated question was how to wait upon God? With the means of grace or without them? Wesley responded:

> It cannot possibly be conceived, that the Word of God should give no direction in so important a point; or, that the Son of God . . . should have left us undetermined with regard to a question wherein our salvation is so nearly concerned. And, in fact, He hath not left us undetermined; He hath shown us the way wherein we should go. We have only to consult the oracles of God; to inquire what is written there; and, if we simply abide by their decision, there can be no possible doubt remain.[18]

While he made clear his position on the necessity of means of grace, it must also be observed that Wesley left no doubt as to why he took this view. It was the position of Scripture, and that for him was determinative.

The second issue with which Wesley continued to grapple after 1729 was the relation of Scripture to the tradition of the Early Church. During the time of his missionary service he was heavily influenced by reading William Cave's *Primitive Christianity*,[19] and for a time apparently began to place the tradition of the first three or four centuries on a par with the authority of Scripture. But while still in Georgia he also read Bishop William Beveridge's *Synodikon*, which convinced him that much of the Early Church tradition was not of apostolic origin, and that he could not place tradition, even that which was closest to the New Testament Church, on the same level of authority as the Scripture.[20] He rejoiced on his return to England that he had been delivered from the error of "making antiquity a co-ordinate rather than a subordinate rule with Scripture."[21]

So by the first of 1738 Wesley had squarely faced the question of the relation of Scripture to both experience and tradition, and he had settled the issue for himself that Scripture was to be the undisputed final authority in all religious matters. He wrote at this time to Lady Cox, "To anyone who asketh me concerning myself or these whom I rejoice to call my brethren, what our principles are, I answer clearly, We have no principles but those revealed in the Word of God."[22] The following year he responded to some reservations about his conduct in promoting the revival, and he clearly justified his actions upon the authority of Scripture:

> If by catholic principles you mean any other than scriptural, they weigh nothing with me. I allow no other rule, whether of faith or practice, than the Holy Scriptures. But on scriptural principles I do not think it hard to justify whatever I do. God in Scripture commands me, according to my power, to instruct the ignorant, reform the wicked, confirm the virtuous. Man forbids me to do this in another's parish; that is, in effect, to do it all; seeing I have now no parish of my own, nor probably ever shall. Whom then shall I hear? God or man?[23]

A convincing demonstration of how the Scripture served as final authority for Wesley at this time is found in the way he dealt with theological issues just prior to his evangelical conversion. As Wesley wrestled from March to May, 1738, with a new definition of faith and a different understanding of justification, his intellectual and spiritual pilgrimage was under the heavy influence of Peter Bohler. Although Bohler was both persuasive and persistent, Wesley was not to be convinced by reasoned argument alone, but began to test Bohler's views against the Bible:

> The next morning I began the Greek testament again, resolving to abide by 'the law and the testimony'; and being confident that God would hereby show me whether this doctrine was of God.[24]

A month later Wesley struggled to comprehend Bohler's assertion that conversion could be instantaneous, and again he turned to the Scripture:

> I could not comprehend what he spoke of an instantaneous work. I could not understand how this faith should be given in a moment. I searched the Scriptures again touching this very thing, particularly the Acts of the Apostles: but, to my utter astonishment, found scarce any so slow as that of St. Paul, who was three days in the pangs of the new birth.[25]

It was this confidence in the authority of Scripture that made it possible for Wesley in future years to invite others to convince him of a different view, but only from the Bible. In the preface to his *Sermons*, which he described as "what I find in the Bible concerning the way to heaven," Wesley indicated by what standard he is willing to be corrected:

> I trust whereinsoever I have mistaken, my mind is open to conviction. I sincerely desire to be better informed. Point out a better way than I have known. Show me it is so, by plain proof of Scripture.[26]

The issue of the final authority of Scripture was settled none too soon. The great revival of the eighteenth century had been going only a few months before major doctrinal questions arose, and as in so many theological disputes the root issue was one of authority, i.e., how was this matter to be settled. This first theological controversy of the revival provided a unique opportunity for Wesley to test his own recently established commitment to the Scripture as the final authority for Christians. It arose in the closing weeks of 1739 and the first half of 1740, when Wesley found himself occupied at the Fetter Lane Society in a doctrinal disagreement with the Moravians.

When he arrived that fall from Bristol, he immediately realized he had a major problem:

> The first person I met there was one (Mrs. Turner) whom I had left strong in faith and zealous of good works; but she now told me Mr. Molther had fully convinced her she never had any faith at all; and had advised her, till she received faith, to be 'still,' ceasing from outward works; which she had accordingly done, and did not doubt but in a short time she should find the advantage of it.[27]

That evening he heard Mr. Bray commending this same "stillness," and speaking against the danger of outward works, attendance at church, and the sacrament. Behind these testimonies stood the influence of Philip Henry Molther, a former tutor to the son of Count Zinzendorf, who had been ordained as a missionary to Pennsylvania. Arriving in London *en route*, he was anxious to bring the society there under stronger Moravian influence. He taught a kind of "Quietism" called "stillness" and persuaded many that the faith they professed was not true faith, and that they must remain "still," without using any means of grace, until they were given faith.[28]

Wesley recognized the problem as a form of antinomianism that was rapidly becoming a threat to all he had designed to promote holines of heart and life, and he took steps to correct it. He had a conference with the Moravian leaders, Molther and Augustus Spangenburg, in order to understand their position, after which he recorded in his Journal the differences between Molther and himself on the nature of faith, the way to faith, the manner of propagating the faith, and the fruits of Moravian effort in England. In addition he wrote what might be called certain "position papers" on his own views "with regard to the questions in dispute with the Moravians" and inserted them in the Journal. He dealt first with the questions of faith and assurance, and then with the doctrine of the true Church.[29]

Because Wesley recognized that the Moravians' position was contrary to Scripture, he immediately began to challenge it, and his attempts at correcting the problem began with a Scriptural base. He recorded that he began the year 1740 by endeavoring "to explain to our brethren the true,

Christian, Scriptural stillness, by largely unfolding those solemn words, 'Be still, and know that I am God.' ''[30] Throughout the spring Wesley continued to explain, in public and private, the Scriptures which had been misunderstood.[31] The base of the Moravian error was bypassing the means of grace in the same manner as the mystics. But Wesley had already worked through the implications of that view at Oxford and in Georgia; so he was not unprepared for the Moravians. From 2 Timothy 3:16, "All Scripture is given by inspiration of God," he explained the ordinances of God as means of grace:

> Although this expression of our church, 'means of grace,' be not found in the Scripture; yet, if the sense of it undeniably is, to cavil at the term is a mere strife of words. But the sense of it is undeniably found in Scripture. For God hath in Scripture ordained prayer, reading or hearing of Scripture, and receiving the Lord's Supper as the ordinary means of conveying His grace to man.[32]

Since the Scripture was final authority, to show that the means of grace were Biblical was to settle the matter for Wesley.

During the last week in June, at the height of the controversy, Wesley delivered a series of morning and evening expositions specifically designed to combat the Moravian influence. In the Fetter Lane Society he began with an account of the work of God in their midst over the past two years, with special reference to the doctrines of salvation, faith and ordinances. He followed this with preaching on obedience after conversion, the confidence of believers, sin in believers, Scripture as a means of grace, and the doctrine of the Lord's Supper. Finally, two of Wesley's "Standard Sermons" from this period, "The Means of Grace" and "The Spirit of Bondage and of Adoption," were directed to the questions raised by the Moravians.

On July 18, a company met with Wesley at his mother's for a Thanksgiving service. Afterwards they "consulted how to proceed with regard to our poor brethren of Fetter Lane. We all saw the thing was now come to a crisis, and we therefore unanimously agreed what to do." On the following Sunday he attended the society's lovefeast, and when it was over, he read a paper reviewing the errors into which they had fallen. He concluded: "I believe these assertions to be flatly contrary to the Word of God. I have warned you hereof again and again, and besought you to turn back to the 'law and the testimony.' I have borne with you long, hoping you would return. But as I find you more and more confirmed in the error of your ways, nothing now remains, but that I should give you up to God. You that are of the same judgment, follow me."[33] Eighteen or nineteen followed him out of the meeting, and five days later he met three or four hundred at the Foundry, and after explaining his position almost all present agreed to join him in a new society.

After the division Wesley detailed his theological differences with the Moravians in a letter to the Church at Herrnhut. Toward the close of the letter he touched their view of the Scripture:

> You receive not the Ancients but the modern Mystics as the best interpreters of Scripture, and in conformity to these, you mix much of man's wisdom with the wisdom of God; you greatly refine the plain religion taught by the letter of Holy Writ, and philosophize on almost every part of it, to accommodate it to the Mystic theory. Hence you talk much, in a manner wholly unsupported by Scripture.[34]

With his brother Charles he was even more pointed: "As yet I dare in no wise join with the Moravians . . . because their general scheme is Mystical, not scriptural,—refined in every point above what is written, immeasurable beyond the plain doctrines of the gospel."[35]

This controversy is relevant to a study on authority and religious pluralism for several reasons. First, it shows that while Wesley did not hastily create division over doctrine, theology was important enough to cause disruption. There was a clear limit to the latitude Wesley was willing to allow on central doctrines like salvation and the nature of faith. The Moravians dealt a blow to these essentials in Christian theology, and for these Wesley was ready to separate. Correct theology no less than a very "practical divinity" was at the center of the dispute.

Second, Wesley began to see the practical effects of false theology on the spiritual life of believers. The Moravian teaching on the role of the Church, prayer, the Scriptures, good works, and the ordinances of God undercut all those "means of grace" which Wesley believed were essential for the cultivation of Christian holiness. The central importance of sanctification in his theology caused him to reject Molther's views as a form of antinomianism. Whatever undermined growth in godliness Wesley saw as contrary to the "Oracles of God," and consequently, to be dismissed out of hand. His theological "tolerance" of divergent views was directly related to whether such a position encouraged or discouraged holiness of heart and life.

Third, Wesley revealed that his standard for judging a doctrine was the Scripture. Whatever did not accord with "the law and the testimony" was not to be received. Further, it was by the Bible that Wesley sought to establish members of the societies in solid theology, and this was the weapon he wielded to correct erroneous doctrines. Wesley thought it quite proper to separate himself from those that refused to recognize the ultimate authority of the Word of God in doctrine and practice.

Finally, these events also indicate that Wesley was patient regarding even doctrinal differences. The fact that almost nine months passed from the beginning of the controversy to the separation shows that Wesley desired to give men time to weigh their theological views. But patience was not indifference, and after a time division occurred because the Moravian position extended beyond the latitude of Scripture.

We may conclude then that the evidence seems to indicate that from 1738 Wesley had settled the question about the relationship of Scripture to other criteria for truth. Scripture is not seen as only the first in a line of co-ordinate criteria, but as the final authority in all religious matters. As

Snyder puts it, Wesley had "Scripture as the 'morning norm' to be placed above all other authority."[36] Because of this Wesley must be classified on the question of religious authority as firmly in the Classical Protestant tradition. Colin Williams, in identifying Wesley with this position, observes, "That Wesley continually subjected tradition and experience to the 'written Word of God' even a casual reading of his works will reveal."[37]

Not only did Wesley begin the revival with his view, but he continued to maintain this conviction throughout his lifetime. Nearly fifty years after the Methodists "began to preach that grand scriptural doctrine, salvation by faith," Wesley could reaffirm his identification with the Reformation position:

> The faith of the Protestants, in general, embraces only those truths necessary to salvation, which are clearly revealed in the oracles of God. Whatever is plainly declared in the Old and New Testaments is the object of their faith. They believe neither more nor less than what is manifestly contained in, and approvable by, the Holy Scriptures. The Word of God is 'a lantern to their feet, and a light in all their paths.' They dare not, on any pretence, go from it, to the right hand or to the left. The written word is the whole and sole rule of their faith, as well as practice.[38]

It is significant for contemporary Methodism to note that this was not only Wesley's personal position, but that it characterized the Methodists as a whole. In 1742 Wesley wrote in the "Character of a Methodist":

> We believe, indeed, that 'all Scripture is given by the inspiration of God'; and herein we are distinguished from Jews, Turks, and Infidels. We believe the written Word of God to be the only and sufficient rule both of Christian faith and practice; and herein we are fundamentally distinguishd from those of the Roman Church.[39]

But if Wesley's position on Scripture was so strong, was there any room in his thinking for other criteria for truth such as reason, experience and tradition? What role, if any, did they play in his thinking? This is a particularly pertinent question to an age that has come to assume the coordinate authority of the so-called "Wesleyan quadrilateral." The answer to the question is that for Wesley all three are quite significant, but only as a secondary means of evaluating truth, never as the primary means. They were viewed always as subordinate criteria, and never as equal authority with that of Scripture. These were always judged by Scripture, never Scripture by them. Thus with regard to the truth given by God Wesley could affirm:

> The Scriptures are the touchstone whereby Christians examine all, real or supposed, revelations. In all cases they appeal 'to the law and testimony' to try every spirit thereby.[40]

As Williams observes about Wesley, "His point is that the final authority in matters of religion is the Bible, and all other writings must be judged in the light of this once-for-all revelation."[41]

Yet, within the parameters of Biblical truth there were many things that needed clarification and others where the Scripture was not explicit in details. This was the place, i.e., under the umbrella of the Word of God, that Wesley saw the proper role for reason, experience and tradition. Since each of these subordinate criteria plays an important role for Wesley, it is appropriate for this study to include an evaluation of the place of each in his thinking. First, is the position of reason, which Wesley saw as a part of the image of God in man. It was a gift from God, and though it had been adversely effected at the Fall, by the grace of God it was still operative. Because it was reflective of the image of God, all true religion Wesley thought would be reasonable in essence. When the Methodists were accused of renouncing reason, Wesley responded:

> It is a fundamental principle with us that to renounce reason is to renounce religion, that religion and reason go hand-in-hand, and that all irrational religion is false religion.[42]

In his sermon "The Case of Reason Impartially Considered" Wesley distinguished himself from both those who undervalue reason and those who overvalue it. To those mystics and others who did not believe in its importance, he pointed out how essential reason was, not only for everyday life, but also to understand the Word of God.

> The foundation of true religion stands upon the oracles of God. Now, of what excellent use is reason, if we would either understand ourselves, or explain to others, those living oracles! And how is it possible without it to understand the essential truths contained therein?[43]

On the other hand, to the rationalists who believed that reason was God's highest gift, Wesley pointed out the dangers of overvaluing it. While it is the handmaiden of faith in that it makes possible the reception of revelation, it can never produce the vital content of the Christian faith. The fact that reason did not produce revelation was the reason Wesley did not make it a coordinate authority with Scripture. But he was willing for it to do all that was possible:

> Let reason do all that reason can: Employ it as far as it will go. But, at the same time, acknowledge it as utterly incapable of giving either faith, or hope, or love; and consequently, of producing either real virtue, or substantial happiness.[44]

Wesley was also vitally concerned that the truth of the Christian faith be actualized in personal experience, and so the place of experience in the structure of authority needs to be considered. Wesley was convinced that Biblical truth does work in everyday life, and if not, something is wrong.

He feared the formalism of the Church of England in which so many had a proper understanding of Christianity, but had no vital experience of it in their lives. He wrote concerning one friend, "The theory of religion he certainly has. May God give him the living experience of it."[45]

Wesley was also willing for experience to drive men back to Scripture to see if they had understood it. This was certainly the situation in his own life when his own experience led him to consider the Scriptural data on the nature of faith and the character of conversion. Further, he thought that experience might clarify and confirm Scripture, but it was never to supercede it.

While Wesley feared any approach to Christianity that overlooked personal appropriation, he was also aware of the danger of making experience normative. Therefore, for him "experience is not the test of truth, but truth the test of experience."[46] Thus he warned fellow Christians against "that daughter of pride, enthusiasm," and the peril of "hastily ascribing things to God" such as dreams, voices, impressions, visions or revelations. His constant counsel was:

> Try all things by the written word, and let all bow down before it. You are in danger of enthusiasm every hour, if you depart ever so little from the Scripture: yea, or from the plain, literal meaning of any text, taken with the context.[47]

In an evaluation of the Quakers Wesley objected to their principle of making the Scriptures "a secondary rule, subordinate to the Spirit." "The Spirit is our principle leader," responded Wesley, "yet He is not our rule at all; the Scriptures are the rule whereby He leads us into all truth."[48] Wesley was convinced that the Spirit of God would never lead in personal experience contrary to the Word of God.

Finally, we must consider the place of tradition in Wesley's criteria for truth. Tradition was important to Wesley for the same reasons that reason and experience were important to him, i.e., because tradition in many ways is primarily a history of the Christian Church's use of reason as well as its experience. For Wesley tradition was never to be taken lightly, and he had a special appreciation, as we have seen, for the positions of the Early Church. He particularly found them helpful in interpreting Scripture, and he would have been quite unsympathetic to those who did not take seriously the history of Biblical interpretation. To the accusation by William Dodd that he rejected all ancient and modern authorities, Wesley replied:

> Sir, who told you so? I never did; it never entered my thoughts. Who it was gave you that rule I know not; but my father gave it me thirty years ago (I mean concerning reverence to the ancient church and our own), and I have endeavored to walk by it to this day. But I try every doctrine by the Bible. This is the word by which we are judged in that day.[49]

So, while Wesley was willing that the great expositors of the Church serve as a check on his own interpretation of Scripture, he was not willing for them to become final authority. This fits with what we have seen earlier regarding his rejection of a position that made "antiquity a co-ordinate rather than a subordinate rule with Scripture."[50] In his tract "Popery Calmly Considered" he made his position clear relative to the Catholic practice of placing the traditions of the Church on an equal base with the Scripture: "The Scripture, therefore, being delivered by divinely inspired men, is rule sufficient of itself: so it neither needs, nor is capable of, any further addition."[51] But not only did he insist that the theology of the Church under the authority of the Bible, but the institution as well. "In all cases, the Church is to be judged by the Scripture, not Scripture by the Church."[52]

Since Wesley is so clear in making reason, experience and tradition not co-ordinate with the authority of Scripture, but subordinate criteria for truth, it may be legitimately asked why did he at times string them together in what would appear to be a listing of equal value? Why does he sometimes imply that he can be convinced of a different view by plain proof from Scripture and reason, or from Scripture, experience and tradition, or from some other combination of the four criteria?[53]

It is obvious from the evidence that whatever purpose Wesley had in mind when he listed several of the criteria together he did not mean to say that they were all of equal authority and that "none could be subsumed under any other." It is obvious that for him Scripture did not just have "primacy" over the other three. Primacy could easily be interpreted as meaning only the first of several equal authorities consulted. Whereas for Wesley there is no question that the Scripture is *the* final authority. The answer to our question must be sought elsewhere.

It would seem that if Wesley saw a legitimate place for reason, experience and tradition, it would not be surprising that he mentioned them repeatedly as significant. The fact that they are sometimes linked with Scripture would suggest Wesley's awareness of two things. First, that Scripture needed to be interpreted, and that these were legitimate, God-given tools for that task. He is not necessarily to be faulted for sometimes speaking in a popular manner and not distinguishing on every occasion the tools from the ultimate authority. He certainly spoke on enough other occasions with the theological precision necessary to articulate his position. Thus he was desirous to see Scripture confirmed in experience. Further, it was obvious to him that understanding of the Scripture was only possible through reason. In addition, he did not see himself isolated from all others who had interpreted the Bible from previous generations. Wesley was willing that all three of these be used to correctly interpret Scripture, and where any one of them came into conflict with Scripture, he was ready to examine the Bible again to see if it had been improperly understood. But when the Scripture was rightly interpreted and still seen in conflict with one of the other criteria, it was the Scripture that prevailed as the final word on any subject.

The second reason why Wesley may have linked Scripture with other criteria was that he was aware that on many things the Scripture does not give guidance, and in many other cases gives only general principles. It was in these situations that Wesley felt it was right to use other criteria for truth. Here it was not a matter of reason, experience or tradition contradicting Scripture, but complementing it; these were not for rejecting its authority but for applying it. Where Scripture is not precise, reason, experience and tradition are the next best means for determining truth or discerning its specific application. Colin Williams has captured Wesley's perspective when he writes:

> Wesley then must be placed with the Reformers in his principle of *sola scriptura,* in the sense that Scripture is the final authority in matters of faith and practice; not in the sense that tradition and experience have no value, but in the sense that these further sources of insight must be congruous with the revelation recorded in Scripture.[54]

Where these insights were congruous rather than contradictory to Scripture, Wesley was prepared to make use of them. Their authoritative status was no doubt more tentative, and they were not to be used in the same absolute sense as principles from Scripture. Nevertheless, they were to be used fully within their limitations.

In conclusion, then, it cannot be said that Wesley views Scripture as a co-ordinate authority with tradition, experience or reason. Whatever the source of the expression "Wesleyan quadrilateral," it is clearly a misleading phrase. It tends to imply that Wesley put all four criteria for truth on the same plane of value and authority, and this is certainly not the case. Accordingly, it would not be possible to legitimately claim Wesley as support for this part of theological pluralism. In reality the opposite would seem to be more true. Not only can he not be referred to as the one who established a pluralism of religious authority, but the evidence strongly suggests that he would resist any theological stance that was contrary to Scripture, or that did not continue the Classical Reformation commitment to *sola scriptura.* If his relationship with the Moravians is any indicator at all, it appears that there could be circumstances in which he would be willing even to separate from those whose theological positions were "flatly contrary to the Word of God." So with regard to the issue of authority, at least, pluralism within the United Methodist Church will have to look elsewhere to justify its existence as a legitimate theological position.

NOTES

1. *The Book of Discipline of the United Methodist Church* (Nashville: United Methodist Publishing House, 1972), p. 70.

2. *Ibid.,* p. 78.

3. *Ibid.,* p. 79.

4. See Samuel Wesley's *The Life of Our Blessed Lord and Savior Jesus Christ: An Heroic Poem, The History of the Old and New Testaments,* and in Latin his *Dissertations on the Book of Job.*

5. *Arminian Magazine,* vol. 13 (1790), p. 214.

6. Martin Schmidt, *John Wesley: A Theological Biography* (Nashville and New York: Abingdon Press, n.d.), I, pp. 76-77.

7. For a fuller discussion of Wesley's consideration of the Articles see Allan Coppedge, "John Wesley and the Doctrine of Predestination," unpublished Ph.D. dissertation at Cambridge University, 1976, pp. 4-6. Also see Susannah's reply, *Arminian Magazine,* vol. 1 (1778), p. 37.

8. Richard Heitzenrater, "John Wesley and the Oxford Methodists, 1725-35," unpublished Ph.D. dissertation at Duke University, 1972, p. 503.

9. John Wesley, *The Letters of the Reverend John Wesley* (London: Epworth Press, 1931), II, p. 70.

10. Gilbert Burnet, *An Exposition of the Thirty-nine Articles of the Church of England* (Oxford: University Press, 1831; 1st ed. 1699), p. 92.

11. *Ibid.,* p. 93.

12. John Wesley, *A Plain Account of Christian Perfection* (London: Epworth Press, 1952), p. 6.

13. Heitzenrater, dissertation, p. 289.

14. Robert Tuttle, Jr., *John Wesley: His Life and Theology* (Grand Rapids: Zondervan, 1978), p. 150.

15. *Letters,* I, pp. 207-08.

16. John Wesley, *The Journal of the Rev. John Wesley, A.M.* (London: Robert Culley, 1909), I, p. 420.

17. John Wesley, *The Standard Sermons of John Wesley* (London: Epworth Press, 1921), I, p. 245.

18. *Ibid.*

19. *Journal,* I, pp. 264-68.

20. Howard Snyder comments, "This meant Scripture and tradition were not an unbroken line, but that the two were sometimes in conflict. And, in case of conflict, tradition must give way." *The Radical Wesley* (Downers Grove, Ill.: Inter-Varsity Press, 1980), p. 69.

21. *Ibid.,* p. 419. January 24, 1738. Baker feels Wesley became convinced "uncorrupted antiquity was the co-ordinate with reason in interpreting and supplementing Scripture." Frank Baker, *John Wesley and the Church of England* (London: Epworth Press, 1970), p. 139.

22. John Wesley, *The Works of John Wesley* (Oxford: Clarendon Press, 1980), Vol, 25, p. 533.

23. *Ibid.,* p. 615. See Snyder's evaluation that Wesley "was always clear as to the priority of Scripture, especially from 1738 on"; *Wesley,* p. 71.

24. *Journal,* I, p. 447. March 23, 1738.

25. *Ibid.,* p. 454. April 22, 1738. Bohler also brought living witnesses to testify to their conversion in this manner. For Wesley the testimony from experience served to confirm Scripture, but not supersede it as final authority. See *Journal,* I, pp. 471-72.

26. *Sermons,* I, pp. 32-33.

27. *Journal,* II, p. 312.

28. *Ibid.* For more on the impact of stillness see MS: Martha Jones to Charles Wesley, and MS: T. Cowper to Charles Wesley, Early Methodist Volume, Methodist Archives, The John Rylands Library, Manchester, and *The Arminian Magazine,* vol, 4 (1781), p. 153.

29. *Journal,* II, pp. 328-31, 333, 335.

30. *Journal,* II, p. 331. See p. 333 Wesley's disagreement with a Bristol man on January 25, 1740: "I cannot approve of your terms, because they are not scriptural. I find no such phrase as either 'faith of assurance' or 'faith of adherence' in the Bible."

31. *Ibid.,* p. 345. See p. 349 his exposition of the book of James the first week in June.

32. *Ibid.,* p. 359-60.

33. *Ibid.,* pp. 354-56, 369-70.

34. *Letters,* I, p. 350. August, 1740.

35. *Ibid.,* p. 353. See p. 32 for his earlier statement to James Hutton: "I think the Brethren

wrong in a few things . . . because I believe the Bible. The chief thing wherein I think them wrong is in mixing human wisdom with divine."

36. Snyder, *Wesley,* p. 71.

37. Colin Williams, *John Wesley's Theology Today* (Nashville-New York: Abingdon Press, 1960), p. 23.

38. *Works,* VII, pp. 198-99.

39. *Works,* VIII, p. 340.

40. *Letters,* II, p. 117.

41. Williams, *Wesley's Theology,* p. 25.

42. *Letters,* V, p. 364.

43. *Works,* IV, p. 354. See Works, VIII, pp. 11-12 for Wesley's "Earnest Appeal to Men of Reason and Religion," in which he says that to decry reason is utterly unscriptural.

44. *Ibid.,* p. 360. See also Williams, *Wesley's Theology,* p. 32: "The importance of reason is not that it provides another source of revelation, but that it is a logical faculty enabling us to order the evidence of revelation"; and *Letters* VII, p. 319.

45. *Letters,* VII, p. 47.

46. Williams, *Wesley's Theology,* p. 34.

47. *Works,* XI, p. 429.

48. *Letters,* II, p. 117.

49. *Letters,* III, p. 172.

50. *Journal,* I, p. 419.

51. *Works,* X, p. 141.

52. *Ibid.,* p. 142.

53. The author has been unable to locate in Wesley's writings any single place where all four parts of the "quadrilateral" are mentioned together.

54. Williams, *Wesley's Theology,* pp. 25-26.

7

FRANCIS ASBURY: THE MAKING OF A BISHOP AND THE AMERICANIZATION OF A LOYALIST

Timothy L. Smith

Dennis Kinlaw is not only a preacher's preacher, he is the Christian scholar's friend. From the day of our first meeting, many years ago, he has given to me, as I know to many others, personal encouragement, and public inspiration for our work. The quality of his intellect, reinforced in every way by the depth of his commitment to the God whom we know in Holy Scripture, leaves me deeply in his debt whenever I hear him preach. Like others, I hope this volume of essays will quicken his enthusiasm for the next great stage of his life, which I suspect will find him leading the troops of Christian scholars and Christian preachers in the cause of biblical and Wesleyan holiness.

In December, 1783, a letter from John Wesley caught up with Francis Asbury in an obscure North Carolina settlement through which he was passing on his annual visitation of the Methodist societies in that primitive country. The letter appointed Asbury Wesley's "General Assistant" in the superintendency of the American churches. It also directed the Assistant not to accept into his fellowship any preacher from England who did not come with Wesley's recommendation and to receive none, however recommended, who would not be fully subject to Asbury and to the American Conference.[1] Thus ended almost twelve years of uncertain and strained relations between the two men. They had not seen each other since 1771, when Wesley had sent young Asbury, then only 26 years old, to help spread Methodism in America. Their misunderstandings stemmed in part from prejudiced reports sent home soon after Asbury arrived, complaining of the latter's insistence that he and his fellow ministers should not settle in cities but itinerate, and criticizing Asbury's overly-zealous administration of Methodist discipline.[2]

Each year thereafter witnessed one or another kind of crisis, both in Asbury's personal ministry and in the Methodist fellowship. Each crisis was symptomatic of differing perceptions of means and ends, both among the ministers and between the ministers and laymen gathered into local societies. The issue of discipline never disappeared, nor did that of evangelism or itinerancy. They were overshadowed for a time by the political crisis of the American Revolution, in which Wesley's intemperate attack upon the rebelling colonists made the Patriot party suspect that every Methodist minister, and particularly any recently from Britain, was a Loyalist agent.

As the war drew to a close, issues relating to the sacraments and to the organization of church life became crucial. Both during and after the War for Independence, Methodist preachers chafed under Wesley's rule which strictly forbad those who had not been ordained deacons or priests in the Church of England to administer the sacraments of baptism and the Lord's supper. Asbury, of course, and nearly all of his fellows in America were not ordained. Their followers usually took communion when they were able in Anglican churches and secured baptism for their infants there. Most Anglican ministers were loyalists, however, and large numbers of them left for Canada or England during the war. The shortage of clergy and the organizational crisis confronting the Anglicans, who had long suffered from the refusal of the Church of England to appoint an American bishop, affected Methodists as well. The desire to provide and to receive the sacraments pushed the Methodist societies toward the establishment of a separate denomination, confronting Asbury with another crisis.

Through his conduct in relation to each one of these complex challenges, Asbury emerged as the true leader of the Methodists in America. In his letter of 1783, John Wesley at last recognized this fact and granted the younger man his fullest approbation. The next year Wesley sent Thomas Coke to America with instructions to organize a separate denomination, to ordain the ministers who were qualified, and to make Francis Asbury co-superintendent with Coke of the Methodist communion in the United States. The proposal required Asbury to reverse his long insistence upon the high-church Anglican position concerning ordination and the sacraments. He spent a month or so praying, thinking, and consulting with his preachers about the plan. He at last accepted it heartily as a formalization of what had, in fact, been the case for many years, only insisting that an election by his fellow ministers ratify Wesley's appointment. He and Coke went a step further. Eager to draw away to the Methodist communion as large as possible a company of American Anglicans willing to make the Methodist discipline their own, they accepted the title of "Bishop." This step was a scandal to some, and it offended the aged Wesley. But Asbury had long since learned to rely upon his own judgment of what seemed God's will for American

Methodists, even if his beloved mentor in England had not yet seen what needed to be done. By that time, moreover, Asbury knew that he had won not only Wesley's approbation but the confidence of his brethren. He had done so by simply being himself, a truly religious man.

I think Asbury's story, like those of other Anglicans, whether Methodist or not, illustrates how religious commitments, made for reasons unrelated to politics, eventually made patriotic Americans out of churchmen who had been British loyalists at the outset of the War for Independence. Neither the rhetoric of the patriot party nor the violence of the revolution was responsible for the remaking. Rather, their emerging identity as Americans stemmed from their decision to stay with the congregations, from their measured response to the new situations that independence created, and from their affection for familiar persons and places and for the institutions and economic enterprises around which their lives of creative work revolved. Conflict set the stage, to be sure—social, political, and military, provoked by that minority of colonists who determined to wage war, if need be, to be free. But conflict did not make the loyalists who opposed independence into patriots. Their conversion was a more deliberate process, and reflected the same moderate way of dealing with changed circumstances that had prompted their original resistance to the movement for independence.

In Francis Asbury's case, the story is a moral and intensely spiritual one. His emergence as the leader of the growing congregations of Anglican Methodists scattered from Connecticut to Carolina and his eventual election as their bishop reflected not political but pastoral realities. Asbury's experience suggests that when a pastor is honestly dealing with his own religious problems, seeking to overcome them by faith in Christ, and when he tries with equal honesty and openness to help others with their problems, the confidence that flows between him and his people may become a stronger bond than ritual or organization or oratory can forge. A bishop, like a pastor, needs charisma. But charisma, understood on Jesus' terms, is not so much a miraculous gift as a consequence of devotedness. It grows out of an apostleship in which one is true to himself, open with his brothers and sisters, and honest to God. That, at least, is the moral I point, in advance of telling the tale, from Francis Asbury's emergence as the founding bishop of American Methodism.

In every case, it seems to me, his conduct and inspiration as a Methodist preacher—what we might call his policy—was a consistent expression of his own inward quest fully to receive and completely to share with those around him the love of the one whom he believed was the Lord, Jesus Christ. Becoming a bishop was incidental to that quest, I think. He could not have anticipated that his peculiar combinations of talents and opportunities for service would lead to such an outcome. That event was in fact one of the lesser fruits of his commitment of his life to larger and essentially religious purposes.

I shall try to make plain the bases of these conclusions by reference to four areas of Asbury's leadership, namely, doctrine, discipline, pastoral care, and the resolution of conflicts.

First, any careful reading of his journal makes clear that the continuous effort to improve his own understanding of his faith was the foundation of Asbury's effectiveness in preaching the doctrines of Christianity to others. He read continuously from a wide range of Christian literature, and dipped occasionally into pagan or secular writings as well. No trip by land or sea found him without some difficult volume to master, and no time of confinement or release from heavy duties passed without his recording in his diary the substance of his reaction to the many things he read.[3] Most interesting to me is not simply the variety of the books but the tenor of his response to them. He was obviously reading both devotionally and critically, searching frequently the writings of Calvinist or of non-Christian authors for insights about truths of the gospel with which he could enrich his own Wesleyan outlook. At the same time, he evaluated all writers by reference to a rigorous standard of what he believed to be Biblical truth.[4] The consequence was that with Asbury, as with Wesley and John Fletcher, devotional and doctrinal pursuits were centered in Scripture, and experience and creed formed a consistent whole. "It is plain to me," he wrote on one occasion, that "the devil will let us read always, if we will not pray; but prayer is the sword of the preacher, the life of the Christian, the terror of hell, and the devil's plague."[5]

Little wonder, therefore, that those doctrines of the Christian faith that Asbury emphasized in his preaching were those which were central to personal religious experience: the incarnation, atonement and resurrection of the Lord, Jesus Christ; the promise to believers of the assurance of salvation, on the ground of their repentance and faith; the saints' inheritance of God's gift of perfect love; the importance of Christians bearing witness to their experience; and the hope of eternal life, which he believed the basis not only of the faith of the church but of the trust and love of each child of God.[6]

Now to be sure, Asbury, like all eighteenth-century ministers, preached a full range of Christian doctrines; the sketches of his many sermons make this point clear. He does not fit the caricature historians have drawn of the circuit-rider who repeated his two or three familiar discourses at each location across a wide area and then moved on to another circuit. Asbury might preach on as many as twelve or fifteen different texts in a single fortnight, even after he had enjoyed great "liberty," as he put it, in preaching on one and might have been, on that account, prompted to repeat that sermon at the next stop.[7] Clearly, his preaching was intended for his own edification as well as that of his hearers. As all good preaching should, it grew out of his devotional approach to the study of Scripture.

The doctrines having to do with the salvation and spiritual development of persons, then, became central in Methodist preaching and remained so for generations to come. This fact has given rise to the remarkable judgment, enforced by incantation rather more than evidence, that American Methodism had little theological substance, being concerned principally with the sanctification of sinners. This judgment stems in fact from the theological bias of European religious thought, which evaluates the strength of a theology according to its originality in dealing with either Calvinistic or rationalistic or sacramental issues. The New Testament, however, like Asbury's sermons, makes the primary meaning of the gospel to be "the power of God for the salvation of everyone who believes."

Asbury learned, as John and Charles Wesley and their colleagues in England had, to preach short sermons, without a manuscript or extensive notes. And he judged each attempt not only by the clarity with which he had been able to enforce a particular teaching but by what he described as the degree of "liberty" he felt when doing so. One inclined to jump to the conclusion that he meant by that word a merely emotional freedom in rhetoric would do well to consider the intensity of Asbury's resistance to sentimentality, and to all forms of what he and Wesley called enthusiasm. Asbury meant by liberty, the degree to which a divinely-inspired conviction of the ultimate significance of what he was preaching flowed between speaker and hearers, breaking up resistance to it. When he wrote, as he often did, that "there was a great melting" while he preached, he meant simply that the minds of his hearers were opened to accept the truth. Whether or not they shed tears was beside the point.[8]

Viewed without preconceptions grounded in either rhetoric or theology, I suppose one would say that the effectiveness of Asbury's preaching lay in the fact that it echoed his praying. At the center of both was his desire to know and to share the love of Christ. He uttered judgments tenderly and made rebuke an act of love. The heart of every sermon was the promise that a God of infinite mercy stood ready to pardon and to cleanse from all sin. Asbury had little patience with what he called the "furious" spirit in which Thomas Rankin sought to enforce the law of the Lord. His own personal salvation, his diary makes plain, was to him each day a wondrous gift of God's loving grace, of which he felt utterly unworthy; what he proclaimed to lost and sinning men was the same loving and hallowing grace. Than such, it seems to me, there is no higher, no more subtle, no more biblical Christian doctrine.[9]

Turning now to discipline, Asbury regarded the willingness of preachers to enforce rigorously the rules Wesley had set forth governing the personal behavior of Methodists as a test of the soundness of their faith. This attitude may appear on first reading as a manifestation merely of organizational loyalty. It proves on closer inspection, however, to have reflected the young preacher's passion for communal discipline. That passion, in turn, stemmed from deep honesty about his own need for that continual correction from Scripture and Holy Spirit and church fellowship that he believed necessary to make him a true disciple of Jesus

Christ. Such discipline, whether personal or communal, was no work for weaklings; Asbury's strength in public tests stemmed from his rigor in self-examination. "It is for holiness my spirit mourns," he wrote some months after his arrival in America; "I want to walk constantly before God without reproof. . . . God hath sent me to this country. All I seek is to be more spiritual, and given up entirely to God—to be all devoted to Him whom I love."[10] Out of this ground sprang his firmness with others.[11] On an early visit to Philadelphia in April, 1772, he recorded that he "preached to the people with some sharpness," and then in the evening "kept at the door, met the society, and read Mr. Wesley's epistle to them." Keeping at the door meant, of course, forbidding participation in the society of those who did not seem truly awakened to their sins and willing to accept Methodist discipline. Later in the week, Asbury wrote that he had "heard that many were offended at my shutting them out of society meeting, as they had been greatly indulged before. But this does not trouble me. While I stay, the rules must be attended to. . . . I cannot suffer myself to be guided by half-hearted Methodists." An elderly member of the Society of Friends thereupon told him that "the opinion of the people was much changed, within a few days, about Methodism," and reminded him "that the Quakers and other dissenters had laxed *their discipline*; that none but the Roman Catholics kept it up with strictness." Asbury confined his response to this criticism to his journal, writing, "these things do not move me."[12]

That he could also accept the discipline of others was continually clear during these early days. When Rankin, who bore the title of Wesley's Assistant in America, forbade him to go back to the Baltimore circuit, where Asbury's work was beginning to bear fruit and where many friends were pleading for him to come, the future bishop found it grievous, but was sure that "all things shall work together for good to them that love God." When Rankin spoke kindly to him the next day, Asbury expressed the hope that "all things will give place to love." He remained in Philadelphia, sharing the pulpit with Rankin, chafing but obeying. On the Lord's day, December 18, 1774, he wrote, "My soul was happy while preaching this morning. Mr. Stringer gave us an old piece at [the Anglican] church; and Mr. Rankin was very furious in the evening." Nevertheless, the following Wednesday, after spending the day reading Neal's *History of the Puritans*, Asbury wrote, "The Lord keeps me from all impure desire, and makes me to abound with divine peace. In prayer meeting this evening, all present were greatly blessed."[13] Again and again, it is clear that the ground of Asbury's administration of discipline in the Methodist community as well as his submission to it was his personal commitment to the will of God, and his persistent quest for growth in Christian holiness.

Since that commitment and that quest transcended allegiance to any man, they may also have reflected or contributed to his sense of alienation. At a quarterly meeting with his fellow ministers in Maryland in 1775, Asbury was depressed by the realization that, as he put it, "my hand appears still to be against every man." The strength of his discipline, which had helped to produce these feelings, stemmed not from physical vigor, for he had been sorely ill, but from a determination, as he put it, "that my few remaining days may be spent to His glory."[14] Methodism was then growing rapidly in Baltimore. Asbury spoke plainly one Monday evening, he tells us, "on the nature of our society," and "the necessity of discipline," a subject which was "not pleasing to some." Nevertheless, he wrote, "I desire to know no man after the flesh. My soul is in peace."[15]

The singular strength of Methodist organization across the ensuing decades, in frontier settlements as well as in the great cities, seems to me to have stemmed from the courage Asbury and his ministerial and lay associates displayed in insisting that the covenant with Christ required radical discipline, inward as well as outward. The preachers seem to have been spared from remorse at the loss of those who were not willing to submit to the rules by their keen awareness of how dangerous it had been to their own spiritual lives to regard temptation lightly or to dally with their vocation to holiness. Not organizational loyalty but the hope of heaven and their earthly experience of the interdependence of holiness and love formed the spiritual basis of their passion for discipline and deepened their attachment to the idea of Christian community.

Consider, now, the evidences of that attachment in Asbury's ministry of pastoral care. If his doctrinal insights and concern for obedience to Methodist rules grew out of his biblical and devotional experience, spiritual identification with the men and women he served was a principal factor in his emergence as bishop. That identification, in turn, stemmed from his efforts to follow closely in the footsteps of Jesus, the great shepherd. Touring Virginia in the fall of 1780, Asbury found himself speaking "with great liberty" at a service attended by several preachers. "They shook whilst I showed the call to the ministry," he wrote,

> how they ought to evidence it, by having the same end in view our Lord had; 'to preach the Gospel to the poor; to bind up the broken-hearted, and to set at liberty them that are bound;' to imitate the prophetic and priestly office of Christ,—thus to set up Christ among the people, or to conclude they had not the call.[16]

Such a pastoral ideal helped Asbury to lay aside very early his initial prejudice against the urban pastorate. In the late fall of 1773, stationed in Baltimore, he found himself preaching to great crowds of people every day, first in the town and then at Fells Point where the docks were located. "Many are under some awakenings here," he wrote, "and they are very kind and affectionate to me."[17] He helped the congregations in both parts of town erect buildings, while visiting and preaching from house to house and leading the way in ministry to the poor, the imprisoned, and the drunken. Before lying down to sleep one Friday night he expressed his overwhelming concern for the people of the city. "I am pressed under them as a cart full of sheaves," he wrote, "and would rather be employed in the most servile offices than preach to them, if it were not from a sense of duty to God. . . ."[18] His love for Baltimore always remained strong, however, and he returned there happily whenever assigned.[19]

Asbury thus learned from brief pastorates in New York City, Philadelphia, and Baltimore during his first two years in America, that a country boy like himself could establish in a large city the base from which to evangelize nearby rural communities. He preached in the smaller places on weekdays, in barns or private homes, establishing a network of Methodist classes around each urban center. He followed this plan regularly thereafter. In the summer of 1775, when stationed at Norfolk, Virginia, he shuttled back and forth by ferry between Norfolk and Portsmouth on Sundays. On weekdays he went sometimes "to the farthermost part of Portsmouth parish," he said, "through such a swamp as I never saw before, and partook of a blessing" with people "of a simple heart."[20] He visited regularly several societies in the country, some of which numbered scarcely a dozen members and met at a farmer's cabin in the woods. Such efforts help explain why the Sunday congregations in Norfolk soon attracted "many people from the country as well as the towns."[21]

When stationed later that year at Philadelphia, Asbury combined a close pastoral ministry to the city congregation with frequent trips to the New Jersey countryside. He conducted class meetings and love feasts, (the latter being services in which those present shared their individual experiences) and encouraged the preachers in the sizable towns to erect houses of worship. Meanwhile he cultivated day by day his own devotion to Christ. In Philadelphia, as Baltimore, he continued to preach often in private dwellings even after church buildings were erected, a habit no doubt enforced by his rural experience where he saw the value of preaching in the intimate surroundings of a home.[22]

In 1788 Asbury wrote Ezekiel Cooper, pastor in Baltimore, brief instructions on how to conduct an urban pastorate. These reveal how mistaken is the myth that the bishop always remained at heart a frontier circuit rider. He told Cooper to call in every home of his society once each two weeks, "for no other purpose than to speak to each in the family about their souls." He counseled him to preach somewhere every other night and to remember that "sermons ought to be short and pointed in town" and that they should "press the people to conviction, repentance, faith and holiness." He continued, "I am sure that the whole method of preaching will be changed as we come near the golden age. So shall we speak not so much by system but by life and application in the heart, little illustration and great fervency in the spark of life."[23]

Asbury's pastoral concern was especially apparent in his insistence upon constantly preaching to poor people, to Negroes, and to persons in prison. On his first appointment for a three-month period in Philadelphia, in the spring of 1772, he wasted no time in going to preach to the "poor mortals in the Bettering-house."[24] Whenever stationed in New York City he went frequently to the cluster of cottages beside Beekman's Swamp, where the hard-pressed tannery workers lived.[25] He preached to Negroes everywhere, and in joint meetings with white people most of the time.[26] But he met Blacks separately also, particularly in Baltimore, where some of their "unhappy masters" forbade them to come for religious instruction. "How will the sons of oppression answer for their conduct," he asked, when the "Proprietor of all shall call them to an account?"[27] His journal shows a remarkable consistency of concern to convert and enroll Black people in Methodist societies; and he opposed slavery always, both before, during, and after the Revolution. On Maryland's Eastern Shore in 1784, he found a Black man who was a Methodist under sentence of death for thefts committed before his conversion. Though "much given up" to his fate, the man was reprieved under the gallows, after "a merchant who cursed the Negro for praying" dropped dead on the spot. "I pity the poor slaves, " Asbury wrote that evening; "Oh that God would look down in mercy, and take their cause in hand."[28]

It is clear also, however, that the young preacher was equally interested in the conversion to Christian faith and discipline of wealthy and socially eminent persons. The summer of 1776 found him ill, and Asbury determined to to to Berkeley Springs, a resort in Morgan County, Virginia, two days journey from Baltimore, to recover his health. Whether the healing powers of the springs had a fair test in his case is questionable. The first Sunday of his six-week stay he injured his throat by trying to preach out of doors loudly enough "that the people who were in their houses might hear." The following Tuesday he "preached again by the side of the hill, near the bath," and the word, he tells us, "had a melting influence on some of the congregation." By Wednesday he sensed "a manifest check to the overflowing tide of immorality" among the crowds of wealthy vacationers. By the end of the week he had established a daily schedule for his holiday: "to read about a hundred pages a day; usually to pray in public five times a day; to preach in the open area every other day; and to lecture in prayer meeting every evening. And if it were in my power," he added, "I would do a thousand times as much for such a gracious and blessed Master. But in the midst of all my little employments, I feel myself as nothing, and Christ to me is all in all."[29]

Nor did this balancing of concern for the poor and the wealthy diminish after Asbury had been elected Bishop. In 1786 his long journey on horseback through the wilds of backwoods Carolina, passing over flooded creeks, occasionally missing appointments from wrong turns taken amidst driving rain, and usually ill himself, revealed the passion of a man driven by concern for poor people settled in the wilderness.[30] He returned by way of Alexandria, Virginia. There he preached Sunday morning in the courthouse and in the evening at the Presbyterian Church, then laid plans for a Methodist meeting house. After a brief visit to Balitmore he headed into Western Maryland and Virginia. Suffering from a swollen and feverish foot, he stayed in miserable lodgings, sometimes rising early to preach when "almost ready to drop for want of sleep."[31] When he got to Friends' Cove in Western Maryland, he wrote, "I have been greatly tempted to impatience and discontent. The roads are bad; my horse's hind feet without shoes; and but little to eat. To this I may add that the lodgings are unclean and uncomfortable." Nevertheless, he preached the next day, Sunday, and, as he put it, "had sweet communion with God in the woods." He stopped a few days later at the Springs in Bath, Virginia, for his annual "vacation," which he spent in reading and preaching to the wealthy planters gathered there while trying to find "the healing efficacy of the waters" for himself. Of the visit he wrote, "more than ordinary in prayer, and spoke in public every other night."[32]

Asbury's pastoral care for children affords another perspective upon his effort to follow the example of Jesus. As early as September, 1772, he held a meeting in New York City "for the better ordering of the spiritual and temporal affairs of the society." Of the sixteen questions he raised dealing with general matters of discipline and organization, one of the several which got an affirmative answer was "Can the preacher meet the children?"[33] In the midst of the Revolutionary War, while still free to travel over his Delaware circuit, he preached persistently on "the education of children, and family duties."[34] In November, 1780, free again after a long period of danger to travel through Virginia and Delaware and help the ministers in charge of the multiplying circuits, he came back to his favorite residence, Dover, and proposed meeting the children. "I appointed a place for them to sit, and desired the parents to send a note with each, letting me know the temper, and those vices to which the child might be most subject." Then, without any indication of a change in subject, he added to his diary for that day, "I love to spend a few minutes every hour in prayer. I see great need of living near to God—the people are so affectionate. Lord, humble me!" He was reading Wesley's *Journal* at the time, preaching frequently on Christian perfection, and conferring constantly with his fellow ministers concerning the danger of a separation of the Methodists in Virginia.[35]

Indeed, this passion for pastoral care, on the model he thought Jesus provided, shaped Asbury's approach to the resolution of conflicts among Methodists, just as it steadily changed him from the high-church Anglican and lover of all things British he had been into an American patriot. These interlocking developments in his work and loyalties were also crucial to his nomination and election as bishop.

The first intimations of an approaching revolt of the colonies from England drew from Asbury a sharp reaction against the involvement of

Methodist preachers in politics. In the fall of 1774 he refused even to think about the consequences of the British attack on Boston. "Alas," he wrote, "what a small matter may interrupt our communion with God; even draw away our affections from him."[36] But the matter would not stay small. In Baltimore in March, 1775, his preaching on the glory of God fell on deaf ears, he thought, because "they were training the militia" and "the town seemed all in confusion."[37] A few Sundays later he heard "alarming military accounts from Boston, New York, and Philadelphia," but comforted himself with the hope that the Lord would overrule "and make all these things subservient to the spiritual welfare of his Church." Nevertheless, back in town Tuesday night after a visit to the country, he "found the people all inflamed with a martial spirit."[38] Throughout the following years Asbury was always unhappy when confined, as he wrote one evening, "to the company of men who were destitute of religion, and full of sin and politics."[39]

Neverthess, the crucial decision to stay in America rather than to join the other British preachers in plans to return to England was for him a clear pastoral duty. In early August, 1775, he received at Norfolk a letter from Thomas Rankin announcing that Rankin and two other preachers had concluded it would be best to return to England. "But I can by no means agree to leave [such] a field for gathering souls to Christ as we have in America," Asbury confided to his journal.

> It would be an eternal dishonour to the Methodists, that we should all leave three thousand souls, who desire to commit themselves to our care; neither is it the part of a good shepherd to leave his flock in time of danger. Therefore, I am determined by the grace of God, not to leave them, let the consequence be what it may.[40]

The consequences were, indeed, formidable. In March, 1776, he came to Philadelphia, having ridden two thousand miles since his last visit there, for a parting conversation with Rankin. The publication in America of John Wesley's denunciation of the rebels had meanwhile complicated Asbury's decision to stay. Although "an affectionate letter from Mr. Wesley" awaited him at Philadelphia, Asbury wrote he was "truly sorry that the venerable man ever dipped into the politics of America. My desire is to live in love and peace with all men; to do them no harm, but all the good I can." He thought it unreasonable for their critics "to censor the Methodists in America, on account of Mr. Wesley's political sentiments," since the Founder had simply revealed by his tract a "conscientious attachment to the government under which he lived." Had Wesley "been a subject of America," Asbury wrote, "he would have been as zealous an advocate of the American cause." In these words, Asbury perhaps unconsciously betrayed his own growing sense of being "a subject of America," though his submission was primarily to his Lord and to his pastoral responsibility.[41]

Asbury spent a great deal of time the following year in Baltimore, endeavoring as much as possible in his work and preaching to ignore the events of the Revolution.[42] In March, 1777, a letter from one of his fellow ministers reminded him that according to the rule adopted by the Methodist conference in England, "the time was drawing near for us to return." Asbury remarked in his diary that since Saint Paul's rule was "that our spiritual children should be in our hearts, to live and die with them, . . . doubtless we should be willing to suffer affliction with them." Then he prayed, "May the Lord give me wisdom sufficient to direct me in this and every intricate case." In the following days he found himself anxious "in respect to the times," and wrote: "My brethren are inclined to leave the continent, and I do not know that something may be propounded to me which would touch my conscience; but my determination is to trust in God, and be satisfied if the souls of my fellow men are saved."[43] Troubled lest his preaching in America seem to support acts of revolution, and informed in September, 1777, that Thomas Rankin and one other minister had at long last left for England, Asbury wrote, "So we are left alone. But I leave myself in the hand of God; relying on His good providence to direct and protect us. . . ."[44]

Retreating from the excitements of Baltimore to Delaware, he concentrated on dealing "plainly and honestly, though affectionately and tenderly" with his people, affirming that, "if we seek to please men, unless it is for their good to edification, we are not the servant of Christ."[45] He buried himself during this time also in John Wesley's works. He found in them "a certain spirituality" which he could "find in no other human compositions." One who "has any taste for true piety, can scarcely read a few pages in the writings of that great divine," he wrote, "without imbibing a greater relish for the pure and simple religion of Jesus Christ, which is therein so Scripturally and rationally explained and defended." In February, 1778, he wrote that he was "under some heaviness of mind." But "it was no wonder," he confided. "Three thousand miles from home—my friends have left me—I am considered by some as an enemy of the country—every day liable to be seized by violence, and abused. However, all this is a trifle to suffer for Christ, and the salvation of souls. Lord, stand by me!" A little later, back in Baltimore, he wrote, "Surely God will stand by and deliver me! I have none other on whom I can depend. And He knows with what intention and for what purposes I came into this distant and strange land, and what little I have suffered for His cause."[46]

Later the same night Asbury received a report that prompted him to leave Baltimore and go into hiding. "I set out after dinner," he wrote, "and lay in a swamp till about sunset; but was then kindly taken in by a friend. My soul has been greatly humbled and blessed under these difficulties, and I thought myself like some of the old prophets who were concealed in times of public distress."[47] In the following days of that summer, he endured patiently what he called his "dumb and silent

Sabbaths." He remembered that he had once thought "it would be death for me to keep silence from declaring the word of God; but now I am in a measure contented, and hope to see a day of liberty once again." Meanwhile, he spent his time in prayer, meditation, and reading.[48] His Delaware host, Judge Thomas White, was jailed for a time for entertaining Asbury. When Asbury was able later to return to the White home, he found himself on a Sunday with a mind "strangely twisted and tortured, not knowing what to do. It seems I know not how to fight, nor how to fly."[49]

During this period of danger and enforced silence, however, Asbury realized that the Anglican population of Maryland, Virginia, and Delaware among whom he was sheltered would never again accept British rule and were, on that account, becoming estranged from the Church of England. The English church and state had refused for generations to grant them a bishop and had shown a remarkable lack of concern to supply them with able and upright clergymen. Asbury realized that his refusal to return to England gave him an opportunity to lead more and more of these Anglicans toward Methodism, if only he could hold back those of his preachers who, desiring to administer the sacraments to their people, wanted to establish at once a separate Methodist sect.

As the worst dangers of the Revolution passed, therefore, Asbury found himself responsible not only for the pastoral guidance of hundreds of lay people but for restraining the enthusiasm of a great company of young preachers, most of them born in America and none of them properly ordained. He assumed the latter reponsibility without realizing that very soon he would become their bishop, preside at their ordination, and with Wesley's blessing lead them in establishing a separate American denomination. Not foreseeing this, his purpose meanwhile was simply to win as many souls as he could, particularly among the Anglicans, and to bring all who would accept it under the discipline of Methodist societies. One by-product of this strategy of restraint, Asbury noted in Delaware in the spring of 1779, was that some of the most wealthy families were attracted to his meetings. "Sundry persons of respectability attend my feeble exercises in public, and express satisfaction," he wrote. "But shall this satisfy, or lift me up? God forbid! If this should be the case, God will punish me for my folly."[50] A few days later, a conference of the Methodist preachers serving north of the Potomac learned they had "great reason to fear" that their "brothers in the south were in danger of separating" from them. Asbury helped compose "a soft, healing epistle" to the Virginia preachers, but at the moment could do no more.[51]

The controversy which then broke out between Asbury and the preachers in Virginia displayed the spiritual side of his emerging powers of leadership: he dealt with contention among the Methodist clergymen in the same way he confronted temptations to pride and self-will in his own life. In the spring of 1779, Asbury received the minutes of the Virginia conference describing what he called "a lame separation from the Episcopal Church."[52] For nearly a year he confined his response to writing frequent letters to the "dissenting brethren in Virginia, hoping to reclaim them." Meanwhile, he continued to preach to rich and poor in Delaware.[53] His affection for his close colleagues, especially Freeborn Garrettson, grew steadily that year, and he prayed each day, morning and evening, for "all the preachers and circuits in America."[54] Often during this period, however, he displayed the wry humor of a man who was constitutionally pessimistic. He called himself once "a true prophet of evil tidings, as it suits my cast of mind."[55]

Asbury worked throughout the spring and summer of 1780 to secure a reconciliation with the Virginia leaders. His occasional reunions with Methodist preachers from afar found him "more moved than ever before, with leaving and meeting my friends." These, he added, were "humbling times," which made the Christians love one another.[56] In April, 1780 the Maryland preachers met in Baltimore. They first concluded to renounce the Virginia secessionists. Asbury proposed instead conditions of union, namely, that the Virginians should not ordain any more preachers; that they should come no farther North than Hanover circuit; that they should not presume to administer the sacraments where there was "a decent Episcopal minister"; and that they should join in plans for a union conference. The Maryland ministers would not agree to these concessions, however, though they acknowledged that "it was like death to think of parting" with the Virginia Methodists. Asbury, almost ready to despair, hit upon the idea of their proposing simply that the Virginians suspend the sacraments for one year while both sides sought a way to restore Methodist unity.[57]

When his colleagues agreed, Asbury and Garrettson journeyed to the Virginia conference, their minds heavy with doubts the plan would be accepted but hoping God's grace would prove "almighty." When permitted to speak, Asbury read Wesley's thoughts against separation from the Church of England; showed his private letters of instruction from the Founder; read the espistles and other expressions of sentiment from the Delaware and Baltimore conferences; and preached a tender sermon. "They wept like children," Asbury wrote, "but kept their opinions." He and Garrettson returned then to their lodgings, "under the heaviest cloud I ever felt in America." The next day they went back to say goodbye and found that while Asbury had been praying alone that morning the Virginians "had been brought to an agreement" to accept the proposal and to suspend their secession for one year.[58] There followed a joyous tour through Virginia, during which Asbury visited Devereaux Jarratt, a Methodist who, being an Anglican clergyman, had taken no part in the separation movement. Asbury preached continuously on the doctrine of entire sanctification, or perfect love, amidst "divine calm and friendly sweetness."[59] The event was crucial, Asbury realized. Forestalling the secession made it possible for John Wesley soon after to send Thomas Coke to bring about the orderly establishment of a separate denomination for all American Methodists, under circumstances that gave at least some chance of drawing a large number of Anglicans into the fold.

Despite poor health, skimpy education and many personal oddities, Francis Asbury became the leader of American Methodists while consciously intending to be only a faithful Christian. In the healing of the Virginia secession, as in the earlier crises which confronted his ministry, the source of his power lay in caring for others, in being open about himself, and in showing a readiness to accept all such corrections and compromises as did not violate his understanding of either the Bible or Methodist discipline. He convinced his associates that he was thoroughly dedicated to the highest aim of Wesley's ministers, namely, to share the love of Jesus, whom he believed to be Christ the Lord, with the people he was sent to serve. He might have been equally successful if he had managed across twenty years of feverish labor merely to seem to be such a man, and to persuade his colleagues to believe it. But his diaries and correspondence argue for the conclusion that he was in fact what his preachers believed him to be—one who became a bishop by being truly religious. Meanwhile, as a by-product of the same processes of spiritual growth, he also became an American patriot and, eventually, a Jeffersonian democrat.

Asbury's story, and the subsequent political behavior of the Methodists in the new nation, contradicts Sidney Mead's picture of the relationships between religion and politics in the period. Mead argued that a temporary alliance of convenience between evangelical pietists and deist rationalists like Thomas Jefferson and Benjamin Franklin sustained the movement for independence, insofar as religion sustained this movement at all. That alliance, Mead says, broke apart after the war had accomplished each group's objectives. The pietist party then withdrew, Mead continues, and formed a new alliance with the conservative heirs of the religious establishments they had once resisted, including the New England Federalists.[60]

I think, on the contrary, that Methodist participation in America's "lively experiment" of nation-founding—and, in my present guess, the participation of other communions that Mead labels "pietists" was deeply rooted in their collective religious experience. Certainly Asbury's followers in America did not draw back from the libertarian ideology he had in such measured strides adopted. Methodists remained throughout the nineteenth century the Protestants most consistently devoted to the political and social aspirations of democracy. Their leaders supported Jefferson's election in 1800, Jackson's in 1828, and, in the North, Lincoln's in 1860.[61]

By the time of the Civil War, America's civil religion, its public faith, owed more to the Methodist formulation of the Christian citizen's duty and the Christian nation's destiny than to any other system of religious belief. If Abraham Lincoln was, indeed, as Elton Trueblood has called him, the theologian of America's anguish, Methodists Matthew Simpson and Gilbert Haven were the preachers who most effectively communicated the hope imbedded in Lincoln's Gettysburg Address and his Second Inaugural to a nation both chastened and reunited by the tragedy of Civil War.[62]

NOTES

All of the references below not otherwise identified are to Francis Asbury, *Journal and Letters*, J. Manning Potts, Elmer T. Clark and Jacob S. Payton, eds., 3 vols. (Nashville, 1958).

1. I, pp. 450; II. pp. 31-32.
2. I, p. 85-86.
3. I, p. 5, 192-98, 263-65, 268-69, 304-05.
4. I, pp. 121, 127, 141, 148-49, 203, 263, 293.
5. I, p. 314; cf. p. 126 and II, p. 479. See also Timothy L. Smith, "How John Fletcher Became the Theologian of Wesleyan Perfectionism, 1770-1776," *The Wesleyan Theological Journal,* vol. 15 (Spring, 1980), pp. 68-69, and *passim.*
6. I, pp. 253, 293, 356, and III, p. 31. On Christian perfection in the later years, see II, pp. 435, 443, 447, 450, 455, 459, 465, 468-69, 475, 483, 494, 499-500, 506, 520-21, and III, pp. 503, 532, 571.
7. See, for example, the sixteen texts he used between May 28 and June 10, 1780, recorded in I, pp. 353-56, and cf. pp. 376-77.
8. See especially I, pp. 353-54, 376-77, and *passim.*
9. I, pp. 141, 245-246, 441, and III, p. 307.
10. I, p. 8.
11. For an example see I, p. 145-46.
12. I, p. 28; cf. pp. 96, 127, 159-61.
13. I, p. 140-41.
14. I, p. 96.
15. I, p. 90.
16. I, p. 16.
17. I, p. 98.
18. I, p. 107.
19. I, p. 140, 150-55.
20. I, p. 157.
21. I, p. 159.
22. I, pp. 184-87.
23. Francis Asbury, Woolard's, Virginia, December 24, 1788, to Ezekiel Cooper, III, p. 66.
24. I, p. 25.
25. I, p. 134.
26. I, p. 9-10, 51, 56-57, 331, 351, 355, and II, pp. 423-24, 449, 456, 487, 494, 501-02, 506, 521.
27. I, p. 190; cf. pp. 200, 323.
28. I, p. 469.
29. I, p. 195; see generally, pp. 191-97.
30. I, pp. 506-09.
31. I, pp. 510-16, *passim.*
32. I, pp. 516-18.
33. I, p. 42; cf. p. 47.
34. I, p. 293.
35. I, pp. 386, 388.
36. I, p. 138; cf. p. 130.

37. I, p. 152.
38. I, p. 155; for comparable events in Norfolk, Virginia, late the same year, see pp. 164, 171, 176.
39. I, p. 156.
40. I, pp. 161-63.
41. I, p. 181. Cf. his later comments on a biography of Washington, II, p. 484.
42. I, pp. 228-29.
43. I, p. 234.
44. I, p. 249.
45. I, p. 263.
46. I, pp. 263-65. For his later reading of Wesley, see II, pp. 470-71, 487, 520, and III, p. 533.
47. I, pp. 265-66.
48. I, p. 267.
49. I, p. 269.
50. I, p. 300; cf. p. 297.
51. I, p. 300.
52. I, p. 304.
53. I, p. 307.
54. I, p. 379; cf. pp. 309, 311, 319.
55. I, p. 376.
56. I, p. 346.
57. I, p. 347.
58. I, pp. 348-50.
59. I, pp. 350-52.
60. Sidney E. Mead, *The Lively Experiment: The Shaping of Christianity in America* (New York, 1963), pp. 33-52.
61. II, 459, 497; Timothy L. Smith, *Revivalism and Social Reform on the Eve of the Civil War* (4th ed.; Baltimore, 1980), pp. 199-203.
62. Smith, *Revivalism*, pp. 220-24.

8

ASA MAHAN ON FREEDOM AND GRACE

Edward H. Madden

For Dennis Kinlaw—whose devotion to philosophy and religion is as deep and rich and fruitful as was Asa Mahan's—with admiration and affection.

Asa Mahan was not a one dimensional man. While nineteenth century America produced many talented people, each genuinely significant in his own specific line—Charles G. Finney as preacher, Mark Hopkins as teacher, James McCosh as scholar, Charles William Eliot as college president, Theodore Weld as abolitionist, Lucy Stone as champion of co-education—Mahan, incredible as it seems, was outstanding in all of these roles. He preached widely in America and the United Kingdom as advocate of New Light theology; and as professor of mental and moral philosophy he taught and wrote effectively at Oberlin and Adrian Colleges. First president of both schools, he advocated the "new education" which was eventually established at Harvard College in 1869 by Eliot. He defended the rights of women to co-education on equal terms with men and engaged in anti-slavery activity long before it became fashionable to do so. His philosophical and religious ideas defined and controlled his reform activities, and the latter enriched his ever developing web of ideas.

Mahan was born and bred in Old School Calvinism, the theology dominant then in the Presbyterian Church in the East and most Plan of Union churches in the West. During the years he developed a philosophical view of human agency which insured freedom of the will and supported Free Will Trinitarianism, a position from which he consistently attacked Calvinism in all its forms. Salvation is a gracious gift of God, he insisted, and man is at liberty either to accept or reject it. On

112

the issue of how to combat one's sinful ways and nature, he later departed not only from Old School Calvinists but also from many New Light theologians in the Congregational fold. He defended and promoted the doctrine of sanctification, or the "second blessing," as the Methodists liked to say. Though his treatment of salvation from sin was uniquely his own, he worked essentially in the tradition of John Wesley's notion of Christian Perfection. His view of combatting sin received much criticism, particularly during the Oberlin years, from Presbyterian and Congregational sources, but his and similar views of sanctification, holiness, full salvation, or the second blessing became increasingly important in American Protestantism from 1850 on, and by the latter part of the century they constituted one of the dominant strands in Protestantism, echoes of which subsequently swelled and receded as religious fashions came and went.

Mahan referred to the development of his ideas and religious experiences from Old School Calvinism through New Light theology to the holiness viewpoint as his journey out of darkness into light. In the present paper, I shall document and discuss the various crucial steps in this somewhat different pilgrim's progress, steps that had experiential and ideational components in equally strong measures.

Asa Mahan was born in Vernon, New York, in 1799, and grew to manhood in the western part of the state, near Warsaw. His mother was a deeply committed Christian and from her Asa accepted the Old School viewpoint, which he implemented by wide reading in theology and discussion with ministers. He was, however, not sustained or nourished by their religious views and even found them demoralizing. He had three close brushes with death which raised in his mind a fear of death and revulsion at the thought of being placed in a coffin and buried in the ground. The fear and revulsion remained with him for years to come—indeed, through college, seminary, and early pastoral days. Part of the cause of his unusual fear was a matter of his early religious training. He had been taught that God graciously saves some undeserving sinners while condemning the rest to eternal damnation. Although he never doubted that his mother was among the happy ones called, he felt that he was hopelessly barred from God's love. Hence his death meant eternal damnation.[1] He accepted the notion that he was religiously passive and had only to wait and see God's inevitable will enacted. He was not responsible for becoming a Christian because it was utterly out of his power. He had no more consciousness of an obligation to become a Christian than he had to become an angel. His fate was already determined, he assumed, and he had no hope of being among those chosen. As far as combatting sin is concerned, he felt that without ability there is no responsibility either. He looked upon sin in the same light as an inherited disease; a person is equally unaccountable for either one.[2] His life seemed hopeless, and he was often near despair over the grimness of his prospects both in this life and the life to come.

When he was seventeen years old Asa taught winter school in the town of Warsaw, and while thus employed he found himself in the midst of a powerful revival of religion. One of his good friends was converted and, much to Asa's astonishment, was transformed into a new person. During this same period he learned that his mother and his friends were praying for his salvation. The young school teacher wondered if there was any point in listening to the old story about the utter depravity of man and the doctrine of the Elect again.[3] With doubts, but impressed by the experience of his friend, Asa decided to try again and listened to the revivalist preacher. What the preacher had to say, what affected the young man so deeply, has not been recorded, but whatever it was the effect was profound. Asa Mahan had his first in a series of deeply religious experiences. He recalled: "I apprehended, with absolute distinctness, God as having ever loved me with a more than parental love, and as having ever been ready to receive me, pardon me, love me, and care for me, as a child, [if] I confessed my sin to Him, implored His pardoning mercy, and sought His favour."[4] He acted according to this refreshingly different religious impulse and knelt in prayer. He emphatically acknowledged that he was totally unworthy of God's grace and simply promised to accept God's will as his own. He pleaded to be spared the deadness and hopelessness of his past religious understanding and asked for the ability to appreciate and respect God's love and glory. In *Out of Darkness into Light,* written many years later in England, Mahan wrote of the result of his prayer. "I had no sooner pronounced these words, than I was consciously encircled in the 'everlasting arms.' I was so overshadowed with a sense of the manifested love of a forgiving God and Saviour, that my whole mental being seemed to be dissolved, and pervaded with an ineffable quietude and assurance. I arose from my knees without a doubt that I was an adopted member of the family of God . . . [and] could and did say, 'My Father and my God.' Such was my entry into the inner life."[5]

Unfortunately, as Asa realized after the first exaltations passed, his intuitions and religious experiences did not fit any part of his Calvinistic theological indoctrination. What, after all, were the implications of his conversion experience? Man is inherently sinful and is saved only by the grace of God. However, man has a role to play in the drama of salvation and should not sit around waiting passively for signs from God indicating whether he is part of the elect or is to be cast into utter darkness. A person is endowed with free will; what he does and what he chooses is "up to him." God offers salvation as a gracious gift to every sinful person. It is up to each individual—undeserving, to be sure—to accept or reject the gracious gift of salvation. Man's destiny hinges on his own free, unforced acceptance of Jesus Christ as his Saviour and Redeemer.

None of these implications, needless to say, were compatible with any of the forms of Calvinism in Asa's time. He was perfectly aware of the implications but lacked the theological and philosophical acumen to defend them against seasoned Calvinistic controversialists. Moreover, he really did not want to abandon the Presbyterian Church because it had constituted his community all his life. He certainly had no desire to be outside the fold when his mother remained inside it. However, he was even less willing to ignore the promptings of his religious experience. He drifted along trying to avoid conflict as much as possible. He came to despise the emphasis on "creeds" and "confessions" and longed for people instead to concentrate on *doing* something in Christ's name. But in college and seminary he was forced into defending one form of Calvinism or another in order to avoid the appearance of being either disinterested in important matters or incapable of effectively arguing for a position. So Asa decided to defend Dr. Emmons' form of Calvinism. Why we do not know—perhaps it was the view held by his mother or the one that allowed for the most direct contact of God with the world. But his heart was not in it since all forms of Calvinism, as far as he could ascertain, claimed that man plays a wholly passive role in conversion. Even when he argued for the system he had selected, he said, his mind shrank back appalled at the difficulties and perplexities presented.[6]

In seminary he was astonished at the arguments used by one of his professors to reconcile the concepts of necessity and responsibility. Said the professor, "We have proved these two doctrines to be true, as matters of fact. That is, these two facts do exist. That is, they exist together. That is, they co-exist. That is, they *co*-sist. That is, they *con*-sist, or are consistent." When the same argument was used again the next year, Mahan reported, "Some of the class came out of the recitation room with their eyes standing out as large as tea-saucers." He wrote that "such abortive attempts to reconcile the palpably incompatible rendered such incompatability more palpable to my mind."[7] He was also embarrassed by passages of Scripture where God expressed astonishment and regret that His children had done what Calvinists had been taught it was impossible for them not to do.

Toward the end of Mahan's seminary training the inherent difficulties he saw in all forms of Calvinism were becoming intolerable to him and a new point of departure needed. Professor Fitch of Yale College published two discourses about that time that proved quite helpful to the struggling student. Asa noted that "in these discourses, the position was taken and verified by proofs . . . that sin proper, that for which the creature is subject to condemnation, consists exclusively in a *voluntary transgression of known duty*." "This doctrine," he continued, "did not deny, but fully admitted, a fallen, or what is called a sinful nature in man, but affirmed that we are accountable, not for the mere existence of this nature, but for our voluntary actions relative to its promptings."[8] In considering the relation of the human will to sin Mahan had reached a very far-sweeping conclusion, one which required him fundamentally to reconstruct his entire system of theology and, as he said, to " 'read with new eyes' the word of God."

Among his reasons for his change of opinion Mahan wrote that Calvinistic determinism not only flatly contradicts the teachings of the leading thinkers of the primitive church but also the reports of ordinary consciousness[9]. But why should I accept a theory over what I directly experience? We are all directly aware that we "could have done otherwise"—that is, we are aware of the ability to do either of two things or, having done one, the ability to have done the other. We are aware not simply that if the circumstances had been different we might have acted differently but rather that in the very *same* circumstances we might have acted other than we did. Unfortunately Old School views make moral responsibility impossible and turn God into an unjust tyrant. If men have no power whatever to will or act differently than in fact they do then the concepts of merit and demerit, and the consequent propriety of reward and punishment, become neaningless and inapplicable. And God is transformed into a tyrant when he admonishes men to give up their sinful ways since He is demanding of them what it is impossible for them to do. God must be seen on Judgment Day as eternally damning certain souls and saving others when none of the lot supposedly could have done other than they did and so merit no judgment at all. Were not such ridiculous consequences a reduction to absurdity of Old School Calvinism? Mahan thought the answer was surely "yes"! He had to work out his view in detail (his critique of Edwards, and other Calvinistic efforts to make determinism compatible with moral responsibility, came later), but he felt he had his bearings and a compass to plot his further course.

During his early pastorates Asa Mahan experienced an "aching void" in his heart. His early experiences of the vivid presence of God had already begun to wear off during his college and seminary years. While he had rejected Calvinistic views of salvation, and felt good about this progress, he still held what he called the legalistic view of combatting sin and felt discouraged by the results it produced. On the legalistic view it was up to man himself to overcome his sinful inclinations and nature, but being spiritually puny and having a carnal nature he was doomed to fail and to continue to disobey God's commandments. To be sure, he had been helped in seminary by Moses Stuart's analysis of Romans 7 that it was a description of the legalistic view, not an endorsement of it. God required, indeed demanded, that man obey His commandments and abandon his evil ways. But how was this possible? Some "legalists" spoke of asking for God's promised help through Christ and the Holy Ghost, the result being a cooperative effort between man and the Holy Ghost in combatting sin. This interpretation was certainly an improvement but again man seemed unable to pull his share of the load, and submitting to sinful inclination seemed the inevitable outcome.[10]

Mahan knew that he himself sinned in various ways—sometimes losing his temper, for example—but he felt that his besetting sin was that of undue ambition and pride. He fought against it, he said, but his legalistic views about how to combat sin and strive after a holy life never led him to victory. In later life he characterized this deficiency in exaggerated terms perhaps, though the deficiency was no doubt nonetheless real.[11]

Moreover, Asa worried a good deal about both public and private matters. Would any headway ever be made against slavery and intemperance? How could he sustain his family in case of further illness like his disability in Rochester that sent Mary and him to his father's farm in Orangeville? Yet if he had such a great belief in the wisdom of God and believed in Providence why should he worry so about the present and future? Further, he found no deep-down consolation in his religious beliefs. He was still as unreconciled to the deaths of his infant children as he had been on the day they died. Yet had they not been lowered into the "lap of God" and should he not be happy that they were with Him? No doubt he should feel this way but he grieved for them as much as ever and wanted them back.[12]

There was, he felt, some crucial religious dimension missing not only in his life but in the lives of the vast majority of Christians. He read Fenelon, Madame Guyon, John Wesley, John Fletcher, and other authors and felt that he was getting close to a crucial insight but hadn't quite got the matter right. The Methodists of Cincinnati apparently thought that whether he knew it or not he had already been granted "the second blessing," the in-dwelling of Christ in his heart, for it had long been clear to them and to many others in Cincinnati that Asa Mahan somehow seemed to preach "with a power beyond his own." They held an annual camp meeting thirty miles from the river city and in 1834 asked their Presbyterian brother to preach to them. It was a memorable experience for Mahan:

> As I took my stand, on my arrival, in the presence of the vast crowd before me, a consciousness of divine power came over me of which I had never had an experience before. During the progress of the discourse the hearts of the crowd were moved by the power of the truth and of the Spirit, "as the trees of wood are moved by the wind." At the close of the discourse, sinners of all classes, and in astonishing numbers, crowded to the places of inquiry. The whole following night was spent by ministers, without sleep at all, in directing inquirers to Christ, and a revival of religion occurred which is spoken of by people in the city and all that region to this day. When I witnessed these results, this sentiment forced itself upon my mind: "He always wins who sides with God," and always wins such victories as his heart most desires. During one of the intervals of worship, I retired into the forest for personal meditation and prayer. While there, with a sense of painful loneliness and isolation which it is impossible to describe, I lifted my eyes and heart above, and said in words to my Father in heaven, that "I was willing, if need be, to be alone and to be despised in the world; but there was one thing that I did desire, and would venture to ask: that I might be conscious that my heart was pure in His sight, that I might *see* God, and live and walk in the manifested light of His countenance. If God would grant me this one infinite good," I added, "I would accept any burdens or afflictions that He might lay upon me." That was the distinctly uttered vow which I took with me from that forest. I have passed through heated furnaces and deep waters since that time, but have never taken back or regretted that

vow. The brightness of the final "rising of the Sun of Righteousness" did not come at that moment. The era was very near, however, when "God did become my everlasting light, and the days of my mourning were ended."[13]

Asa Mahan carried to Oberlin the aching void in his heart. Even though he had never lost the sense of being saved by freely accepting the gracious gift of God, he had become increasingly discouraged by his own efforts to combat sinful inclinations. To be sure, as we have seen, at the Methodist camp meeting near Cincinnati he had had joyful intimations of things to come, but the complete results were not forthcoming.[14] It was at Oberlin that the result he hoped for finally appeared.

Mahan's aching void was filled as a result of several distinctly different experiences. During his second summer at Oberlin he and Finney took the tabernacle tent to Mansfield, Ohio, and preached to "great congregations of unregenerate persons and [to] Christians." While the camp meeting was in progress he picked up a copy of *Clarke on the Promises,* which "providentially lay by me," and on the title page he read this passage: "Whereby are given unto us exceeding great and precious promises: that by these ye may be partakers of the divine nature, having escaped the corruption that is in the world through lust." Dr. Mahan was thunderstruck. "No words can describe the effect which the reading of that passage had upon my mind. I seemed at once to be fanned by 'the wings of the morning' whose everlasting light was about to dawn upon my waiting spirit."[15] He now believed that all things pertaining to a holy and godly life are given in the knowledge of Christ. But, as he later frequently stressed, there are two crucially different ways of knowing—knowing *about* something and being directly aware or acquainted with it. After reading this book he knew *about* holiness: he believed that God would grant a person release from every specific sin whenever by faith he asked Him to do it, for God does not promise things He is unwilling to do; and he further believed that the purpose for which the promises were given was, upon supplication, to transform man's nature so there was no longer a predilection or disposition to transgress God's law and the moral law.

While Mahan felt all these views to be true, he still lacked the feeling of the immanent presence of God. He had discursive knowledge about God but was not directly acquainted with Him. Feeling that God was for him "still far off in Heaven," he prayed after his return to Oberlin, as he had done at the Methodist camp meeting, to *see* God and feel his inner presence. He "entreated the Father of mercies, for Christ's sake, to lead me out of darkness into the light after which I was seeking." The next day he entered the room of a faculty member who was living in his home and discussed the nature of St. Paul's "undying and all-constraining flame" of devotion. "While thus speaking upon the subject, I suddenly rose from my seat with the joyful exclamation, 'I have found it!' and without uttering another word, I returned to my study, and again falling upon my knees, returned most fervent thanksgiving to God." Asa was convinced that while talking about Paul he had seen God and felt his inner presence.

> In the depth of my inner being, I felt an instantaneous enlargement, expansion, and invigoration of all my receptive capacities. There then opened upon my mind a direct apprehension, an open vision, as it were, of the infinite and ineffable love and glory of Christ, a love and glory which filled and occupied the entire compass of my being, and warmed, and quickened, and vitalized all the powers and activities of my mental nature. The rock of the heart was struck with the rod of love divine.[16]

However, Mahan was struck with loathing several days later when he thought of his enslavement to his temper, appetites, and secret ambition. Near despair, he prayed earnestly that he might be fully searched, cleansed, and led in the way everlasting. He felt that his plea was heard. "After the process of searching and self-revelation was completed, the waters of life seemed to flow through every department of my nature, rolling down as the river of life into the Dead Sea of the propensities, and everywhere with the same healing and vitalising efficacy."[17] Soon after this experience, upon retiring to his bedroom, he received what he described as a personal manifestation of the presence of Christ. "I did not 'fall at his feet as dead,' the manifestation being too mildly loving for that. My breathing, however stopped in an instant, and it was some time before I could recover it again." His joy, he wrote, was full, and he later described this manifestation as his "first full baptism of the Spirit."[18]

Preaching from this new standpoint Mahan and Finney, also an advocate of the holiness view, were immediately asked by a student at a public meeting,

> What *degree* of sanctification do the Scriptures authorize us to trust Christ for? May we, or may we not, trust Him to save us from *all* sin, and to sanctify us *wholly*, and to do it in this present life? I would very earnestly appeal to our beloved instructors, President Mahan and Professor Finney, for a specific answer to this question.[19]

Mahan and Finney were initially taken aback. To reply "yes" might suggest that a sanctified person was no longer capable of sinning, the terrible heresy of antinomianism present in John Humphrey Noyes' Perfectionism. Mahan replied that he would give the question prayerful and careful attention and would, the Lord permitting, furnish in due time a full and specific answer. With this question in mind Mahan and Finney spent the winter off-term in New York City preaching and searching the Scriptures for an answer. The writings of John Wesley and James B. Taylor on Christian Perfection were helpful at this time.

Mahan's "full and specific answer" was published in 1839 as the *Scripture Doctrine of Christian Perfection*, "a series of discourses designed to throw light on the way of holiness." This book proved to be immensely influential in the holiness movement.[20] It was first published by D. S. King in Boston and was reprinted by this firm and its successor, Waite and Peirce, ten times. In 1850 J. M. Fitch of Oberlin reprinted it for the eleventh time.

In his influential book Mahan distinguished between salvation from sin and the continuous battle against sin. Theologically speaking, the first is a matter of justification through faith; the latter a matter of perfection, holiness, or sanctification. Protestants in general hold the standard Reformation doctrine concerning the former: man is an inherently sinful creature and can never merit salvation; however God, out of grace, saves some. For free-will Trinitarians it is up to each individual to accept or reject God's gracious gift; those who do are saved, those who do not are damned. In short, man's role in salvation is limited to choosing freely one way or another; God's role is to actually provide Salvation when it is chosen even though the agent is unworthy of it.

Christian perfection, or holiness, on the other hand, refers to man's capacity for following God's commandments. Is it possible—and if so, how?—to wage successful warfare against the ever present enemy, sinful dispositions and tendencies? Here the ranks of Protestantism are markedly split and two quite different answers—let us call one the legalistic and the other evangelistic—are given, which have significantly different results. The legalistic answer says that overcoming sin is quite different from salvation. A sanctified life is not a gracious gift of God to be sought by earnest prayerfulness but is something that man must heroically struggle to achieve for himself. However, given the sinful nature of man, such efforts are bound to fail and such failures dishearten the Christian until he makes a sort of piety out of inevitable wickedness. "Oh, dear, how sinful I am! Thankfully I am saved by the grace of God in spite of my inherent shortcomings!"[21]

The evangelistic alternative, Mahan averred, is the only successful way to combat sin. According to this view, sanctification is quite similar to salvation. It is just as hopeless for man to think he can overcome sin by his own effort as it is to think he can earn salvation through good works. Victory over sin, like salvation, is a gracious gift of God. The in-dwelling Christ, the Spirit of God in man's heart, is the victor over sin, not man himself. The role of man in receiving this second gracious gift of God is to pray sincerely and earnestly for it: "If you will open the door, the Son of God will enter in, and confer this blessed inheritance upon you." "Ask and it shall be given you."[22]

However, Mahan emphasized, one must ever be alert to avoid the opposite error, namely, antinomianism, the notion that once "the Son of God enters in" a person becomes incapable of sinful behavior—by definition, so to speak, since it is now the Spirit of God acting. According to Mahan, the presence of the Spirit does *not* supplant the agency of the human being; it is present only because a person freely, and without constraint, sincerely sought its presence. And the continuing presence of the Spirit is dependent upon the constantly renewed decision to ask for and prayerfully seek that presence. The human being can always succumb to his previous sinful ways and thus lose the Spirit's domination of his life. Our first parents and the fallen angels were once completely pure, or entirely sanctified, and still they were tempted and fell. A fully and wisely instructed sanctified believer "is perfected in watchfulness, as well as in other Christian virtues, and, like the prudent general, is never for a moment off his guard." Finally, the antinomian view of perfection is wrong, Mahan claimed, since it is perfectly possible for a person to have a *will* that is "perfect in holiness" and yet *act* imperfectly. A will is perfect in holiness when a person loves God with all his heart and his neighbor as himself. It does not follow from this fact, however, that a man's *action* is perfect since man, even with the in-dwelling Spirit of Christ, unlike God does not possess perfect wisdom and may wrongly interpret his duty in complicated cases.[23]

Mahan's commitment to Christian Perfection, his espousal of "the way of holiness," had profound consequences both for him and his family. As we have seen, he had long considered his chief sins to be pride, ambition, and loss of temper. With his new religious convictions he prayed specifically for the removal of each of "these evil propensities" and sincerely believed that they "were crucified" by the in-dwelling Spirit of Christ. Mahan also lost, he felt, many fears that had haunted him through the years, including his horror of dying and repugnance at the thought of being put into a coffin and lowered into the ground. He also became reconciled to the loss of loved ones and was relieved of his tormenting grief over the deaths of his infant children. He never ceased to think about them but now joyfully looked forward to seeing them again. Now he could dream that his infant son, grown to manhood, greeted him in Heaven, "It is my father come at last."

NOTES

1. E. D. Eaton, "Asa Mahan" entry, *Dictionary of American Biography* (New York: Scribners, 1933), XIII, p. 209; "Asa Mahan" folder, Alumni Records, Bosworth Hall, Oberlin College; Asa Mahan, "Reminiscences and Reflections, Part VI," *Divine Life*, vol. 13, February 1980, especially pp. 213-15; Mahan, *Autobiography: Intellectual, Moral, and Spiritual* (London: T. Woolmer, 1882), pp. 1-39.

2. Mahan, *Autobiography*, pp. 1-39.

3. *Ibid.*, pp. 40-57.

4. Mahan, *Out of Darkness into Light* (New York: Willard Tract Repository, 1876), p. 11.

5. *Ibid.*, p. 13; *Autobiography*, pp. 50-55.

6. Cf. *Autobiography*, chs. 6-11, and *Out of Darkness into Light*, Part I.

7. *Autobiography*, p. 120.

8. *Ibid.*, p. 203.

9. *Ibid.*, pp. 204-14.

10. *Ibid.* pp. 289-92; *Out of Darkness into Light*, pp. 90-122.

11. Mahan, "Reminiscences and Reflections, Part II," *Divine Life*, vol. 13, October 1889, pp. 87-88.

12. *Out of Darkness into Light*, pp. 91-92.

13. *Ibid.*, pp. 119-20.

14. *Ibid.*

15. *Ibid.*, p. 125.

16. *Ibid.*, p. 135.

17. *Ibid.*, p. 149.

18. *Ibid.*, p. 158; Mahan, *The True Believer* (New York: Harper, 1847), pp. 276-77.

19. *Autobiography*, p. 323. Cf. *Out of Darkness into Light*, pp. 123-55 and Timothy Smith's Introduction to C. G. Finney, *The Promise of the Spirit* (Minneapolis: Bethany Fellowship, 1980), pp. 16-17.

20. Mahan, *Scripture Doctrine of Christian Perfection* (Boston: D. S. King, 1839). This text was reprinted eleven times. In 1849 an English edition was published by Partridge and Company with an Introduction by John Stevenson. A new edition entitled simply *Christian Perfection* was published in London in 1875 by F. E. Longley. It contains a prefatory letter by Mahan in which he endorsed all that he had written thirty-six years before, and an Introduction by George Warner, one of Mahan's colleagues in the holiness movement in England. Mahan lived the last fifteen years of his life in England.

21. Mahan, *Scripture Doctrine*, pp. 77-79, 98-104, 129-32, 136-39; *Autobiography*, pp. 281-364.

22. *Ibid.*, pp. 162, 172, 186.

23. *Ibid.*, pp. 70-73, 162, 172, 186; *Autobiography*, pp. 293, 372-74, 382-86, 387-89; *The Banner of Holiness*, vol. 1, September 23, 1875, p. 4; Mahan, *Doctrine of the Will* (New York: Mark H. Newman, 1845), especially pp. 84-85, 103-04; *Divine Life*, February 1878, pp. 193-95.

PART THREE

Old Testament Studies

9

EBLA AND GENESIS 11

Cyrus H. Gordon

Dedicated to Dennis Kinlaw, gifted disciple and loyal friend.

It is regrettable that new discoveries are often misunderstood, misrepresented and then discredited. This may happen not so much because of evil motives, but good intentions tainted by misguided enthusiasms. We need not play down the significance of the Early Bronze Age archives from Ebla because of bad "PR." For example, early estimates of the number of tablets found have ranged between 16,000 and 20,000. We now hear that these figures may be about twice the actual number. But the fact remains that a library of say 8,000 documents is not rendered unimportant by statistical inflation. We have in any case to reckon with Ebla as a thriving intellectual city in Syria-Palestine, in contact with Mesopotamia, Anatolia, Cyprus, Canaan and Egypt. Ebla fostered an academy that trained scholars bilingually in Sumerian and Eblaite.

The correct readings and identifications in the Ebla tablets have an enduring significance that should not be downgraded because of other mistaken readings. The latter have simply saddled us with the additional task of separating the wheat from the chaff. How the five cities of Genesis 14 (Sodom, Gomorrah, Admah, Zeboim and Zoar) were announced as definitely in a single Ebla tablet, and then definitely not in the tablet, is part of a series of mispronouncements which has bequeathed a murky legacy.

The allegation that the Eblaite village of Ga-sa is biblical Gaza has been properly repudiated on phonetic and topographical grounds.[1] But such corrections of blatant errors in no way change the picture concerning

Uru-Salim[2] = Jerusalem. It has been known for a long time that Jerusalem is called Uru-Salim in cuneiform tablets; e.g., in the Amarna Letters[3] and Assyrian Annals.[4] The Sumerian name[5] points to the founding of biblical Jerusalem by traders of the Sumerian Order in Early Bronze times long before the advent of the Hebrews. The occurrence of a city called Salim (= Salem as Jerusalem is called in Genesis 14:18) in the Ebla archives is of great interest, even though it refers to another city of the same name.

Although we must sweep out the nonsense from the Augean Stables, we must resist the temptation to denigrate the value of the Ebla material because of some highly publicized bad judgment. Were it not for such misleading enthusiasm, the progress of science would be much slower, albeit with less foolishness along the way. Let us not forget that many decades of wild science fiction stimulated and expedited the coming of the space age.

This article aims at outlining a new vista that Ebla is opening in biblical pre-history.[6] This development is not affected in its broad outlines by half-truths and outright errors given out by professional scholars in learned journals or by popularizers in the media.

The firm fact we are dealing with is that in the Semitic Levant, around 2500 B.C., Sumerian was used as the lingua franca in urban administrative centers such as Ebla.

Linguae francae are employed for communication among members of different speech groups. Thus India is full of mutually unintelligible native languages. However, a lasting benefit of British rule is the use of English throughout India. Accordingly, at a meeting of the Cabinet, Tamil-speaking ministers discuss matters of state with their Hindustani-speaking colleagues in the English lingua franca. Far beyond the confines of India, English now serves as the main (though not the only) lingua franca globally. A Persian and a Mexican, or even a Chinese and a Japanese, are likely to communicate in English at the UN or in the marketplace.

The biblical Hebrews were exposed to a number of linguae francae. We start with Aramaic and then go backward in time. In dealing with ancient history it is sometimes advisable to start with the later "known" and go from there back to the earlier "unknown."[7] Aramaic as a lingua franca in later biblical times is quite well known. While it is of interest to review some of the data pertaining to it, it does not have to be proved or established as a fact.

During Sennacherib's invasion of Judah in 701 B.C., the general public in Jerusalem spoke only Hebrew, though their diplomats could also use Aramaic as the lingua franca in negotiating with foreign officials.[8] When the spokesmen of King Hezekiah wanted the Assyrian representative to speak Aramaic so as to keep the public from understanding the alarming Assyrian ultimatum, the Assyrian insisted on using Hebrew precisely so that the public would know what was going on.[9]

Aramaic made steady gains internationally. The Achaemenian Empire of the Medes and Persians (6th-4th centuries B.C.) used it as the interprovincial medium beyond the Iranian homeland. Thus in the Fifth Century B.C. it was used by the agents of the Achaemenian emperors even in the distant province of Egypt.[10] The Jewish colony at Elephantine in Upper Egypt, functioning as an outpost of the Achaemenian Empire, used Aramaic for their correspondence and other documents. The Achaemenian Age also evoked the Aramaic portions of Ezra and Daniel.[11]

The extension of Aramaic as a lingua franca grew apace so that in addition to being the medium of much of rabbinic literature, it simultaneously became the language of much of eastern Christianity. Pagans also fostered Aramaic dialects; e.g., note pagan Syriac literature and the whole corpus of Mandaic writings.[12]

The wide use of Aramaic was always familiar in learned Judeo-Christian circles. But it was not until 1887 that the Amarna Letters began to come to light in Egypt. Those letters from the reigns of Amenophis III (ca. 1417-1379 B.C.) and Amenophis IV (= Akhenaton, ca. 1379-62) are in Babylonian even though they were exchanged between the Pharaoh on the one hand, and the rulers of a wide variety of Near East regions on the other. Those regions covered Syria-Palestine, Mesopotamia, Anatolia and Cyprus. Many familiar sites, now in Israel, are included: Jerusalem, Megiddo, Taanach, Ascalon, Gaza, Acre, etc. Babylonian was neither the language of Egypt, nor of Syria-Palestine, nor Anatolia, nor Cyprus. But it had gained the status of a lingua franca throughout widely diversified speech areas.[13]

The Amarna Tablets are far from the only witnesses of the Babylonian lingua franca during the Late Bronze Age (1600-1200). One of the best documented witnesses is Ugarit (ca. 1400-1200) on the north Syrian coast. The cuneiform tablets from Ugarit fall into two main categories: (1) the alphabetic texts in the local Ugaritic language, and (2) the syllabic archives in Babylonian. Diplomatic correspondence and treaties are normally in the international medium: Babylonian.[14] The lingua franca of Canaan when Joshua conquered the Holy Land was still (albeit waning) Babylonian.

The classical language of Babylonia was Sumerian, and as long as Babylonian survived (into the first century, A.D.), its scribes looked upon Sumerian much as Western Europe looks back on Latin.[15] In Ugarit the scribes copied and studied quadrilingual vocabularies in which words of the same meaning were entered, each in four parallel columns: Sumerian, Babylonian, Hurrian and Ugaritic.[16] Ugaritic was the main, and Hurrian the next most important, language spoken by the local and regional population. Babylonian was the lingua franca, but Sumerian was still cherished as the classical tongue of a by-gone era.

The Early Bronze Age archives of Ebla are mainly (about four-fifths) in Sumerian and point to a Sumerian lingua franca, antedating by a millennium the Amarna Age, by which time Babylonian had become the international language of the Near East. How are we to account for this role of Sumerian? Syria is far from Sumer, in southern Iraq. There are two ways of approaching the Sumerian problem, and we can learn from both of them. First, the conventional way: Sumerian developed into a written medium in Sumer (= southern Babylonia), flourished throughout the third millennium B.C., and thereafter was fostered as the classical language of the Assyro-Babylonian World. During the third millennium, certain rulers of Sumerian city-states embarked on spectacular conquests extending to the East Mediterranean. The best known example is Lugalzaggesi of Umma, whose empire reached the Mediterranean, and who was vanquished by Sargon of Akkad around 2400 B.C., around the time when tablets of the Ebla archives were being inscribed. We can hardly attribute the Sumerianism of Ebla to Lugalzaggesi's conquests in Syria which would in any case be too recent to account for the depth of Sumerian tradition at Ebla. It is likely that Sumerianization had been gaining momentum for some time under the initiative of Mesopotamian merchants famed for their initiative in foreign trade. Yet there is always the possibility that armies had to some extent paved the way for traders. We must not deny some kernel of historicity to Mesopotamian traditions that earlier rulers of Sumerian city-states, notably Lugal-anne-mundu of Adab, had carved out an empire stretching to the Mediterranean about six generations before Lugalzaggesi.

There is also a quite different way of approaching the Sumerian problem. The Sumerians could not have originated in Sumer. Their language is unrelated to any speech in the region and their way of life required minerals, both metals and stones, that never existed in Sumer. A suggestive discovery was made early in the 1960's at Tartaria in Romanian Transylvania. Archaeologists found there a few inscribed clay tablets, whose shapes and writing are associated with the most archaic tablets of Sumer. The date of the Tartaria tablets was at first announced as ca. 3000, but carbon-14 tests later pointed to ca. 2700. The minerals of Transylvania, including gold, provide a possible inducement that would have attracted the Sumerians. While Sumer required gold (whether from Nubia, Arabia, Transylvania, or anywhere else), it also needed an assortment of stones, such as lapis-lazuli which was presumably imported from Badakhshan in eastern Afghanistan, near the Soviet and Chinese borders. That the essentials of Sumerian civilization required raw materials from great distances in different directions confronts us with a view of Sumerian origins like the following: There was a loose, far-flung network of operational outposts for securing various raw materials to be processed at a "national" center. In pre-historic times the center shifted, eventually to be located (ca. 3500) in the land we call Sumer.[17]

The selection of Sumer was favored by a number of basic considerations. The land is well watered by the Tigris and Euphrates. Those rivers and the canal systems along and between them provided boat lanes as well as fish and agricultural products. Sumer is bordered on the south by the Persian Gulf which opens on to the Indian Ocean with all its maritime trade. The limited natural resources of the land itself were compensated by the proximity of the mineral wealth of Iran, Arabia and the mountainous terrain to the north. The Twin Rivers were gateways to many desiderata; thus the Euphrates provided the water routes for a good part of the way to the forests of Lebanon, Anti-Lebanon and Amanus mountains. Aside from the agricultural wealth of Sumer, that land had one abundant though unprepossessing product: mud. The Rivers bring down from the north vast quantities of silt. The Sumerians used mud brick as their primary building material, and clay tablets as their main writing material. Whenever Sumerian (or its off-shoot, Babylonian) civilization spread, the clay tablet inscribed with a stylus went with it.

Ebla by about 2500 B.C. had become a major outlier[18] of the Sumerian Order. Simplification of the complex Sumerian problem has a useful place provided that we remember it is only a first step in the quest for understanding something bigger than we can now fully envisage. The standard way of viewing the outposts of Sumerianism (which explains much, if not all of the story) starts with the Sumerians in Sumer, with an economy that required foreign trade for securing raw materials which it processed. In exchange it exported agricultural and animal products as well as manufactured wares. To maintain such a system, mercantile colonies had to be set up in peripheral areas. In the more remote colonies, the Sumerianization tended to be more attenuated. Hand in hand with the spread of Sumerianism through the foreign outposts, the latter introduced elements of the peripheral cultures to the Sumerian homeland.[19]

The colonies required personnel to keep the business records. For the cuneiform scribes, Sumerian remained the ultimate classical language, even though they might apply Sumerian script to various "barbaric"[20] languages. Among the latter, Semitic Akkadian was foremost. Hittite comes next in importance. Hurrian must also be rated high on the list, for it was the language of the powerful Mitanni Kingdom during the early part of the Amarna Age. Hurrian texts have also been found at major sites such as Mari, Ugarit and Amarna. The Nuzi population was essentially Hurrian, while at Alalakh and Ugarit there were large Hurrian minorities. Clay tablets inscribed with cuneiform, include records of lost languages such as the Semitic dialects of Ugarit[21] and Ebla.[22]

We have noted that in the first millennium B.C., Aramaic was a lingua franca in the Bible World; and that it was preceded by Akkadian as the lingua franca in the second millennium. And now, Ebla points to an earlier age when Sumerian was established in the Levant as a lingua franca beyond the borders of Mesopotamia.

Genesis 11:1-9 records a tradition about developments "after the Deluge" (Genesis 10:32) which means in modern terms "at the dawn of history." It narrates that in the land of Shinar,[23] the construction of a great city and tower[24] was being accomplished by a vast working force united through a single language[25] used throughout the earth.[26] In modern parlance this means "an international lingua franca." This does not mean there was only one language in existence up to that time, because just previously, we read Genesis 10:5, 20, 31 that the various groupings of mankind, living in different countries, had each its own language. Accordingly, the "one language" does not mean that only one speech was used at home by all members of mankind but rather that in the entire ecumene,[27] there was a lingua franca that made international projects possible.

The legend has it that insufferable arrogance went with such mighty projects, whose builders were out to reach the very heavens.[28] God put an end to such hubris by breaking up the ecumene through terminating the lingua franca. Lacking the means of communication, that international order split into its component parts.[29]

What was that lingua franca? For plain historic reasons known to the classical Hebrews, the Aramaic lingua franca was too late for wonderous Mesopotamian constructions just "after the Flood." A conceivable candidate would be the Babylonian lingua franca which we can document from numerous extrabiblical sources. Yet a tradition about the state of affairs "after the Flood" (long before Abraham) should refer back to a still more remote antiquity. The Ebla tablets strongly suggest that the lingua franca "after the Flood" was Sumerian.

While the Semitic languages of Western Asia on the one hand, and Sumerian on the other, belong to two entirely different divisions of speech, they were in contact with each other before the first texts appear around 3000 B.C. Sumerian, which was written before any known Semitic text, already has Semitic loanwords imbedded in it; e.g., *silim* "well being, peace" (cognate with Hebrew *šālôm* and Arabic *salâm*). Sumerian *damgar* "merchant" (pronounced *tamkar* in Akkadian) is regarded as an early loan from Semitic (i.e., MKR "to sell or buy"; usually "to sell" in Hebrew). Early Sumerian loans in Semitic are familiar. Thus Sumerian *é-gal* (= é "house" + *gal* "big") "palace, temple," comes into Akkadian as *ekallu* and into Hebrew as *hêkāl*. Until recently Sumerian gu-*za* "chair, throne" was considered as borrowed into Semitic (Akkadian *kussû*, Hebrew *kissê'*, Aramaic *kursî*, etc.) Now, some scholars consider it a Semitic loan in Sumerian. Either way, it attests prehistoric contacts between the Semites and Sumerians.[30]

Sumerian *má-lah₄* "sailor" (= *má* "boat" + *lah₄* "to go" or "cause to go") is borrowed into Semitic (Akkadian *mallâhu*, Hebrew *mallâh*, etc, "sailor"). Sumerian *na(n)-gar* "carpenter" has been borrowed into Semitic; e.g., Hebrew *naggâr*, Arabic *najjâr*; and so forth with other Sumerian loans and native Semitic roots in the *qattâl* formation (patterned after such Semitic loans) to indicate *nomina agentis* or professions; note, for example, Hebrew *gazzâr* or Arabic *jazzâr* "butcher," Arabic *baqqâl* "grocer," Hebrew *pehâr* (from **pahhâr*) "potter" or *nahâg* (from **nahhâg*) "driver, chauffeur." This formation is interesting in that it is Sumerian in origin and became a common nominal type in Semitic.

Whatever the contribution of the Semites to early Sumerian civilization, it cannot diminish the primacy of the Sumerians as the first known speech-group in the world to establish a literate culture and, moreover, one that was to remain classical for a galaxy of important offshoots for three thousand years. The Sumerian legacy in fact goes on through its loanwords in Hebrew. Sumerian loanwords in Arabic keep spreading with the growth of Islam among Turkic, Persian, Urdu, Indonesian and other speech-groups in the Eastern Hemisphere.

That the first element (*yᵉrû-*) of "Jerusalem" is the word for "city" not in Canaanite (for the Hebrew is *ʿîr*) but in Sumerian (*uru*) is clear from the Hebrew YRWŠLM against the background of its rendition in Sumero-Akkadian literature (*uru-salim*). The capital of Israel was probably given its Sumerian name over 1500 years before David occupied it. To state matters in terms of Genesis 11, Jerusalem was founded and given its lasting name when Sumerian was the lingua franca.[31]

We cannot speak of the Hebrew language or of the Hebrews during the period of the Ebla archives, any more than we can speak of Spanish or the Spaniards when the Roman legions occupied the Iberian Peninsula. Indeed we should not speak of Spaniards or Portuguese prior to the impact of the Arabs and Jews. As Americo Castro noted, the Jewish and Arab components of Spanish character are so basic that whatever we call the people of the Iberian Peninsula before the Judeo-Arabic impact, they cannot be described as "Spaniards," as the term is applied to modern Spaniards.[32]

By the same token, in our quest for a meaningful terminology concerning Hebrew and the Hebrews, we should start with Abram "the Hebrew" in Genesis 14:13, who marked a break with the pagan past to which his father, Terah, belonged. The transition from father to son even marked a linguistic break, from Aramaic to Canaanite.[33] The Sumerian Age, attested at Ebla, contributed much to the background of the land, people and even language of Israel. But it would be a delusion to imagine that any of the forerunners and ancestors of the Hebrews were essentially the same kind of people that numbered Abram, Moses, the heroes of the Conquest, David, Solomon and the kings and prophets of Israel and Judah.

When we speak of "Jews" we run into a still more complex set of problems. Why Hillel and Shammai are "Jews" is obvious, however different they were from medieval and modern rabbis. We can even see familiar "Jewish" traits in Nehemiah: a prominent leader of the Diaspora, using his influence to help his struggling coreligionists in the Homeland secure Jerusalem and their survival on their ancestral soil. But can we describe Samson as a Jewish leader: a muscleman whose heroic violence and heedless sense of honor left many a corpse on the ground, all because a woman was withheld from him?[34] That not only an ancient Achilles, or even a latter-day "Texan badman," could behave that way is conceivable, but not a "Jewish leader," from Nehemiah's time to our own.

There was no one resembling a "Hebrew" on earth during the Early Bronze Age. When we come to the biblical Hebrews, we must recognize that just as much a part of their make-up as their original or distinctive features[35] are the elements they borrowed from their neighbors in an arc of 360°. And exactly when the biblical Hebrews evolved into types that we can recognize as "Jewish" is a moot question for which there may never be a clear-cut answer.

The importance of Ebla for biblical studies is that it provides us with written documentation for a major development, with lasting effects, on Palestine before the Hebrews[36]—on the Holy Land, before it was sanctified by God's promise to Abram.

NOTES

1. *Ga-sa*, in the vicinity of Ebla, was not a city but a village ruled by a mere *ugula* "overseer" (Alfonso Archi, "Notes on Eblaite Geography," *Studi Eblaiti* vol. 2, (1980), pp. 1-16, 4 plates; see pp. 5-6.

2. It is the "Ebla Age" that accounts for the Sumerian name of Jerusalem (= Sumerian Uru "city" of the deity Salim).

3. In the Amarna tablets, "Jerusalem" is spelled *U-ru-sa-lim* (texts 287:25, 61, 63; 289:14, 29; 290:15; the numbering is the same in the earlier German edition of Knudtzon *et al.* and in the later English edition of S.A.B. Mercer, The *Tell el-Amarna Tablets*, II (Toronto: Macmillan, 1939).

4. In Sennacherib's Annals, it is spelled *Ur-sa-li-im-mu* (var. *-ma*); see Third Campaign, col. III, lines 8 and 20. The cuneiform text is on p. 67 of Friedrich Delitzsch, *Assyrische Lesestücke*, 5th ed., Leipzig: Hinrichs, 1912.

5. It should be noted that uru "city" (which comes into Hebrew as yᵉrû-) is written quite differently from the city-name Ur (which appears in Hebrew as '*ûr*; note '*ûr kaśdîm* "Ur of the Chaldees"), which is written ŠEŠ-UNU-KI (ideographically). Outside of the name of Jerusalem, the prefix yᵉrû- occurs only in the toponym yᵉrû-'ēl (2 Chronicles 20:16). The phonetic and other aspects of yᵉrû- (vis-à-vis Sumerian *uru*) will be discussed in detail elsewhere.

6. The legendary character of Genesis 11:1-9 must not shut our eyes to the genuine features embodied in the tale, such as the construction of baked-brick cities and ziggurats in Babylonia, and the breakdown of an old order which had been made possible by the use of a lingua franca.

7. We use the term "unknown" in the algebraic sense. We set out to solve "x" ("the unknown") on the basis of "knowns" ("a," "b," "c," etc.).

8. 2 Kings 18:26 contrasts the Aramaic lingua franca with the "Judean" vernacular. "Judean" = the dialect of Jerusalem and the Judean Kingdom. The term "Hebrew" is not used linguistically in the Old Testament.

9. 2 Kings 18:27-28.

10. Cf. Cyrus H. Gordon, "The Origin of the Jews in Elephantine," *Journal of Near Eastern Studies*, vol. 14, 1955, pp. 56-58.

11. The Aramaic portions of Ezra are documents of the Achaemenian Age. The Book of Daniel, however, has Greek loanwords and veiled references to Alexander and the Diadochi, which suggest a Hellenistic date. Yet the Aramaic of Daniel is a legacy of the Achaemenian Age and is linguistically to be classified as Empire Aramaic (the official lingua franca used provincially throughout the Empire).

12. For orientation, see Kurt Randolph, *Mandeism* (Leiden: Brill, 1978).

13. See the index of geographical names listed by Mercer, *Tablets,* II, pp. 892-900.

14. Jean Nougayrol, *Palais royal d'Ugarit* (Paris: Imprimerie Nationale), III (1955) and IV (1956).

15. The comprehensive analysis and description in all its stages, remains Arno Poebel's *Grundzüge der sumerischen Grammatik* (Rostock: privately printed by the author, 1923). There is a more recent grammar of New Sumerian by Adam Falkenstein, *Grammatik der Sprache Gudeas von Lagasch,* 2 vols. (Rome: Pontifical Biblical Institute, 1949-50).

16. Nougayrol, *Palais royal d'Ugarit* III (1955) and IV (1956).

17. It is reasonable to suppose that the Sumerians arrived in the Uruk Period (ca. 3500) when the seal cylinder, ziggurat, beginnings of Sumerian writing and other characteristic features of Sumerian civilization suddenly appear.

18. The term is used here in the sense of an outpost or colony in a peripheral region.

19. For an attempt to summarize what happened, see Geoffrey Barraclough (ed.), *The Times Atlas of World History* (Maplewood, N.J.: Hammond, 1979), pp. 54-55.

20. "Barbaric" is not used pejoratively. From the standpoint of an enlightened Greek like Herodotus, "barbarians" (so-called simply because they spoke languages other than Greek) could be highly civilized. Cf. Herodotus, *Histories,* Book II (on Egypt).

21. Cyrus H. Gordon, *Ugaritic Textbook* (Rome: Pontifical Biblical Institute, 1967).

22. The dialect of Ebla is contributing to the study of the complex interrelationships among the Hebrew, Ugaritic, Minoan, Egyptian and other Semitic languages. This does not mean that it should be classified narrowly with any one of the latter; see Cyrus H. Gordon, "Eblaite and its Affinities," *Current Issues in Linguistic Theory 11: Festschrift for Oswald Szemerényi* (Amsterdam: John Benjamins B.V., 1979) I, pp. 297-301.

23. "The Land of Shinar" (Genesis 11:2) designates "Babylonia." However, the term "Babylonia" is only accurate when applied after the emergence of Babylon under the First Dynasty of Babylon early in the second millenium B.C. Before then, the country was called "Sumer and Akkad" and, still earlier, before the rise of Sargon of Akkad (ca. 2400), it was called "Sumer."

24. Genesis 11:1.

25. Called *śāfā 'eḥāt* in Genesis 11:1. In the Table of Nations (Genesis 10), *lāšôn* is the word for "language."

26. *Kol-ha'āreṣ* (Genesis 11:1) refers to "the known world" which we could call "the ecumene" (as spelled out in Genesis 10). Contrast *kol-ha'āreṣ* with *'ereṣ šinᶜār* "(the specific) Land of Shinar."

27. The concept of an ecumene is inherent in Genesis 10 where all the nations are listed as interrelated.

28. Genesis 11:4.

29. The legend obliges us to consider the phenomenon of Empire Art. When craftsmen from different regions of an empire contribute their combined skills, they produce Empire Art. Nebuchadnezzar carried off artisans of the nations he conquered (2 Kings 24:14) to construct the composite of Empire Art of Babylon. Later, Cyrus the Great built his capital at Pasargade; it is an example of the National Art of Persia. But Persepolis, constructed mainly under Darius I and Xerxes I through pooling the talents of the satrapies, exemplifies Achaemenian Empire Art. When the central authority is destroyed, the component work forces disband, some returning to their native lands, and in any case the Empire Art disintegrates because there is no leadership to hold it together. Genesis 11:9 reflects this in noting that the "Old Order" ended with the cessation of the lingua franca so that the component peoples were scattered abroad.

30. Sumerian loans in Ugaritic (thus *hkl* = biblical Hebrew *hêkāl; ngr* = postbiblical Hebrew *naggâr*) show that the borrowings precede the recorded history of the Hebrew language.

31. Early ceramic remains at Jerusalem go back to about 3000. The Sumerian name of Jerusalem suggests that the settlement first became significant as a trading outpost of the "Sumerian Order" as reflected in the Ebla archives. Jerusalem is located in a saddle of the watershed ridge. It is therefore a crossroads, north-south and east-west. In remote antiquity

it was technically impossible to use the heights overlooking Jerusalem for attacking the city because they were beyond bow-shot and catapulting. (Long before the airplane, artillery rendered Jerusalem vulnerable.) Jerusalem was also desirable because it has its own water supply that remained sufficient as long as the city had a small population. Later, in Roman times, an adequate water supply for the large population could be brought by gravity by aqueducts from higher land (notably from Hebron).

32. The late Americo Castro of Princeton University developed this point convincingly; his work went through several editions of which the most recent is *The Spaniards: An Introduction to Their History* (rev. ed., 1971).

33. Genesis 31:47-48 is explicit in identifying the language of Laban as Aramaic (and he still lived in the ancestral Aram Naharaim) and Jacob's as Hebrew/Canaanite.

34. In *The Common Background of Greek and Hebrew Civilizations* (New York City: Norton, 1965), I have shown that Achilles and Samson (who were roughly contemporaries, ca. 1100 B.C.) resembled each other more than Achilles resembled a classical Athenian, or Samson a classical Prophet.

35. The concept that, above all else, God demands from the individual, as well as from society as a whole, kindness and mercy for the underdog is distinctively Hebraic. So too is the Tenth Commandment that it is wrong, not only to steal, but even to covet. On the other hand, most aspects of Hebrew culture, far from being unique, were shared with some of Israel's neighbors; e.g., the worship of one god, prohibitions against crimes like murder, perjury, theft, etc.

36. Understandably, Emmanuel Anati's *Palestine Before the Hebrews* (New York City: Knopf, 1963) provides no inkling of what the title of his book would convey since the discoveries at Ebla.

10

A MYTH IS A MYTH IS A MYTH: TOWARD A WORKING DEFINITION

John N. Oswalt

It is with particular pleasure that I offer this essay in tribute to Dennis Kinlaw, since it was he who first introduced me to the study of myth and planted in my mind the seeds of many of the ideas contained herein.

When Alice chided the March Hare for his improper use of a word, he assured her with considerable dignity that any word meant precisely what he wanted it to mean. It appears that we are in a similar situation with the word "myth." The word crops up on every hand in both religious and literary studies and with a bewildering variety of definitions. G. B. Caird has recently isolated nine definitions, while J. W. Rogerson had previously identified twelve.[1] The result is that while the user of the word may be clear enough about his or her intended meaning, the hearer or reader is frequently left in considerable doubt.

It may be that the very vagueness of the word is a part of the reason for its widespread usage. Precisely because it does not have a generally-agreed-upon meaning it can be pressed into service in many different ways without the user's becoming open to the charge of linguistic abuse. This essay will hardly settle the issue of the most appropriate definition of myth. What it does seek to do is to sensitize the reader to some of the critical issues in the discussion.

In my opinion, the definitions of myth currently in use may be grouped into four classifications. They are the etymological, the sociological, the literary, and the phenomenological types. The etymological definitions, based on the Greek *mythos,* stress the falsehood of the material. To the Greeks a myth was "an invented story, fable, tale or legend understood to be the opposite of *logos* or truth."[2] This is, of course, the definition of the average person. If that person is told that the resurrection of Christ is a myth, he immediately assumes that the speaker takes the story of the resurrection to be a false legend which teaches matters contrary to the truth. Nor can he be blamed for holding such a definition. It has been the prevailing one for many years.[3] It will not do for those who do not accept this meaning to dismiss it lightly as being the territory of the unenlightened.[4] The burden of proof is upon them to demonstrate why the generally-held meaning is not correct. Furthermore, it is incumbent upon them to explain why not only the Greeks but also the New Testament writers used the term in this way.

Those scholars who affirm an etymological definition of myth generally do so on the ground that myths rest upon a pre- or non-scientific world-view. So, for instance, Theodore Gaster describes myth as "a story of the gods or other superhuman beings or one told to account for a custom, institution or natural phenomenon."[5] Such a definition assumes a rigidly naturalistic understanding of the world. Any accounting for events, institutions or customs which is not strictly based on natural causes is false and thus mythical.

Millar Burrows says much the same when he defines myth as

> treating as the acts of a personal being or beings what a scientific world-view sees as the operation of impersonal forces and laws. . . . In this sense, it is at the same time false, or at best only a poetic, figurative expression of truth.

Another example of this kind of etymological definition is that of Hartlich and Sachs. "Occurrences are designated as 'mythical' insofar as the statements concerning such events arise from a pre-scientific and uncritical, naive stage of consciousness."[7]

What is fundamental to all of these definitions is the concept of a world which is removed several steps, if not absolutely, from the possibility of the direct intervention of a personal Deity. According to this position, any view which permits such intervention is of necessity "pre-scientific" and false. The difficulty here is in the conclusion that the "falseness" of myth stems from its "pre-scientific" world-view.

However, suppose the conclusion of the representatives of the "scientific" world-view, namely that we live in a closed system into which the Deity cannot penetrate on any but a psycho-spiritual plane, is itself false? What then? Simply because a given world-view may express itself in pre-scientific terms says nothing about its perception of ultimate truth.

Thus, it becomes important to determine in what respect a piece of literature is false before designating it as myth. C. S. Lewis demonstrates this in typically incisive fashion through his story of "horrid red things." A little girl reports that poison will kill a person. But when asked why, she replies that it is full of horrid red things.[8] Her understanding of causation is undoubtedly pre-scientific. Are her conclusions therefore false? By no means. By the same token, it is a *non sequitur* to suggest that belief in a bodily resurrection is pre-scientific and that therefore Jesus did not rise from the dead. The correspondence or non-correspondence of any account with reality must be judged on other bases than whether it is couched in "scientific" terms or not. If the religious perceptions of Egypt or Babylon or Israel are false, it is not merely because they use pre-scientific terminology and it is inappropriate to term them "myths" solely because they employ such terminology.

It is probably fair to say that this very concern has given rise to what is here called the sociological definition. Far from equating myth with falsehood, it equates it with perceived truth.

The "history of religions" school has given rise to this definition in its attempt to be fair to the various religions of the world, each of which has claimed to represent ultimate truth through a given set of images. So, for example, E. O. James says

> Myth . . . gave expression to the fundamental experience of a divinely ordered world in which a conflict of supernatural powers and forces was immanent, the one hostile and the other beneficial to their well-being. To fulfill its proper functions it must always be symbolic representation of the ultimate reality, however this may be conceived and interpreted, concerning the essential meaning and the facts of existence and of human destinies.[9]

Rudolf Bultmann has identified himself with this school by defining myth as "the use of imagery to express the other-worldly in terms of this world and the divine in terms of human life, the other side in terms of this side."[10] Similarly, Millar Burrows says,

> Myth implies not falsehood, but truth, not primitive, naive misunderstanding, but an insight more profound than scientific description and logical analysis can ever achieve. The language of myth in this sense is consciously inadequate, being simply the nearest we can come to the formulation of what we see very darkly.[11]

What all this comes down to is that myth is the central theory of any religion which its adherents regard as true.[12] James Barr is expressing this position when he declares,

> In a way the recognition that the Bible offers the classic primitive model of faith brings us back, perhaps surprisingly, to the literary character of most of the Bible: its allusiveness, its circumstantiality, its many-sidedness; all these make it fit to be the material upon which the church reflects and, if readers are willing to use the word *myth* in its most positive sense, to be understood as the basic foundation myth of Christianity—which qualities it has, as we have seen, precisely because it is in fact such a basic foundation myth.[13]

As several scholars have pointed out, the problem with such definitions is in their breadth.[14] Under such terms, any statement about God becomes mythical because it must express truth perceived about the other world in this worldy terms. This is a bit like saying that an automobile is a vehicle with wheels. The definition may be true enough as far as it goes, but it would be possible in those terms to label as automobile many items which are manifestly *not* automobile.

A second objection to such definitions is the ease with which they separate this-worldly truth and other-worldly truth. At first it appears that such a ploy could save the faith. The vehicle by which the truth is conveyed may be grossly false, but the truth itself is still true. The body of Jesus of Nazareth may well have rotted away long centuries ago, but the truth which that story conveyed, namely that God has conquered sin and death, remains untouched.

To be sure, this is precisely the route which most of the world religions have traveled. The physical world is not real, nor is it true. Truth is a concomitant of the real, or divine, world, of which ours is but a shadow.[15] Plato's cave story gives us perhaps the most developed form of such an understanding. In this light, it is positively wrong to expect to demonstrate ultimate truth by appeal to this world. Bultmann appears to agree with such a position, for he says that an attempt to support ultimate truth from the facts of history is only idolatrous.[16]

A modern example of such a world view is found in the works of Carlos Castaneda. Castaneda describes his apprenticeship to a Yaqui Indian sorcerer named Don Juan. In the course of the apprenticeship, Don Juan's goal was to separate present reality from ultimate reality in Castaneda's mind. One part of the regimen was aimed at making it possible for the sorcerer to fly to some distant spot where he could exercise power over some other person. Finally, in a drug-induced trance, Castaneda feels himself flying. When he comes out of the trance he excitedly inquires of Don Juan whether he has really flown. Don Juan assures him he has indeed. Not quite content, Castaneda asks whether his body actually left the chair. Don Juan replies harshly, "That is a foolish question."[17] What he means is that reality cannot be demonstrated by appeal to this world.

But can the vehicle be false and yet convey ultimate truth? (This is different from our earlier discussion of pre-scientific language. It is an entirely different thing to say that there was no flood than it is to say heaven does not have windows. The earlier definitions would suggest that since heaven has no windows, there was no flood. These definitions suggest that whether there was a flood or not is immaterial. The important matter is that God judges sin, but keeps covenant with those who love him. What must be asked is: on what basis shall the teaching of God's justice and mercy be judged true if the vehicle which purports to teach this is false?

This conflict is heightened in the Bible by the fact that everywhere it bases its claims to religious authority upon the attestations to be found in this world. Over and over it argues that this world is reality and that God's reality is to be perceived through His actions in this world. It may be possible to save some sort of faith by cutting it loose from the facticity of this world, but it will not be the Biblical faith. From Deuteronomy to I John, the claim is one: "Do not forget the things which your eyes have seen . . . make them known to your children." (Dt 4:9); "That . . . which we have heard, which we have seen with our eyes, which we have looked upon and touched with our hands . . . we . . . proclaim to you" (I Jn 1:1, 2).

To sum up the argument thus far, we have said that the etymological definitions are inadequate in that they tend to equate falsehood with any account which goes beyond a closed view of nature, whereas the sociological definitions fail in that they assume there need be no connection between the truth of the vehicle and the truth it supposedly conveys.

The literary definitions seek to avoid the issue of truth and falsehood altogether. Here the term merely applies to a type of symbolic language which is heavily evocative. The use of story to convey values is frequently referred to here. C. S. Lewis uses the term in this way at times. So, for instance, in *Miracles* he writes

> This involves the belief that Myth in general is not merely misunderstood history . . . nor diabolical illusion . . . nor priestly lying . . . but, at its best, a real, though unfocused gleam of divine truth falling on the human imagination.[18]

Lewis' own Narnia tales as well as J. R. R. Tolkien's *The Hobbitt* and *The Lord of the Rings* are often referred to as modern examples of myth in this sense.[19] So also large parts of the Old Testament are said to be mythic in nature because the theological values are taught in story form.

However, the issues of truth and falsehood cannot be laid aside so easily, especially in view of the generally accepted definition. Why use the term at all unless one intends thereby to say that the facticity of the stories is really of no importance to their value? If this is indeed the case, as I suspect it is, then the literary definition is only a species of the sociological one.

Furthermore, this definition runs the danger of being so broad that it blurs distinctions between pieces of literature which are really quite different. Is it legitimate to lump together the *Epic of Gilgamesh*, the story of Abraham, the *Odyssey*, *The Search for the Holy Grail*, and *The Lord of the Rings* under the heading of myth? One cannot help but wonder whether a more useful, because more narrow, definition can be found.

The definitions of the fourth type seem to meet this criterion. They are more descriptive and less prescriptive, attempting to analyze actual literatures with a view to discovering common or distinguishing characteristics. For this reason, I am labeling them with a term borrowed from Brevard Childs, as phenomenological definitions. Childs himself has offered such a definition when he says,

> Myth is a form by which the existing structure of reality is understood and
> maintained. It concerns itself with showing how an action of a deity, conceived
> of as occurring in the primeval age, determines a phase of contemporary world
> order. Existing world order is maintained through actualization of the myth in
> the cult.[20]

Childs correctly stresses the common element of control and
maintenance through actualization in mythical literature. He could
perhaps go further along the lines laid out by Henri Frankfort and others
in indicating that this control is achieved through the personalization of
natural forces. In Frankfort's words, "The mainspring of the acts,
thoughts and feelings of early man was the conviction that the divine was
immanent in nature and nature intimately connected with society."[21]
Arthur Weiser says much the same: "[myth] usually arises in the soil of
natural religion in which those processes of nature which are impressive
by their regular recurrence or their peculiarity are explained by means of
personifying them and representing them as the fortunes of the gods."[22]
  This identification of nature with divine reality, which is characteristic
of myth, has a number of implications. One of these is determinism.
Yehezkel Kaufmann maintains that determinism is the central feature of
myth. He says,

> Myth describes the unfolding destiny of the gods, giving expression to the idea
> that besides the will of the gods there are other independent forces that wholly
> or in part determine their destinies. . . . The god is . . . a personal embodiment
> of one of the seminal forces of the primordial realm. His nature and destiny are
> determined by the nature of this force.[23]

Furthermore, this deification of nature which is at the heart of myth
means that myth is specifically not interested in the unique, non-recurring
events and persons in locate-able time and space. "Ignoring the fetters of
time and space, its nature is to gaze into the widest vistas and to launch out
into the exalted and immense."[24] It is interested in the recurring and the
cyclical, in principles and forces. It is an "attempt to relate the actual to
the ideal, the punctual to the continual."[25] Since the nonrecurring is least
related to the ideal norm, it is therefore of least worth and interest. The
issue is not how to move forward; rather, it is how to keep from moving
backward. In the ideal world chaos is continually being conquered by
order. But in the actual world chaos seems always on the point of
destroying hard-won order through the agency of change. It is thus the
function of myth to reproduce the benefits of the ideal world in the actual
world. It does so by devaluing this changing actual world in favor of the
reality of the unchanging ideal world.
  This latter point brings us to what some consider the heart of myth.
Frankfort calls it coalescence or identity.[26] Kaufmann entitles it
continuity.[27] This is the idea that the human realm and the divine realm
are continuous with, or identical to, each other, just as nature and the

divine are continuous with each other. Thus, the function of religion is to insure that the identity or continuity is indeed intact so that the benefits of the ideal world may be actualized in this world. This continuity is preserved and made effective through precise performance of ritual. Such elements as trust, faithfulness or ethical responsibility are really beside the point. The desired results will be achieved through mechanical means. If the worshippers act out the behavior of the god or goddess, then that behavior must be duplicated in the natural realm whatever the worshipper's attitudes. Thus it may be said that myth is a form of thought in which the deity is understood to be continuous with the natural and human realms and by means of the expression of which thought the physical and social benefits believed to inhere in divine power are procured for the natural and human realms. In short, myth identifies deity with this world in order to control deity.

An understanding of the centrality of the principle of continuity in mythic thinking explains the great common features found in completely unrelated myths around the world. Some of these are: 1) Matter is eternal and is the source of existence; 2) The gods are derivative from the Absolute, which is impersonal power, and are fated by that power and can be manipulated through it; 3) There are as many gods as there are natural and social forces; 4) Although the universe has no origins, the gods do and to understand their origins is to understand ourselves and our world; 5) Creation is only possible through conflict between creative and dis-creative powers; 6) Sexuality is at the source of life and is the means whereby life continues; 7) Symbol and reality are inseparable; therefore, what is done to the symbol is done to the reality itself; 8) The great desideratum of life is the harmonious, cyclical functioning of existence.

Whence come these commonalities? They are manifestly not the result of borrowing. Rather they are the result of a common method of understanding the world. They are all the result of reasoning from the given to the divine. The given is the universe as we know it and when ultimate truth is derived from the universe certain conclusions follow inevitably. Although the universe had no beginning, *we* did and therefore the gods did. Since the universe has no evident purpose in its existence, neither have the gods. Since we find an admixture of good and evil in ourselves, so there is such an admixture in the gods. Since nature is arbitrary, so are the gods, etc. Since persons the world over have the same set of givens, reasoning from those givens to the divine will lead to the same general conclusions the world over.[28]

Given this phenomenological understanding of myth, it is not difficult to see why such scholars as Weiser,[29] Childs,[30] Bright,[31] and Frankfort argue that the Bible cannot be correctly defined as myth. Frankfort's statement is particularly cogent.

> When we read in Psalm xix that 'the heavens declare the glory of God; and the firmament sheweth his handiwork,' we hear a voice which mocks the beliefs of

the Egyptians and the Babylonians. . . . The God of the psalmists and the prophets was not in nature. He transcended nature—and transcended, likewise, the realm of mythopoeic thought.[32]

It is possible to detect the reflection of Egyptian and Mesopotamian beliefs in many episodes of the Old Testament; but the overwhelming impression left by that document is one, not of derivation, but of originality.[33]

What are the marks of this originality? They are seen in the overt denial of the common elements just cited. Matter is not eternal.[34] God has no origin. God is not identified with any natural element, nor can he be represented by any image of anything in creation. God is one. God is wholly good and utterly faithful. Creation is solely the product of God's will, no conflict between good and evil entered into the process.[35] God is a-sexual and sexuality has no cosmic significance. God cannot be manipulated by means of magic. The means whereby God's blessing is procured is through commitment, trust and ethical obedience. Symbol and reality are not continuous.[36] Thus manipulation of a symbol will not produce automatic results. Rather, as our handling of the symbol indicates certain personal and ethical responses, that handling becomes significant. Unique events in time and space become significant in themselves. No longer is their significance determined by some magical correspondence to an ideal. Life has meaning by reference to its conformity to the Creator's purposes for it.

We could go on, but these are enough to establish that, in John Bright's words, "the Bible is really quite free of the *mind* of youth. . . . Whatever it is that we have in the Bible, it is certainly not myth as we have it elsewhere."[37] To speak of the Bible as myth, meaning thereby that it speaks of God in imagery, or through the use of legend, is simply an irresponsible use of the term "myth." It is a bit like saying that since a man and his dog both have brown eyes both are canine or both are human. Identity of "accidents" (used in the technical sense) says nothing about identity of essence—except to the mythopoeic mind.

Why should the Bible differ so radically from myth at these essential points? It is because the Bible operates on a different principle, the principle which Frankfort labels "transcendance." God is not continuous with creation. He cannot be manipulated through it, nor His being be determined by it. He is neither contigent upon it nor contained by it. He is other than the created system.

The great paradox of the mythical world-view is that by defining ultimate meaning in terms of this world, it only succeeds in devaluing this world. It creates an ideal world in this world's image and then ascribes to that ideal world meaning and denies it to this world. Modern philosophies have followed much the same path and have achieved much the same result: man is the measure of all things, but since man is not self-existent, he is without purpose and meaning.

By contrast, the Bible takes the paradox in the opposite direction. God is radically discontinuous with this world. He cannot be known by projecting the characteristics of this world on the canvas of the stars. It is impossible to find the meaning of life in some divine realm continuous with ours. Rather, the Transcendant One has intersected our realm and has chosen to manifest Himself through unique events of time and space. Suddenly this realm is invested with tremendous significance. Our unique response to what God has shown us of Himself becomes terribly important. For those responses are not determined by reference to past existences or other kinds of continuities. Just as He transcends humanity, so we can transcend our past, our conditionings, our emotions in response to Him. It is no longer our origins which determine our meaning. It is what we do here and now in relation to the Other who confronts us with a call for ethical commitment. No longer do ideal persons, places and events in some primeval "otherworld" devalue persons, places and events in this world. Now persons, places and events take on their own significance in the light of responsible choices made in relation to the purposes of the Creator.

What I am saying, of course, is that the Bible has a historical concern which is utterly lacking in mythical literature. Responsible ethical choice in this world which results in certain unique developments and movements is at the very heart of the concept of history and it is of little or no concern to the mythmaker. To speak of the Bible as substituting history myth for nature myth is to play at word games which must ultimately reduce language to meaninglessness.[38]

To say that the Bible has a unique historical consciousness is not to approve automatically the "revelation as history" motif. To root the divine revelation merely in some unusual, but still ambiguous, events is not enough. The neighbors of Israel could also speak of divine acts on their behalf, as B. Albrektson and H. W. F. Saggs have shown.[39] But to demonstrate this similarity is not to have shown that the Bible and the literatures of Egypt, Babylon and Canaan are operating from the same premises. They are not. And although the history writing of the Bible is markedly different from modern history writing, nonetheless they share concerns which are of no significance in the other literatures: the concerns for human responsibility and influence in the course of developing human affairs. The uniqueness of those concerns cannot be gainsaid.

In all of this, the argument has not been to prove the Bible "true" and therefore non-mythic. That is another matter, although I am personally firmly convinced of that truthfulness. Rather, the purpose has been to show that those definitions of myth which rest upon attribution of truth or falsehood, including the literary, are hopelessly ineffective because of the difficulty of making that attribution in an unbiased way. Of much greater usefulness, I have maintained, are those definitions which seek to describe the actual literatures and their world-views. It is in that light that the Bible seems unique. If these observations are correct, then however we do define the Bible, we ought not to define it as myth.

NOTES

1. G. B. Caird, *The Language and Imagery of the Bible* (Philadelphia: Westminster Press, 1980), pp. 219-24; J. W. Rogerson, *Myth in Old Testament Interpretation* (Berlin: Walter De Gruyter, 1974), pp. 174-78.

2. *Interpreter's Dictionary of the Bible, s.v.* "Myth in the New Testament," by E. Dinkler.

3. The *Oxford English Dictionary's* definition is entirely unambiguous: "A purely fictitious narrative usually involving supernatural persons, actions, or events and embodying some popular idea concerning natural or historical phenomena" (1933, *s.v.* "Myth").

4. As Caird seems to do (*Language,* pp. 219-20).

5. *Interpreter's Dictionary of the Bible, s.v.* "Myth, Mythology," by Theodore Gaster.

6. Millar Burrows, *An Outline of Biblical Theology* (Philadelphia: Westminster Press, 1946), p. 115.

7. C. Hartlich and W. Sachs, *Der Ursprung des Mythosbegriffes in der modernen Bibelwissenschaft* (Tubingen: 1952), p. 148, cited in B. Childs, *Myth and Reality in the Old Testament* (London: SCM Press, 1960), p. 14.

8. C. S. Lewis, *Miracles* (Collins: London, 1947), pp. 75-76.

9. E. O. James, *Myth and Ritual in the Ancient Near East* (London: Thames and Hudson, 1958), p. 307.

10. Rudolf Bultmann, *Kerygma and Myth,* I, ed. H. Bartsch, tr. R. Fuller (London: SPCK, 1953), p. 10, n. 2.

11. Burrows, *Outline,* pp. 115-16.

12. cf. J. L. McKenzie, *Myths and Realities* (Milwaukee: Bruce Publishing Co., 1953), p. 185.

13. James Barr, *The Bible in the Modern World* (New York: Harper and Row, 1973), p. 137.

14. cf. Childs, *Myth and Reality,* pp. 3-29, and J. Bright, *The Authority of the Old Testament* (London: SCM Press, 1967), pp. 128-31.

15. Joseph Campbell, *The Mythic Image,* Bollingen Series C (Princeton: Princeton University Press, 1974), p. 493.

16. Bultmann, *Kerygma,* pp. 196ff.

17. Carlos Castaneda, *The Teachings of Don Juan* (New York: Ballantine Books, 1969), p. 183.

18. C. S. Lewis, *Miracles,* pp. 137, 8, n.1 See also E. M. W. Tillyard, *Myth and the English Mind,* pp. 11-12, cited in Caird, *Language,* p. 223.

19. So, for example, Chad Walsh, "The Literary Stature of C. S. Lewis," *Christianity Today,* vol. 8 (June 1979), p. 23. For a more critical view of such assertions see Donald T. Williams, "A Closer Look at the 'Unorthodox' Lewis," *Christianity Today,* vol. 21 (December 1979), pp. 24-27.

20. Childs, *Myth and Reality,* pp. 29, 30.

21. Henri Frankfort, *et al., Before Philosophy* (Baltimore: Penguin Books, 1949), p. 237. Rogerson's critique of Frankfort is somewhat mystifying; *Interpretation,* pp. 85-97. He is at great pains to show that Frankfort is dependent upon Ernst Cassirer, which may or may not be so. But then he seems to believe that he has discredited Frankfort if that be the case, which is hardly so. Apart from any supposed dependence on Cassirer it must be plain to anyone who has read ancient Near Eastern literature that Frankfort's point on the personalization of natural and psycho-social forces is a key factor in those peoples' view of the world.

22. A. Weiser, *Introduction to the Old Testament* (London: Dartman, Longman and Todd, 1961), p. 57.

23. Y. Kaufmann, *The Religion of Israel,* tr. and abridged by M. Greenberg (Chicago: University of Chicago Press, 1960), p. 22.

24. Weiser, *Introduction,* p. 58.

25. Gaster, *Myth.*

26. Frankfort, *Before Philosophy,* p. 21.

27. Kaufmann, *Religion*, p. 36.

28. See Campbell, *Mythic Image*, pp. 76-100, for further discussion of these commonalities.

29. Weiser, *Introduction*, p. 58.

30. Childs, *Myth and Reality*, p. 98.

31. Bright, *Authority*, p. 179.

32. Frankfort, *Before Philosophy*, p. 237.

33. *Ibid.*, p. 241. This is not to say that the Bible never makes use of myth. That it certainly does (e.g. Ps 74:13, 14; Isa 51:9-11). But the Bible does not accept the worldview of the myths it uses. They only supply the imagery which is adapted in a thorough-going way to the Biblical program. See the writer's "The Myth of the Dragon and Old Testament Faith," *Evangelical Quarterly*, vol, 49 (1979), pp. 163-72; see also Caird, *Language*, p. 232.

34. While it is not illegitimate to translate Genesis 1:1 as "When God began to create . . . the earth was without form and void" (cf. NEB), the classic translation of the Septuagint (followed by the KJV) is equally permissible. Even if the NEB translation were accepted, the eternality of matter cannot be drawn from one verse.

35. Satan is a creature, not a cosmic principle. Nor is there any creative tension between God and Satan. Evil only enters creation when the process is complete.

36. The prohibition of imagery is a clear statement in this direction, as are the various attacks on manipulative cult. The symbols may not be used to influence reality in a mechanistic way.

37. Bright, *Authority*, p. 179.

38. W. T. Stevenson, *History as Myth* (New York: Seabury Press, 1969).

39. Bertil Albrektson, *History and the Gods* (Lund: Gleerup, 1967), p. 41; H. W. F. Saggs, *The Encounter with the Divine in Mesopotamia and Israel* (London: The University of London, 1978), pp. 64-92.

11

RECENT STUDIES IN *LEVITICUS* AND THEIR CONTRIBUTION TO A FURTHER UNDERSTANDING OF WESLEYAN THEOLOGY

Victor P. Hamilton

It is a deep pleasure to dedicate this paper to Dr. Dennis Kinlaw on the happy occasion of his sixtieth birthday. During my seminary days it was Dr. Kinlow who introduced me to the critical study of the Old Testament in general, and to the study of the Semitic languages in particular. Such classes enforced in my mind the absolute necessity of a linguistic control of the biblical language as a precondition for serious exposition of Scripture, not as a fringe benefit or luxury.

The book of Leviticus has not gone unnoticed by Dr. Kinlaw, not only as a part of the biblical canon, but as one of the constituent factors in our Wesleyan heritage.[1] In more instances than not Leviticus has been a closed book to Christians. If we have studied it at all it has been through the back door via the Epistle to the Hebrews. But is it possible to allow Leviticus to speak for itself first? The answer to that question must be a resounding yes. No book of the Old Testament has influenced subsequent Judaism more than it. Rabbinical literature informs us that it was the first book taught to school children. And approximately one-half of the Talmud is based on Leviticus.

A perusal of the commentary sections in libraries and religious book stores reveals copious treatments of Genesis, Exodus, and Deuteronomy. Trailing far behind are commentaries on the other two books of the Torah, Leviticus and Numbers. Happily in the case of Leviticus this situation has been changed with the recent appearance of two

146

commentaries by evangelical scholars, G. J. Wenham and R. K. Harrison.[2] Either volume would be an excellent addition to the pastor's and scholar's library. But in my judgment Wenham's is the better of the two. It is more creative and innovative, displays a greater theological dexterity, and explores to a deeper dimension the relationship between Leviticus and the New Testament.

Apart from these commentaries I might also mention other materials such as monographs and articles in the academic biblical journals. These are more technical in their approach, and normally are available only in the libraries of theological seminaries. One thinks of the recent monograph by Baruch Levine.[3] It is a penetrating analysis of the burnt and peace offerings of Leviticus 1 and 3, and more extensively of the concept of atonement through sacrifice. I have severe misgivings, however, about the presence of magic and apotropaic rites to ward off the demonic that Levine claims to detect in these cultic rites.

Although it deals with matters more post-biblical than biblical, note should also be made of Jacob Neusner's *The Idea of Purity In Ancient Judaism*.[4] Neusner is a prolific scholar in the area of Judaica and Talmudic thought, and the first chapter of this book is a brief discussion of purity in Scripture.

The contributions of a third Jewish scholar must also be included. No author has written more compellingly on Leviticus and Numbers than has Jacob Milgrom. He is the author of two books and a very high number of journal and encyclopaedia articles in this area.[5] I have discovered Milgrom's writings to be most lucid and suggestive. Most of this article will demonstrate my heavy indebtedness to him.

One final bibliographical note. Often it is the person who does not operate professionally as a biblical scholar per se who brings to Scripture a different and often more successful perspective than those who operate within the mainstream of biblical scholarship. For example, it would be difficult to discover a more illuminating study of themes in the Psalter than in *Reflections On The Psalms* by C. S. Lewis, a teacher of English and medieval literature.

In the study of Leviticus some very incisive observations have been made by Mary Douglas, professor of Social Anthropology at University College, London.[6] To a good degree her observations have focused on the dietary laws of Leviticus: animals that are edible and those that are not. On what basis is the distinction made? Is it aesthetic? Some animals by appearance are repulsive. Is it theological? Often animals were associated with pagan religions, the bull for example. Is it hygienic? Those animals that are carriers of disease or scavengers are disallowed for health reasons.

Douglas appeals to the criteria of Leviticus 11 itself. Animals acceptable for consumption by humans must part the hoof, be cloven-footed, and chew the cud (Lev 11:3). Acceptable aquatic creatures must have fins and scales (Lev 11:9). The point is that the dietary code "rejects creatures which are anomalous, whether in living between two spheres, or having defining features of members of another sphere, or lacking defining features."[7] What is unacceptable to God, then, is hybrids.

Ranging beyond the dietary code Douglas, on examining all of Leviticus, is able to say that, "Much of Leviticus is taken up with stating the physical perfection that is required of things presented in the temple and of persons approaching it. . . . We can conclude that holiness is exemplified by completeness. Holiness requires that individuals shall conform to the class to which they belong."[8] The emphasis is that to limit sanctification to the idea of separation, or being set apart for service not only seriously diminishes the force behind sanctification, but clearly repudiates what Leviticus is saying. To be holy and acceptable before God means to be conformed to His standards, to meet His criteria of acceptability.

Certainly at the heart of the Christian faith is the concept of sacrifice, and most supremely Christ's sacrifice of Himself. Such a sacrifice was necessitated by the sins of man. A radical problem—sin—called for a radical solution—atonement—provided by God's Son. In light of this there has been at the heart of Wesleyan theology a strong emphasis on the biblical teaching of sin.[9] And, we might add, an emphasis that is more ethical than legal. But more on this later.

If the center of New Testament faith is the sacrifice of Christ then it must be stressed that the Old Testament more than adequately laid the groundwork for that emphasis to emerge. The first seven chapters of Leviticus give a succinct presentation of the Old Testament sacrifical system. Of course, the ritual literature is not the only place one may turn to for information on sacrifice. An examination of historical, prophetic, and poetical sections of Scripture would unearth much helpful detail. However, this paper is concerned mainly with the Leviticus material, and more particularly with chapters 1-7.

In this sub-unit the contents may be divided into two general categories: (a) chaps. 1:1—6:7 (b) chaps. 6:8—7:38. Both sections address themselves to the subject of sacrifice, but with this difference. Lev 1:1—6:7 is introduced with "speak to the people of Israel and say to them" (1:2). On the other hand, 6:8—7:38 is introduced with "command Aaron and his sons" (6:9). Thus 1:1—6:7 treats sacrifice with the interests, needs, and duties of the laity in mind. Conversely, 6:8—7:38 covers the same area, but this time from the perspective of the officiating clergy, not the lay donor and participant.[10] In both sub-units five sacrifices in all are discussed, but the order in which they are discussed in each is different. Thus, in 1:1—6:7 the order is: burnt, cereal, peace, sin, and guilt offering. In 6:8—7:38 the order is: burnt, cereal, sin, guilt and peace offering.

Why a different sequence in back-to-back sections? Anson Rainey has suggested that the first grouping is a didactic order, the order in which the people were instructed about the sacrifices. The second grouping he calls an administrative order; i.e., the order in which the materials brought for the sacrifice were entered in the tabernacle/temple log book.[11] Wenham has taken a different approach and has opted for the idea that the first grouping is theologically motivated—fellowship offerings precede expiatory offerings. The second grouping, by contrast, is arranged in order of frequency, from the daily to the optional.[12]

In my opinion more important is Rainey's detection of a third order of sacrifices. This he calls the procedural order.[13] For documentation of this we must turn outside Lev 1-7. The important element is that when several offerings are brought to the Lord priority of place must always be given to the sin offering. At the ordination of the priests the sequence of sacrifices presented by the candidate is sin (Lev 8:14-17), burnt (Lev 8:18-21), and peace (Lev 8:22-29, here called a "wave" offering). At the high priest's ordination Aaron offers for himself first a sin offering (Lev 9:8-11), and then a burnt offering (Lev 9:12-14). As an extension of this particular service the high priest next offers for the people a sin offering (Lev 9:15), a burnt offering (Lev 9:16), a cereal offering (Lev 9:17), and a peace offering (Lev 9:18). Always the sin offering is first.

This procedural order is demonstrated most graphically in the case of the Nazirite upon the successful completion of his vow of separation. The offerings he is to present follow this order: burnt, sin, peace (Num 6:14). But the order in which they are actually presented to the Lord by the priest is: sin, burnt, peace (Num 6:16, 17). In the presentation, then, the sin offering has moved from second position to first position. All this surely is the Bible's way of saying that if sin is not first of all brought into God's presence, and dealt with, then to speak of other concerns such as worship or fellowship or service is to put the cart before the horse. Indeed, it renders them, for all practical purposes, void.

Thus far I have divided Leviticus 1-7 into two sub-units. Now we need to go beyond that and take a deeper look at this first sub-unit, Lev 1:1—6:7. When one mentions the word "sacrifice," the first idea that probably enters his mind is sin. After all, Christ sacrificed His life because of our sins. And at the heart of sacrifice is (substitutional) death.

Apart from some keys in Lev 1:1—6:7 there are other items in Scripture that should alert us about over-simplifying and defining too narrowly the function of sacrifice. I am thinking of phrases such as bringing "the sacrifice of praise" into the house of the Lord (Jer 17:26), or offering the "sacrifice of thanksgiving" (Ps 107:22; 116:17), an emphasis that is carried into the New Testament, as demonstrated by Heb 13:15.

There is in Lev 1:1—6:7 one give-away clue that underscores the "double-bladed edge" of Old Testament sacrifice vis-à-vis purpose. This clue is the isolation of two key phrases that occur throughout this section.

Three times the burnt offering is described as a "pleasing odor to the Lord" (Lev 1:9, 13, 17). Five times the cereal offering is described with exactly the same phrase (Lev 2:2, 9, 12, and also 6:15, 21). The peace offering similarly is twice described as a pleasing odor to the Lord (Lev

3:5, 16). A total, then, of ten times. By contrast, the phrase appears only once in the sin offering legislation (Lev 4:31), and not at all with the guilt offering.

If we look at the last two offerings, this phrase is consistently used: "he/they shall be forgiven." Six times it is used in the sin offering section (4:20, 26, 31, 35; 5:10, 13) and three times in the guilt offering (5:16, 18; 6:7).[14] Here, then, a total of nine times, but not once with the first three sacrifices.

Obviously the first three sacrifices move to their climax in the impact they have on God. To Him they are a sweet aroma, something to be inhaled. The last two sacrifices, by contrast, move to their climax in the impact they have on the offerer. His sins are forgiven. Atonement is made on his behalf by the priest.

Two other differences between these two categories of sacrifices need to be noted. One is that in none of the first three sacrifices is any specific occasion earmarked for the presentation of this particular offering. They simply begin, "when any man brings an offering . . ." or, "if a man's offering is . . . ." Not so with the sin and guilt offering. The sin offering is required in the following situation: "if any one sins unwittingly in any of the things which the Lord has commanded not to be done" (Lev 4:2, 13, 22, 27, RSV). Covered here is the "inadvertent" (RSV, "unwittingly"; KJV, "in ignorance") doing of an act prohibited by God's commandment. Similarly the guilt offering is mandated when one "commits a breach of faith and sins unwittingly in any of the holy things of the Lord" (Lev 5:14, RSV). The fact that both the sin and guilt offering are targeted to cover certain kinds of trespass, both sins of omission and of commission, should indicate transparently the distinction between the categories. The first category—burnt, cereal, and peace—includes sacrifices of praise and thanksgiving, and has nothing to do with atonement.[15] The latter two sacrifices—sin and guilt—are aimed directly at the question of sin and its removal.

In addition to significant phrases, and the presence or lack of a stated occasion for the offering of these sacrifices, a third distinction needs to be underlined. That is, in the sin offering (but not the guilt offering) there is a much heavier emphasis on the use of the blood. And this is to be expected where the forgiveness of sin is at stake.

In the burnt and peace offerings the blood is shed only around the outer altar of the tabernacle complex, the bronze altar. See Lev. 1:5 and 3:2 for example. This holds true for the sin offering of the tribal leader (Lev 4:22-26) and the commoner (Lev 4:27-35). But when it is the sin of the priest (Lev 4:1-12) or the sin of the whole congregation (Lev 4:13-21) part of the blood is sprinkled seven times before the veil, part is splashed over the inner altar, the altar of incense, and the remainder of the blood is poured around the outer bronze altar.[16]

Why this distinction? Why more blood? And why the blood sometimes here and sometimes there? My interpretation is that Leviticus is scaling sinners in a kind of hierarchy. The greater the sinner the greater the sin. And the greater the sin the nearer the blood needs to be poured to the presence of God. The sins of the priest or the whole congregation (following their religious leader's unwise counsel?) are more obnoxious and odious, and thus in need of a demonstrably more shocking blood rite.[17]

A further evidence of the greater criminality attached to the sin of the priest/whole congregation is that the animal they present is not consumed, but rather is carried forth "outside the camp to a clean place" and there incinerated (Lev 4:12, 21).[18] In the case of the sin offering of the tribal leader or commoner, however, the animal is to be eaten by the priest (Lev 6:26, 29, and note especially 6:30). This distinction, by the way, provides the background to Moses' query to Aaron's sons, "why have you not eaten the sin offering in the place of the sanctuary, since it is a thing most holy?" (Lev 10:16ff.).

Now that we have separated the sacrifices of thanksgiving from the sacrifices of expiation it is time to turn our attention to these last two sacrifices, the sin and the guilt offerings.[19]

It is not my purpose to add to the amount of ink that has been used in attempts to differentiate the sin offering from the guilt offering. I am interested rather in a phrase that is common to both. Again I quote from the RSV, "if anyone sins unwittingly" (Lev 4:2 *inter alia*). The Hebrew word, herewith translated "unwittingly," appears in the following passages—in addition to Lev 4:2—Lev 4:13, 22. 27; 5:15, 18; 22:14; Num 15:24-29; 35:11, 15; Jos 20:3, 9; and Eccl 10:5, plus other passages in related forms.

The verdict on how this expression is to be translated has not always been unanimous. Preponderantly the RSV opts for "unwittingly" except for the references in Num 35 and Jos 20 to the manslaughterer who has killed "without intent." The KJV prefers the translation "through/in ignorance" and for the manslaughter passages "unawares." Other modern versions of the Bible translate the word in the Leviticus passages at least as follows: "unwittingly" (The Torah—A New Translation, Jewish Publication Society); "unintentionally" (New International Version); "ignorantly" (Berkley); "without intending to" (Good News Bible); "inadvertently" (Jerusalem Bible and New English Bible).

I shall not pause, at least at this point, to argue the merits of one of these renderings over the others, although I think some considerably more commendable than others. I am interested, however, in underscoring the fact that the two expiatory offerings within the Old Testament's sacrificial system are to provide atonement for inadvertent sins, not for intentional sins (the classical passage of which is to be found in Num 15:30, 31—"anyone who does anything *with a high hand* ['sins defiantly,' NIV] . . . shall be *cut off*").[20]

Before we jump to the conclusion, as not a few Christian expositors have done, that it is precisely here where the superiority of Christ's sacrifice emerges, we had better take a second look. It simply is a distortion of the facts to say that in the Old Testament there is sacrifice only for inadvertent sin, but that Christ's death is for both inadvertent and intentional sin. If nothing else, Heb 10:26 affirms that not even Christ's death is efficacious for the forgiveness of intentional sin (of the believer), if liberty in Christ is changed into license in Christ. In essence, then, Heb 10:26 is echoing Num 15:30, 31. The passage states, "For if we sin *deliberately* after receiving the knowledge of the truth, there no longer remains a sacrifice for sins."

All of this emphasis within both testaments on sacrifice to cover or not to cover inadvertent and intentional sin is of particular interest for those who identify theologically with the Wesleyan tradition. Wesley's frequently quoted sin definition is: "Nothing is sin, strictly speaking, but a *voluntary* transgression of a known law of God. Therefore, every *voluntary* breach of the law of love is sin; *and nothing else,* if we speak properly."[21]

It is not my purpose to explore all the implications of Wesley's definition of sin. To be sure, it is not the only word he said on the subject. At times he could quote with approval the Westminster catechism on the topic, in spite of its Reformed emphasis. One suspects that Wesley's unique definition was informed not only by biblical principles, but also by a lethargic eighteenth century Christian community which lived under the canopy of an Anglican-Calvinism, in which sinfulness was almost equated with humanity. To err was human and inevitable. Thus the massive temptation to self-exoneration.[22]

One of the questions facing us is how does one fit Wesley's emphasis on voluntary, deliberate transgressions into the categories of Leviticus 4 and 5? For here the emphasis is on sins committed inadvertently, either through negligence or ignorance.[23] There is atonement provided for them. Did Wesley miss the mark so widely as to suggest a category of sin for which in fact there is no atonement? The answer is simply that Leviticus itself says that God has provided atonement both for sins of inadvertence and sins of intention. We need go no further than Lev 4-6 to notice this.

The sin offering is discussed in 4:1—5:13. The legislation contained, however, within 4:1-35 is different considerably from that contained in 5:1-13. For one thing, the phrase "sin inadvertently," used four times in 4:1-35, is absent totally in 5:1-13. (The reason for this absence will become evident shortly.) Secondly, the sin offering in 4:1-35 is geared to a person's status: "if it is the anointed priest who sins" (4:3); "if the whole congregation of Israel sins" (4:13); "when a ruler sins" (4:22); "if any of the common people sins" (4:27). By contrast, the sin offering of 5:1-13 is geared to the financial means of the offerer: "he shall bring . . . a female from the flock, a lamb or a goat, . . . but if he cannot afford a lamb, then he shall bring . . . two turtledoves or two young pigeons" (5:6-7).

What is of supreme interest here is that at least a few of the sins listed in

5:1-13 seem to be more in the category of conscious acts than in the category of unconscious acts. For example, to withhold testimony from a court, to refuse to be an informer (Lev 5:1), can hardly be called an inadvertent sin. And what about touching an unclean animal or person (Lev 5:2-3), or uttering a rash oath (Lev 5:4)?

The guilt offering continues this conundrum. As we have already seen, it too is designed for sins committed inadvertently (5:14, 18). And yet again the list of sins in 6:1-7 is most graphic in terms of intentionality. Can deceiving one's neighbor be termed inadvertent, especially if such deceit involves lying and robbery (Lev 6:2)? What about "oppression" (Lev 6:2b)? And what makes the sins listed in 6:1-7 so detestable and obnoxious is that the perpetrator tries to conceal his thievery by appeal to an oath he has made to God. This is the force of the phrase "swearing falsely" in 6:3 and 5. That is, a man has something illegally, perhaps stolen or borrowed from somebody else but never returned. To make his (false) claim to ownership appear even more convincing he says: "this belongs to me, and so help me God, I am telling you the truth."

Here then is the issue. First, in staccato-like fashion, "if a man sins inadvertently . . . he shall be forgiven." But then comes in both Leviticus 5 and 6 a catena of sins that could hardly be more deliberate and voluntary, especially those listed in chapter 6.[26] And yet either the presentation of a sin offering or a guilt offering provides atonement for such transgressions![25]

It is my belief that Milgrom has successfully made sense out of this paradox, and indeed has shown it to be no paradox at all.[26] He has observed that in Leviticus and Numbers four times, and four times only, *confession* over sin is mandated. And most interesting of all, each time the context under discussion is *deliberate* sin. The four passages are: (1) Lev 5:5, ". . . he shall *confess* the sin he has committed." The context is offering a sin offering to atone for intentional sin. (2) Lev 16:21, "And Aaron shall . . . *confess* over him all the iniquities of the people of Israel, all their transgressions, all their sins." The context is the Day of Atonement and the cancellation of venal sins. (3) Lev 26:40, "But if they *confess* their iniquity. . . ." The context again is a sermon on the blessings of obedience and the punishments of disobedience. But "confession" can bring to a halt God's wrath. (4) Num 5:7, "he shall *confess* his sin which he has committed." And the context is a commentary on the guilt offering. As such Num 5:5-10 is the Numbers parallel to Lev 5:14—6:7.[27]

The only conclusion that can be drawn from the above evidence is that confession turns voluntary sin into the category of involuntary sin, and for this there is sacrificial expiation.[28] This is, in a nutshell, the doctrine of repentance articulated in Leviticus and Numbers.

It is not the deliberate sinner who is excluded from possible atonement. Rather it is the unrepentant sinner (or believer, I might add) who is excluded. Even under the old covenant God's grace is extended to the voluntary transgressor, the wilful sinner. It is not extended automatically to be sure. But whenever that individual reaches the place of contrition, open acknowledgement of his sin, and repentance, he is guaranteed a reconciliation with his Lord.

Thus, in defining sin as a voluntary transgression of a known law of God, Wesley was in no way stepping outside the parameters of the priestly teaching on sin and its forgiveness.

NOTES

1. D. F. Kinlaw, "Leviticus" in *Beacon Bible Commentary,* vol. I (Kansas City, Missouri: Beacon Hill Press, 1969), pp. 317-95; and, "Old Testament Roots of the Wesleyan Message" in *Further Insights Into Holiness*, Compiled by K. Geiger (Kansas City, Missouri: Beacon Hill Press, 1963), pp. 41-53.

2. G. J. Wenham, *The Book of Leviticus,* New International Commentary on the Old Testament series (Grand Rapids: Eerdmans, 1979); and R. K. Harrison, *Leviticus: An Introduction and Commentary,* Tyndale Old Testament Commentaries series (Downer's Grove, Ill.: Inter-Varsity, 1980).

3. B. Levine, *In The Presence of the Lord* (Leiden: E. J. Brill, 1974).

4. J. Neusner, *The Idea of Purity In Ancient Judaism* (Leiden: E. J. Brill, 1973).

5. J. Milgrom, *Studies in Levitical Terminology,* I (Berkeley: U. of California, 1970); and *Cult And Conscience: The Asham and The Priestly Doctrine of Repentance* (Leiden: E. J. Brill, 1976).

6. M. Douglas, *Purity and Danger: An Analysis of Concepts of Pollution and Taboo* (London: Routledge and Kegan Paul, 1966); "Deciphering a Meal," *Daedalus,* vol. 101 (1972), pp. 61-81; *Implicit Meanings* (London: Routledge and Kegan Paul, 1975). Professor Douglas has also provided a response to Neusner's *The Idea of Purity* at the end of that volume, pp. 137-42. See most recently G. J. Wenham, "The Theology of Unclean Food," *Evangelical Quarterly,* vol. 53 (1981), pp. 6-15. Douglas' observations have been applied to the Old Testament concept of sacrifice by D. Davies, "An Interpretation of sacrifice in Leviticus," *Zeitschrift für die altestestamentliche Wissenschaft,* vol. 89 (1977), pp. 387-99.

7. Douglas, *Implicit Meanings,* p. 266.

8. Douglas, *Purity and Danger,* pp. 51, 53.

9. R. S. Taylor, *A Right Conception Of Sin* (Kansas City, Missouri, Beacon Hill Press, 1945).

10. This separation is even clearer in the chapter division of the Hebrew Bible. In the Hebrew Bible the first seven verses of chapter six (the guilt offering) are part of chapter five. So then, 6:8 (the start of sub-unit #2) is 6:1 in the Hebrew text.

11. A. Rainey, "The Order of Sacrifices in Old Testament Ritual Texts," *Biblica,* vol. 51 (1970), pp. 485-98.

12. G. J. Wenham, *Leviticus,* pp. 118-19.

13. A. Rainey, "The Order of . . . ," pp. 494-98.

14. Levine, *Presence,* pp. 65-66, astutely observes that the thrust of putting the verb about forgiveness consistently in the passive voice is to stress that one receives forgiveness from God not because he performs certain rites—however indispensable they may be—but because it is God alone who bestows forgiveness. Levine's translation of the standard "and he shall be forgiven" is "with the result that he is granted forgiveness."

15. To be sure, we do read of the burnt offering (Lev 1) that it is to provide atonement for the donor of the animal (Lev 1:4). Additionally, in Lev 9:7 it is coupled with the sin offering again for atonement. Job offers this offering to the Lord on behalf of his sons in case "they have sinned and cursed God in their hearts" (Job 1:5). The Lord urges Job's "friends" to do the same (Job 42:8). However, the significant phrase "and he shall be forgiven" is not present in Lev 1.

16. It is beyond the scope of this paper, but not totally inappropriate, to draw attention to the fact that on the Day of Atonement alone the blood is brought even beyond the veil and

the altar of incense, and into the Holy of Holies (Lev 16:14, 15). The reason for this radical departure from otherwise normal procedure is plain enough. Only on this day does God provide atonement for sins called "transgressions" (Lev 16:16, 21), i.e., sin in its most defiant manifestation. See the observation, in terms of higher critical terminology, by G. von Rad, *Old Testament Theology*, vol. I, p. 263n. The word occurs nowhere else in Leviticus except for chapter 16.

17. I am much happier here with Milgrom, "Two Kinds of *hattā't*," *Vetus Testamentum*, vol. 26 (1976), pp. 333-37, than I am with Levine, *Presence*, p. 103ff., at this particular point.

18. "Outside the camp" does not *a priori* designate a God-abandoned area. Morally, the site is neutral. There is such a thing as a "clean place" outside the camp just as there is "an unclean place" (Lev 14:40, 41, 45).

19. I am aware that I am using traditional translations for "sin offering" and "guilt offering". Almost all modern translations of the Bible follow these designations, but there are a few exceptions. For "sin offering" Milgrom prefers "purification offering"; and for "guilt offering," "reparation offering," for here there is to be repayment for the misappropriation of sacred property. Observe that the sin offering is mandated for recovery from childbirth (Lev 12:6), the dedication of a newly built altar (Ex 29:36), and the successful completion of the vow of the Nazirite (Num 6:14-16). Patently none of these instances have anything to do with sin. The correct translation can only be "purification offering." But I prefer that "sin offering" be retained for Lev 4-5. See Milgrom, "Sin-offering or purification-offering?" *Vetus Testamentum*, vol. 21 (1971), pp. 237-39.

20. D. J. Wold, "The Kareth Penalty in P: Rationale and Cases," *Society of Biblical Literature Seminar Papers*, vol. 1 (1979), pp. 1-45.

21. W. Arnett, "The Wesleyan Arminian Teaching on Sin," in *Insights Into Holiness*, Compiled by K. Geiger (Kansas City, Missouri: Beacon Hill Press, 1962), p. 61; and M. B. Wynkoop, *A Theology of Love* (Kansas City, Missouri: Beacon Hill Press, 1972), pp. 150-53; italics mine.

22. In my opinion no one has demonstrated more convincingly that both the ethical view of sin (Wesleyan) and the legal view of sin (Lutheran/Reformed) are Scripturally authentic, and both are essential as a check on the possible extremes of the other than has K. Kinghorn, "Biblical Concepts of Sin," *Wesleyan Theological Journal*, vol. 1 (1966) pp. 21-26.

23. J. Milgrom, "The Cultic Š͏ᵉGĀGĀ and its Influence in Psalms and Job," *Jewish Quarterly Review*, vol. 58 (1967), pp. 115-25.

24. I am therefore unable to agree with the logic of Harrison's observation: "there is no ritual here or elsewhere in the Pentateuch to cover the sins of deliberate and conscious rebellion against God. . . . Had the levitical system covered every form of sin . . . there would have been no room for the work of Christ"; p. 68.

25. W. Eichrodt, *Theology of the Old Testament*, vol. I (Philadelphia: Westminster, 1961), p. 161, n.6, reflects sensitivity to this fact in his suggestion that the phrase "unwittingly" be translated "in human frailty," and so to be contrasted with sins "of a high hand." His suggestion is hardly an improvement but his subsequent sentence is to the point: "the difference between the two kinds (of sins) could be tested by the person's willingness to confess his sin and his effort to make reparation."

26. Milgrom, *Cult and Conscience*, p. 108ff.

27. Milgrom in *Cult and Conscience*, p. 109, n. 407, quotes Saul Lieberman's observation (*Hellenism in Jewish Palestine*, p. 140, n. 11) that the Greek Septuagint translates this four-fold use of "confess" in Leviticus and Numbers not with the more normal New Testament word *homologeō* but the rarer *exagoreuō*. This word, which is not used in the New Testament, means "to speak, to declare, to betray a secret by blurting it out." To confess one's sins then is not something done privately in a closet of a confessional booth. But the confession envisioned here is a public, clearly articulated confession. (Shades of an early Wesleyan class meeting?) I might also add that the Hebrew word for "confess" used here—*yādâ*—also means "to give thanks, to praise." How interesting that Hebrew can use the same verb for confessing sins and giving praise to the Lord. Can they be separated existentially?

28. I have discovered happily that Milgrom's observations were anticipated by the evangelical scholar Leon Morris in his article "ASHAM," *Evangelical Quarterly*, vol 30 (1958), pp. 196-210. For instance he says on p. 201, "It is the defiant, unrepentant sinner for whom there is no atonement, and in view of the teaching in other parts of the atonement, and in view of the teaching in other parts of the Scriptures, it would seem that if and when his attitude changes to one of repentance the whole situation is altered."

12

REMARKS ON SOME RECENT WRITING ABOUT LITURGICAL EVIDENCES IN JEREMIAH

John F. X. Sheehan

In 1960, I embarrassed Dr. Kinlaw by telling him that my association with him was one of the finest things that had ever happened to me, that I considered him to be "one of the obscure great men of the twentieth century." The statement, of course, is no longer true. There is no longer anything obscure about Dr. Kinlaw.

I. Introduction

The title of this essay has been chosen with care. The essay is largely based on the reading of three fairly recent works by Berridge,[1] Bright,[2] and Reventlow.[3] Each of these works has had insights to offer on the reading of the great prophet. Each of them—at least occasionally—has overstated its case. The failure of their methodologies has had this in common. None of them has had a particularly modest thesis. This present paper would avoid that fault; hence our thesis: *there are some evidences in Jeremiah for an earlier liturgical dimension of some of the texts.* For the author, this adds a special note to the gracious love of that God Who makes His revealed word known to us.

What is the nature of that liturgical dimension? It is a secondary thesis of this paper that a valid answer to that question lies beyond the capabilities of present methodologies. This is a disappointment, perhaps, but it is something that must be reckoned with. None of the three writers seems adequately to have grasped the impossibility of answering the questions that they were positing.

One of the advantages of our modest thesis is this: it provides a handle for treating the very valuable but disparate insights offered by the three authors.

Reventlow offers a quote from the work of Skinner which comes close to stating his own thesis:

> There is nothing quite like [the confessions] in the range of devotional literature. Communings of the soul with God as tender and intimate, meditations as profound, prayers as fervent and sincere, may be found in the Psalms and the great classics of the spiritual life; but Jeremiah's experience is unique in this respect, that it springs out of a prior official relationship to God which he had in virtue of his prophetic vocation.[4]

Where Reventlow moves beyond Skinner is in his judgment that this "official relationship" to God involved certain cultic activities which gave him the opportunity to preach and to pray in a liturgical context and that much of the present Jeremiah is directly derived from that cultic preaching and prayer.

This brings us to the heart of the question. Once having determined that a text is liturgical in form (and we can almost stipulate that in most of the questions under discussion) does it follow that the text was composed and used always in a liturgical context? Reventlow seems at times to presuppose this. With reason, Bright has some problems with this. He notes:

> The assumption that forms of address must remain anchored to the institution in which they have their original setting has already been attacked by Fohrer.[5]

He goes on to amplify Fohrer's remarks by saying that prophets have used all sorts of forms (e.g. songs of the minstrel-bard) and it "is absurd to suppose that they employed each in some official institutional capacity."[6]

But cult is by its nature conservative. In discussing the linguistic nature of texts that were demonstrated to be liturgical, Gordon has written that all liturgical texts tend to be linguistically "archaic or archaised."[7] One is tempted to have recourse to the recent history of the Roman Church. Efforts to reform the liturgy met considerable opposition from both laity and clergy as both groups tended to stay with the basic conservatism of the cult that they had always known.

Lady Drower offers more evidence of the innate conservatism of cult:

> Many of the technical terms employed in the OT for the different sacrificial rites are found also in the texts from Ras Shamra; it may be assumed that the Israelites adopted much of their ritual of offering from the Canaanites, and also some of their festivals, for references to seasonal rites in the poems correspond with those performed at early Hebrew festivals such as the Autumnal Festival . . . and the Feast of Weeks.[8]

Evidences for the conservatism of cult abound also in recent writing of Baruch Levine.[9] Finally, there are at least some stray lines throughout the

Hebrew Bible that make more sense if they are interpreted as liturgical rubrics that persisted even in contexts where they no longer made a good deal of sense.[10]

Getting back to Bright, one could note that there is little evidence for the innate conservatism of the minstrel. (In fact, it is the part of the minstrel to be imaginative and creative in his use of received material while everything about the cult, on the other hand, is conservative.) The argumentation is not perfect here, but one may ask the question: if cult is so conservative that even rubrics pass unchanged from Ugaritic to Hebrew, is it likely that a demonstrated liturgical form could pass from liturgical to nonliturgical use without some difficulty and some possibility of offense to the audience—the ultimate arbiter of what is possible or not possible in the social composition that marks the world of the OT? Let us then examine some basic ideas.

II. Going Out and Coming In

In this merism, it should be noted that in opposition to *yṣ'* the verb *bw'* has the meaning of going or coming in. Berridge[11] suggests that the phrase of 1 Kgs 3:7 is the best illumination of Jer 1:6. *na'ar* is the common denominator of the two. Jeremiah is a *na'ar* and therefore cannot be a prophet. Solomon notes in his prayer that he is a *na'ar* and finishes: *l' 'd' ṣ't wb'* (I am a *na'ar;* I do not know how to go out and to come in). Berridge suggests that the meaning of the phrase has to do with warfare, not cult. (One could ask if warfare without a related cult was possible in the ancient Near East, but let us put that question to one side for the moment.) Rather, there is some evidence that this phrase is itself cultic. In this one imposition, we do not have a Ugaritic root cognate. We do have a cognate idea. The Ugaritic *'rb* means "to enter." In its nominative form, it has the common meaning of "cultic personnel."[12] How is this possible?

> With the eventual building of the temple, the sacred place becomes limited and with the construction of the holy of holies, the sanctuary was even more limited. It was not always that way. The land itself, the "holy land" is in its entirety both temple and sanctuary. . . . Because of all this, the Deuteronomic concern with the act of entering the Holy Land is more than a mere geographic or historical description. The very act of entering the land is itself sacral. With the building of the temple, with the evolution of a more specialised priesthood, some of this notion may have been lost or rather transferred. In the later New Testament letter to the Hebrews, Christ is described as the high priest par excellence precisely because he entered once and for all the sanctuary of Heaven. (Heb 9:11)[13]

The entire Hebrew people had long since staked out its claim to royal priesthood by entering the sanctuary of Palestine.

As the priest enters the sanctuary, as the liturgical procesion (so described) of
the holy people enters the land, so the Divine Son enters "heaven." Since all
this is clearly known, it is more tha interesting that one of the Ugaritic texts
describes cultic personnel as 'rbm the "enterers."[14]

Further work in the notion of the act of entering as one that is basically
sacral has been done by Taft[15] who has researched the idea in the
Byzantine liturgy. He had begun with the question of why the "great
entrance" had developed such importance in the Eastern liturgy and
turned to Psalm 24 as a partial solution to the problem.

But what do we do with the $s't$ of the above phrase? Is there any
evidence for a cultic meaning of this? Claude Lévi Strauss would note that
"the whole structure of primitive thought is binary."[16] If it can be
demonstrated that to enter is a cultic dimension, then to go out must be a
cultic dimension.

Let us pause here for a moment. If this seems a bit much to the reader,
note that we began with an ambiguous phrase. "I am a youth who does
not know how to go out or to come in." In that ambiguity, we have so far
anchored one of the two phrases. Is it a wild guess to conclude with Lévi
Strauss that the polarity of Hebrew thought demands that the second of
the two also be cultic?

III. Jer 4:11-12

In treating this passage, Berridge[17] focuses on the word sh.

The sh wind portrayed in v. 11 has traditionally been translated with *Glutwind*.
In light of the recent discovery that sh is a Canaanite month, Soggin has noted
that from Jer 4:11, we learn that the name of the month can also be used to
designate the east-wind. Since in Jer 4:11 this wind is mentioned in association
with the winnowing of grain, which was usually effected by the gentle
west-wind, it is apparent that both winds could be suited for such winnowing.[18]

Berridge goes on to say

The image of the east-wind is occasionally used in the Old Testament in
association with Yahweh's judgment. Hosea in particular favored this imagery
and it is not improbable that Jeremiah has here been influenced by Hosea.
However, although in 4:11 an east-wind once again represents Yahweh's
judgment, this is now the unexpected! The sh wind, which could be expected to
have the positive function of winnowing grain, now represents devastation
instead.[19]

But is it really possible to separate the notion of threshing from that of
cultic judgment?

The threshing floor, then, conveniently served as a general meeting place. On a
more poetic level, the notion of the eschatological judgment evident in the

threshing floor imagery, an idea picked up in the New Testament (Mt 3:12 and Lk 3:17) the division of wheat and chaff, the storage of one and the destruction of the other, lent itself easily to notions of primitive worship.[20]

With this observation, then, we note both the strength and the weakness of merely citing cultic imagery. No one has suggested that the communities which composed the gospels of Matthew and Luke were made up exclusively of "cultic personnel." What the use of the imagery in Jeremiah does suggest is that both the speaker and his intended audience were acquainted with the cultic imagery so that even an allusion (the *sh* wind) was enough to alert both of them to the meaning intended. Or to put it another way, the speaker was familiar enough with the image so that it came readily to mind; he did not censor it as too obscure for his audience since they were familiar with the liturgical backdrop of his words as he was. Someone might object that what we have here is surely eschatological imagery, but that is far removed from the world of the cult. Perhaps one of the basic insights of the Scandinavians is helpful here. Those actions which take place in "Heaven" always have their correspondence in the cult:

> To "what happens" in the cultic drama corresponds what happens in heaven; he that sits enthroned in the Temple is the one who sits enthroned up there, and sends thunder and rain and "renews the surface of the earth" and with awe, all kings and peoples ought to recognise that he is at the same time the God of Israel.[21]

To prove our point (that the language of Jeremiah is so cultic as to demand some kind of cultic background for its composition) would perhaps require this: a detailed listing of all the metaphors in Jeremiah and a mathematical calculation of the percentage of them that are best explained in a cultic context. That is beyond the scope of the present paper. What we shall continue to do is to cite a number of passages and expressions that our three authors have recognized (or as here occasionally failed to recognize) in their cultic dimension.

IV. Joy and Sadness

Berridge has detailed treatment of the words *śśon* and *śmḥ*.[22] He concludes:

> The combination of these words in Jeremiah is probably rooted in the cultic thanksgiving rites. D. W. Harvey concludes that "the part which the people play in Israel's public worship, in singing, giving thanks, and joining in the feast, comes out plainly in the meanings of *śamaḥ* and *halal*." The same may undoubtedly be said of *śśon* and *smḥh* and of the corresponding verbs *śuś* and *smḥ*.[23]

In light of the work of Lévi-Strauss which we have already cited,[24] it is not a surprise that Reventlow argues analogously from the words in Jeremiah for sadness and weeping. He is treating 14:1—15:9 and says:

> Über das kultische Weinen hat Hvidberg eine Monographie verfasst, auf die Kapelrud verweist. Ursprünglich ein Trauerritus aus der Totenklage, hat der Akt des Weinens offentlich als Klage um den gestorbenen Gott eine wichtige Rolle im Vegetationskult gespielt. . . . Ausserdem spricht dafür, dass diese Termini in (den) erwähnten alttestamentlichen Texten, auch Jer 14:2-6 im Zusammenhang mit der Schilderung von Dürreerscheinungen auftreten. Kapelrud hat das für Joel 1:8-12 sehr deutlich herausgestellt.[25]

Reventlow concludes that it is likely to expect a "cultic dimension" to much of the writing in Jeremiah, as there is a long tradition of "cultic response" on the part of the prophets. In this he follows Mowinckel who is convinced that there is evidence for a liturgical response on the part of prophets in general. (If this were demonstrated beyond cavil, then, there would be an easy progression to the statement that what we have recorded in some of the Jeremianic statements are simply some of his more memorable responses which his disciples had heard in the liturgy.)

> Dass nun diese Tempelpropheten bei gewissen kultischen Handlungen geradezu verpflichtet waren, ein dem Inhalt der Kultfeier angemessenes Orakel zu geben, und zwar in Übereinstimmung mit dem Glauben und den Erwartungen der Mehrzahl der Gemeinde oder der Machthaber, dürfen wir aus mehreren Erzählungen folgern.[26]

Reventlow goes on to quote Mowinckel to the effect that the means for effecting the prophecy frequently lay in the hands of the prophet and his hearers (which would make their preservation for subsequent generations all the more likely.)

> Wir gehen kaum irren, wenn wir annehmen, dass man Mittel gehabt hat, die Antwort in den meisten Fallen günstig gestalten zu können.[27]

He quotes Johnson as making an analogous statement:

> It should be realized that it was the function of the cult prophets to create the *šalom* or "peace" which they were apparently promising so glibly.[28]

If this is so, then what is more logical than that the prophets should use their authoritative pulpit as the opportunity to preach in a cultic situation and to get then the *qahal* to cooperate with them in what would be a self-fulfilling prophecy?

For those personalities that are otherwise defined as "cult prophets" the work of Widengren is helpful here. He has written comparing those prophets to the "dervish fraternities" of the Arab countries.[29] One of the side effects of the cultic atmosphere of their work is that the congregation is then inclined to cooperate in the work of the self-fulfilling prophecy.[30] It lies outside the scope of this paper to discuss prophecy as a God-directed "relation" between the prophet and the *qahal*.

V. The Secret

The word *sod* is used among other places in Jer 15:17 and in Jer 23:18. The word is best explained in conjunction with Amos 3:7. The word has both the meaning of "the Council of the Deity" and "the secret." This last is what is discussed in the Council of the Deity. It is the prophet and he alone who has access to the Council, its deliberations, and the results of those deliberations—the secret.

Von Rad observes:

> Later Israel knows Yahweh as the one who is ready to speak and even to have questions put to him (Is XLV.11); he does nothing without taking his prophets into confidence. (Am III.7).[31]

What more logical place to put those questions and to receive the answers than in the cult?

Reventlow notes that there takes place in the cult what a later tradition might call the discernment of spirits—the distinguishing between the spirits of Good and Evil.

> Doch Auch die Form selbst, das liturgische Formular . . . in dem die Gerichtsankündigung von Jer. 4.11 erscheint, führt über eine so einseitige Auffassung hinaus. Die Fürbitte, das sahen wir, gehört in diese Liturgie hinein. Wie verhält es sich aber nun mit dem Orakel, das auf die Klage bzw. Fürbitte antwortet? . . . Im Prinzip des Orakels liegt grundsätzlich die Doppelseitigkeit: es kann sowohl eine günstige wie auch eine ungünstige Antwort der Gottheit erfolgen.[32]

VI. "Calling of the Name"

The expression the calling of the name (Jer 15:16), says Reventlow, is otherwise found only in the clearest of cultic contexts: in the Temple, before the Ark, or in cultic assemblies of besieged peoples.[33]

But Bright says that it is "unthinkable" that the expression (addressed to God) "you are indeed to me like a deceitful brook" could ever be found in a liturgical context.[34]

He is even more forceful with another objection.

> Even more damaging are the opening words of the piece (v.10): *'wi li 'immi.* The expression occurs only here; the prophet apostrophizes his (presumably) long-dead mother. Such words could not possibly introduce a liturgical text, or even be used in the course of it. In a prayer uttered publicly in the cult, by a cultic official, address must *always* be to God—as in fact it invariably is in the Pss. Lam. A distressed individual might cry out, 'O mother, why did you bring

me into the world?' but a liturgist making public intercession for the people would never do so.[35]

Why not?

One would avoid flippancy here, but what argument has Bright advanced for his position other than the statement that these phrases are "unthinkable" in the liturgy? Unthinkable for whom? From the subjective viewpoint of the present writer, these outcries are quite thinkable in many liturgical settings of his personal experience. The question, of course, is not whether they suit my experience or that of John Bright. Are they suited to the experience of Jeremiah? As was noted in the opening paragraphs of this paper, a definitive answer to that question is not to be found with any presently available methodology. Still, we can make two statements. First, many liturgies allow for considerable spontaneity on the part of the cultic leader. Secondly, Jeremiah was a man of profound personal passion. If he presided at any kind of liturgy, one would expect that passionate outbursts (that a more sober individual might find liturgically "unthinkable") would take place. More than that, unfortunately, cannot be said at this time on the question.

VII. Memory and the Lament

As far back as the work of Gunkel, the motivation of the Laments was seen to be the marvelous works of God done in the past. It was judged that those memories would make the prayer of the present more efficacious.[36] Reventlow writes:

> Die Erinnerung an die früheren Wundertaten Jahwehs ist . . . ein typisches Motiv der Klage, die damit eine gnädige Antwort Jahwehs herbeiführen will.[37]

In talking of Jer 14:1 ff. Reventlow uses the above as part of his argument that what we have here is a real liturgy, not an imitation.[38] One turns immediately to the work of Childs on the re-creative power of memory.[39] We have in this passage an appeal to the "Savior of Israel" (v. 8), an invocation of the divine presence, "Why should you be a stranger in your own land?" (v. 9) and finally a summary memory of the works of the covenant (v. 21). In such a context it is difficult to see such expressions as "Then said the Lord unto me . . ." as any but cultic answers to a cultic plea.

According to Childs' definition, the above is a good example of the desire on the part of Israel not to "actualize" the past, but to make its saving effects "present."

> God is in no sense confined to the past within the barriers of time and space. He is always present. The question at issue in the cult is whether God will continue to act in Israel's behalf as he did in the past or withdraw his aid because of her disobedience.[40]

For Reventlow, intercession and response are simply the stuff of cult and prophecy. Requests, reasonable and unreasonable, answers, favorable or unfavorable—these are things that happen in the cult.[41] Perhaps it is partially because these things were so well known to the readers and hearers of the earlier Jeremianic redactions, that the rubrics of the cultic dimension were not more clearly pointed out.

VIII. Cultic Judgments—Just and Unjust

If one has a problem in seeing the bifurcation of the cultic oracle—favorable or unfavorable—Reventlow would have him note that this is but a variant on a very common cultic practice, the judgment that a man is just or unjust.[42] He cites the locus classicus, Ex 18:9, "He is just; he shall surely live."

Reventlow speaks of this liturgy as a "Beichtspiegel" or "Torliturgie." The judgment must be made *now;* is this man worthy to participate further in the liturgy? Ja oder nein?

Since the cultic role here offers the cultic president the opportunity of giving good news or bad news, we should not be distressed by the fact that:

> der Prophet in seiner Wächterfunktion auf der einen Seite der Bote des kommenden Gerichts ist, dass er nun auf der anderen Seite als der Fürbitter gerade die entgegengesetzte Aufgabe übernimmt die drohende Gefahr abzuwvehren.[43]

Rather

> Diese wechselnde Rolle des Propheten entspricht dem Ablauf der Stadien in der Liturgie, in denen der Prophet einmal den Part der einen, dann weider den der anderen Seite übernimmt.[44]

IX. Overholt's Remarks

A couple of judgments offered by Overholt[45] may be useful here.

> It is not the notion of cultic prophecy which (Jeremiah has) under attack. On the contrary the call to intercession . . . becomes a test of true prophecy and is in effect a call to perform a liturgical action. Such intercession is not an unconditional proclamation of peace, but is an appropriate action precisely because, as Rudolph points out, the prophetic threat is never unconditional for Yahweh is always free to change his plans for his people.[46]

Two of Overholt's judgments are worth citing:

> On the basis of visions, laments, and other passages found in the book of Jeremiah, Henning Graf Reventlow has recently argued persuasively that intercession on behalf of the people forms at least part of the prophet's function.[47]

and finally

> By comparing some passages with the ritual pattern of lamentation followed by
> an oracle of salvation known from other portions of the Old Testament and by
> taking the cultic *Sitz im Leben* very seriously, he is able to point to a number of
> passages which reflect Jeremiah's performing of this function.[48]

Here, too, it may be appropriate to invoke one argument from
authority. Reventlow following von Rad notes that:

> die konfessionen Jeremias nicht seine ausserdienstliche Religiosität losgelöst
> von seinem prophetischen Auftrag weidergeben, sondern in sein Propheten-
> amt mitten hineingehören "dass sie unmittelbar ex *munere prophetico*
> stammen."[49]

Since myth is only the libretto of cult,[50] we should look at one position
which Reventlow espouses in the matter of myth in Jeremiah:

> Damit kommen wir zu der mythologischen Deutung des "Nordens" die zuerst
> von Gressmann begründet und systematisch dargestellt worden ist. Schon
> Gressman stellt die zwei Vorstellungen klar heraus, in denen der "norden" in
> mythisch gefärbter Bedeutung in Alten Testament erscheint: 1. Als die
> Vorstellung von dem Gottesberg im Norden, dem Sitz der Götter, 2. Als die
> Anschauung von dem unheilsdrohende Norden, dem Sitz alles Böen, aus dem
> auch der schreckliche Zerstörer der Endzeit erscheint. In beiden Fällen handelt
> es sich um mythische Voerstellungen, *die erst verhältnismässig spät* ein fast
> politisches Gewand erheilten.[51]

This is, unfortunately, one more issue that cannot be satisfactorily
resolved. Berridge writes:

> This thesis has rightly been rejected by B. Childs who argues that there are no
> elements in the various pre-exilic prophetic descriptions of this enemy which
> must be considered as indicating an enemy of a mythical nature. "Rather
> throughout the enemy [retains] the characteristics of the human agent."[52]

Unfortunately, philology is not conclusive here.

The Ugaritic *ṣpn* is invariably endowed with mythic meaning; in texts
so far attested, it never means anything but "the dwelling of the god."[53]
On the other hand, the Hebrew language throughout its long history
never did come up with a word for "north" which was not derived from
the root ṣpn.[54]

X. Jer 6:25

Beridge comes close to an insight when he discusses the *magor
missabib*. Believing that two things equal to the same thing are equal to
each other, he argues that *magor missabib* is equal to *tᵉruʿah* which is
equal to holy war and therefore that *magor missabib* is equal to holy war.[55]

Let us suppose for the moment that *magor missabib* is equal to *t̆ru'ah*. Among other argumentation, he quotes the conclusion of H. J. Kraus that the expression:

> könnte eine landläufige Redewendung gewesen sein—ein Ausruf der die Ausweglosigkeit einer Gefahr kennzeichnete.[56]

He cites also the parallel passage of Jer 49:29 as proof that the expression is indeed an "outcry." "Terror is on every side" and suggests that this outcry, as did the "*t̆ru'ah*," began the battle. It was a shout of a whoop from the troops as they began to fight.

True enough.

But what was the force of the expression *t̆ru'ah?* Years ago Mowinckel understood this as a reference to the oncoming presence of Yahweh.

> the cry of homage means 'royal homage,' 'homage to the king' (*t̆ru'ath melekh*) for Yahweh; when this cry is heard in Israel it is evidence that 'Yahweh her God is with her' (Num 23:21).[57]

In other words, a serious imposition of the *t̆ru'ah* is that it is an invocation of the presence of the deity.

To prove conclusively that *t̆ru'ah* involves an invocation of the divine presence is beyond the scope of this paper.[58] We can say this much here. It is at least interesting to reflect on *t̆ru'ah* in connection with Nu 10:34-5. "And it came to pass when the ark set forward that Moses said, Rise up Lord and let thine enemies be scattered; and let them that hate thee flee before thee.

And when it rested, he said, Return O Lord unto the many thousands of Israel." (King James Version)

What is the connection? This is another side of Nu 23:21. Yahweh is among them *when* the shout of the king is among them. In the earlier passage, Moses invokes the divine presence in one way. The latter passage describes the invocation of the divine presence obliquely. In light of Berridge's insightful reading of *magor missabib,* it is interesting to note the effect of the divine presence. The enemy flees in terror "Terror on every side!" may well be a war cry but it is a war cry which invokes the divine presence that occasions the terror for the foe or—on occasion—for the rebellious Israel.

Berridge in this section, though, seems to presuppose a strict demarcation between holy war and cult. But war is holy because God is present; God's presence is the heart of cult; many cults are simply the reenactment of the holy war or the preparation for the next one.

The classic case for the union of War and Cult is, of course, Joshua 6. In light of what we have already said, it would be no surprise that the "walls came tumbling down" precisely when the people shouted, (*yari'u*). The city fell because Yahweh was present. In the cultic reenactment of this,

Yahweh is also present. On both occasions, "Terror was on every side."[59]
Now in light of all that has preceded, a lengthy citation from Berridge may
be useful:

> Although only v. 6 can be termed a call to flight, it is clear that this *Gattung* has
> influenced Jeremiah's formulation of v. 5. Verses 5b and 5c are closely related
> to v. 6, with their "blow a horn in the land, call aloud and say: 'Assemble
> yourselves, and let us go into the fortified cities' " . . . .

> The call to flight *Gattung* has its *Sitz im Leben* in the practice of holy war. It was
> originally directed to a third party, distinct from those who were themselves
> threatened with judgment. Jer 4:6 thus deviates from the original form of the
> Gattung. Nevertheless, as we have noted earlier, for Jeremiah, the "Enemy
> from the North" represented Yahweh's agent in His holy war agaist Judah.
> Thus, a bond with the original *Sitz im Leben* of this *Gattung* is still evidenced
> here.[60]

Perhaps the most insightful general idea that Reventlow had was this:
"Kunst als Selbstzweck ist eine in der antiken Sakralliteratur unbekannte
Erscheinung."[61] We have already seen Lady Drower's remark on the
tenacity of rubrics from Ugaritic to Hebrew. The sober witness of
archaeology is this: that holy place is built on holy place. In Palestine it is
the normal thing for pre-Hebraic shrines to be located in the same spot
where later are found Hebrew shrines, the shrines to Greek and Roman
gods, Christian sites, and perhaps later Mohammedan places of worship.
Only part of this is convenience. (At least some of the shrines came to be
located, as human traffic patterns moved, in out of the way places.)
Rather, this trend continued because of the human conviction that the
places had been made holy by previous worship. Is it such a long distance
from this to the conviction that certain forms are sacral and that they
ought not be used for another purpose? Rather their sacredness, even in
the worship of another god, demanded that they be reserved as "holy
forms."

There are other evidences, of course. For example, Berridge notes that
the formula *'ad mathay* (Jer 4:14) appears generally elsewhere in cultic
contexts where the distress that is being alleviated through the cult has
already existed for some time.[62]

Under pressure of time and space, we choose to conclude here. With
what conclusions do we end? Perhaps the wisest sentence of the three
works is found on the last page of Reventlow where he notes that "das
letze Wort noch nicht gesprochen [ist]."[63] Berridge had graciously written
earlier in his work:

> Reventlow's study undoubtedly offers a necessary corrective to an under-
> standing of Jeremiah, which as he notes, is too often rooted in psychological
> presuppositions and considerations."[64]

Perhaps the most important conclusion that we can reach is this. The God Who lives revealed Himself to Israel and to us in many ways. The gentlest of school teachers, He remembers that we are but dust and begins wherever we are. In the case of Israel, this meant that it was good pedagogy for Him to utter His sacred revealing word in the cult where it would be accessible to the Hebrews. With similar love, He made sure that the word was recorded in the Holy Bible where it is available to us after all these centuries.

NOTES

1. J. Berridge, *Prophet, People, and the Word of Yahweh* (Zurich: EVZ-Verlag, 1970).

2. J. Bright, "Jeremiah's Complaints—Liturgy or Expressions of Personal Distress?" in *Proclamation and Presence*, eds. Durhama and Porter (London: SCM Press, 1970), pp. 189-215.

3. H. Reventlow, *Liturgie und prophetisches Ich bei Jeremia* (Tübingen: Gütersloh Verlagshaus, 1963).

4. Reventlow, *Liturgie*, pp. 205-06.

5. Bright, "Jeremiah's Complaints . . . ," p. 192.

6. *Ibid.*, p. 193.

7. C. Gordon, "Review of von Soden's *Grundriss der Akkadischen Grammatik*," *Orientalia* 22 (1953), p. 231 makes the point that ritual texts are generally either archaic or "archaised."

8. M. Drower, "Canaanite Religion and Literature," in *Cambridge Ancient History*, Vol. II, part 2, (Cambridge: University Press, 1975), pp. 149-50.

9. This point is developed in some fairly recent work of B. Levine: "Ugaritic Descriptive Rituals," *Journal of Cuneiform Studies*, vol. 17 (1963), pp. 105-11; "The Descriptive Tabernacle Texts of the Pentateuch," *Journal of the American Oriental Society*, vol. 85 (1965), pp. 307-18.

10. This may explain, for example, the stray words *'yšbtrw* in Gen 15:10 in the Kittel text. We have a historical account of Abraham performing a ritual action coming together with cultic instructions for the re-performance of the act. In the latter, "each man brings his portion" and places it as Abraham is described as placing his portion.

11. Berridge, *Prophet*, p. 47.

12. C. H. Gordon, *Ugaritic Textbook* (Rome: Pontifical Biblical Institute, 1965), *sub verbo*.

13. J. Sheehan, *Let the People Cry Amen!* (New York: Paulist Press, 1977), pp. 66-67.

14. *Ibid.*, p. 90.

15. R. Taft, "Psalm 24 at the Transfer of Gifts in the Byzantine Liturgy: "A Study in the Origins of a Liturgical Practice," in *The Word in the World*, eds. Clifford and MacRae (Weston: Weston College Press, 1973), pp. 159-79.

16. Cf. E. Leach, *Claude Lévi-Strauss* (New York: Viking, 1970), p. 92. See also pp. 65-67, where the notion is developed in some detail.

17. Berridge, *Prophet*, pp. 111-12.

18. *Ibid.*

19. *Ibid.*

20. J. Sheehan, *The Threshing Floor* (New York: Paulist Press, 1972), p. 36.

21. S. Mowinckel, *The Psalms in Israel's Worship*, trans. D. R. Ap-Thomas (New York: Abingdon Press, 1967) I, p. 174.

22. Berridge, *Prophet*, p. 121.

23. *Ibid.*

24. *Ibid.*, n. 17.

25. Reventlow, *Liturgie*, p. 157.

26. *Ibid.*, p. 130.

27. *Ibid.*

28. *Ibid.*

29. G. Widengren, *Literary and Psychological Aspects of the Hebrew Prophets* (Uppsala: Lundquistka Bokhandelin, 1948), p. 96.

30. *Ibid.*

31. G. von Rad, *Old Testament Theology*, trans, D. Walker (New York: Harper and Row, 1965) II, p. 359.

32. Reventlow, *Liturgie*, p. 132.

33. *Ibid.*, p. 220.

34. Bright, "Jeremiah's Complaints . . . ," pp. 204-05.

35. *Ibid.*

36. Reventlow, *Liturgie*, p. 128, so summarizes Gunkel.

37. *Ibid.*, p. 145.

38. *Ibid.*, p. 152.

39. B. Childs, *Memory and Tradition in Israel* (Naperville: Allenson, 1962).

40. *Ibid.*, p. 74.

41. Reventlow, *Liturgie*, p. 144.

42. *Ibid.*, p. 133.

43. *Ibid.*, p. 126

44. *Ibid.*

45. T. Overholt, *The Threat of Falsehood* (Naperville: Allenson, 1970).

46. *Ibid.*, pp. 36-37.

47. *Ibid.*, p. 42.

48. *Ibid.*, p. 42, n. 34.

49. Reventlow, *Liturgie*, p. 144.

50. J. McKenzie "Aspects of Old Testament Thought," in *Jerome Biblical Commentary*, eds. Fitzmyer and Murphy (Englewood Cliffs, N.J.: Prentice-Hall, 1968), p. 752.

51. Reventlow, *Liturgie*, p. 103; italics mine.

52. Berridge, *Prophet*, p. 82.

53. Gordon, *Ugaritic Textbook,* glossary, *sub verbo*.

54. At any rate, no words for "north" except those derived from *spn* appear in the comprehensive *The Complete English-Hebrew Dictionary*, Reuben Alcalay (Tel Aviv: Massada, 1965), *sub verbo* "north."

55. Berridge, *Prophet*, pp. 90-91.

56. *Ibid.*, p. 80.

57. Mowinckel, *The Psalms*, I, p. 122.

58. Although I think that I can do so and have done so in graduate class lectures, but not in published writing.

59. One thinks of the major thesis of Rudolph Otto in *The Idea of the Holy*, 2nd ed., trans. J. Harvey (London: Oxford University Press, 1950). Throughout the book he develops the theme that the essence of "the holy" as touched in cult is that it is *quid tremendum*, "something to be trembled at." This is far more than the English word "awe" or "awful" frequently means.

60. Berridge, *Prophet*, pp. 94-95.

61. Reventlow, *Liturgie*, p. 96.

62. Berridge, *Prophet*, p. 53; in this he follows Westermann and gives the reference as ZAW 66.

63. Reventlow, *Liturgie*, p. 260.

64. Berridge, *Prophet*, p. 17.

13

NEHEMIAH, A MODEL LEADER

Edwin M. Yamauchi

I count it a special privilege to have been a fellow graduate student with Dennis Kinlaw in the Mediterranean Studies Department at Brandeis University. In his distinguished career Dr. Kinlaw has exemplified the ideal Christian leader, a man of compassion and vision. It is therefore fitting that the following study should be dedicated to him, as it is a sketch of another model leader, Nehemiah.

I. The Historical Situation

Nehemiah's ministry can be dated to the latter part of the fifth century B.C. by two chronological references (the 20th year of Artaxerxes I = 445 B.C., Neh 1:1; the 32nd year, Neh 13:6).[1]

Artaxerxes I, nicknamed Longimanus, was the third son of Xerxes and Amestris. Shortly after he came to the throne in 464 he was faced with a major revolt in Egypt which was to last a decade. The rebellion was led by Inarus, a Libyan, and by Amyrtaeus of Sais. They were aided by the Athenians, who sent 200 triremes to the rebels.

In 456 Megabyzus, the Persian satrap of Syria, began a campaign to suppress the revolt. Later Megabyzus himself rebelled against the Persian king from 449 to 446. If the events of Ezra 4:7-3 took place in this period, Artaxerxes I would have been suspicious of the building activities in Jerusalem. How then could the same king have commissioned Nehemiah to rebuild the walls of the city in 445? By then both the Egyptian revolt and the rebellion of Megabyzus had been settled.

Artaxerxes I ended his long 40-year reign by dying from natural causes in the winter of 424—a rarity in view of the frequent assassinations of Persian kings. He was buried in one of the four tombs, probably the second from the left, at Naqsh-i-Rustam, north of Persepolis.[2]

II. A Man of Responsibility

Though we are not told anything about Nehemiah's prior background, we can be certain that like Joseph, Moses, and Daniel he had proved himself to be trustworthy before God and man. His position as "cupbearer" to the king (Neh 1:11—2:1) could have been entrusted only to someone who was completely trustworthy.

Classical sources give us detailed descriptions of cupbearers at the Persian court. Xenophon's *Cyropaedia* I.3.9 describes one of their main duties as follows:

> Now, it is a well known fact that the cupbearers, when they proffer the cup, draw off some of it with the ladle, pour it into their left hand, and swallow it down—so that, if they should put poison in, they may not profit by it.

From varied sources we may assume that Nehemiah as a royal cupbearer would probably have had the following traits:

a) He would have been well trained in court etiquette (cf. Dan 1:4 ff.).[3]

b) He was probably a handsome individual (cf. Dan 1:4, 13, 15; Josephus *Antiq.* XVI.230).

c) He would certainly know how to select the wines to set before the king. A proverb in the Babylonian Talmud (Baba Qamma 92b) states: "The wine belongs to the master but credit for it is due to his cupbearer."

d) He would have to be a convivial companion with a willingness to lend an ear at all times. R. North is reminded of Saki, the companion of Omar Khayyam, who served wine to him and listened to his discourses.[4]

e) He would be a man of great influence as one with the closest access to the king, and one who could well determine who got to see the king (Xenophon, *Cyropaedia* I.3.8-9).

f) Above all Nehemiah had to be an individual who enjoyed the unreserved confidence of the king. The great need for trustworthy attendants is underscored by the intrigues which were endemic to the Achaemenid court.

III. A Man of Vision

The distressing news which was brought to Nehemiah was the report that "The wall of Jerusalem is broken down, and its gates have been burned with fire" (Neh 1:3, all citations from the NIV). Now the walls had been broken down by Nebuchadnezzar's attack in 586.[5] But what apparently set off this present report was the frustration of a recent attempt to rebuild the walls (Ezra 4:23).

The situation must have seemed hopeless to the Jews. They had passed daily by the broken gates and the heaps of rubbish (Neh 4:10) and had become accustomed to the sight. This is the way things had stood for 141 years (586 to 445 B.C.)!

After arriving in Palestine, Nehemiah made a secret inspection tour of the city walls at night (Neh 2:13-16). K. Kenyon's excavations between

1961-67 on the eastern slopes of Ophel, the original hill of Jerusalem, shed light on the situation Nehemiah must have faced:

> The tumble of stones uncovered by our Trench 1 is a vivid sample of the ruinous state of the eastern side of Jerusalem that baulked Nehemiah's donkey. The event shows that the sight of this cascade of stones persuaded Nehemiah that he could not attempt to restore the quarter of Jerusalem on the eastern slope of the eastern ridge, or the wall that had enclosed it.[6]

Nehemiah was a man with a great vision of who God was and what He could do through His servants. He could not remain apathetic to the situation. He was so moved by the report that he "sat down and wept," "mourned and fasted and prayed" (Neh 1:4).

Though a man of vision, Nehemiah was not a visionary but a man who planned and then acted. He did not act impulsively but waited some four months (Neh 2:1),[7] before he seized the opportunity to gain permission from the king to rebuild the walls which this same monarch had ordered left alone.

IV. A Man of Prayer

Nehemiah's immediate resort was to prayer (Neh 1:5 ff.). His prayer is steeped in Scripture. He reminds God of His steadfast love *(ḥésed)*.[8]

His was not just a concern for his private spirituality but for the corporate concerns of all God's people. It was a burden which prompted him to pray day and night very much like the intercessions of Paul (cf. Neh 1:6 with 1 Thess 3:10; 2 Tim 1:3).

Nor was Nehemiah's prayer life restricted to stated times of prayer three times a day (Dan 6:10). He prayed spontaneously and constantly during the course of the day, even in the presence of the king. "Then I prayed to the God of heaven, and I answered the king" (Neh 2:4-5) is a beautiful collocation which also illustrates what Nehemiah did first before opening his mouth in public.

In spite of his trepidation Nehemiah knew that he stood not only in the presence of an earthly monarch but before the King of the heavens. As W. F. Adeney has aptly expressed it:

> The brief and sudden prayer reaches heaven as an arrow suddenly shot from the bow; but it goes right home, because he who lets it off in his surprise is a good marksman, well practised. This ready prayer only springs to the lips of a man who lives in a daily habit of prayer.[9]

V. A Man of Action and Cooperation

After Nehemiah ascertained what needed to be done, he explained this clearly to the others (Neh 2:16-17). He realized that no leader can do everything by himself. He must enlist others to join him and he must inspire others by sharing what God has said to him (Neh 2:18).

Nehemiah carefully organized the work. He enlisted as many people as possible to aid him and gave them clearly defined tasks (Neh 3).[10] There were, of course, a few people like the leading men of Tekoa (Neh 3:5) who refused to do their share,[11] but the common people of the same town did twice their share (Neh 3:27).

In spite of harassment and opposition the people responded so enthusiastically to Nehemiah's leadership that they were able to mend the wall in but 52 days (Neh 6:15).

Josephus *Antiq.* XI.168 gives 440 B.C. as the date of Nehemiah's arrival and dates the completion of the wall in Dec., 437, two years and four months after Nehemiah's arrival.[12] The longer period of time for the rebuilding of the wall has been favored by W. F. Albright and John Bright. But the archaeological investigations of K. Kenyon confirm the biblical text. Her discoveries indicate that the circuit of the wall in Nehemiah's day was much reduced.[13]

A striking parallel to Nehemiah's project occurred a half century later in Greek history. After the walls of Athens had been dismantled at the end of the Peloponnesian War in 404 B.C., the people of Athens began to rebuild the walls. The project, however, lagged until Conon, an Athenian admiral, came with sufficient funds and used the men from his fleet to finish the work in 393 (Xenophon, *Hellenica* IV,viii.10).

Nehemiah, a layman, was able to cooperate with his contemporary, Ezra, the scribe and priest (Ezra 2:2; Neh 8:9; 12:26, 36; 10:1),[14] in spite of the fact that these two leaders were of entirely different temperaments. In reaction to the intermarriage of the people, Ezra plucked out his own hair (Ezra 9:3) whereas Nehemiah pulled out the hair of the offenders (Neh 13:25)!

Historians have noted that one mark of a great president is his ability to choose able men for his cabinet. Nehemiah knew how to delegate authority wisely. He gave responsibility to his own brother Hanai,[15] and to Hananiah,[16] who is described as "a man of integrity" (Neh 7:2). The latter phrase, Heb. *'îš 'émet*, is used one other time in the plural at Exod 18:21, that is in Jethro's advice that the overworked Moses should enlist the aid of faithful men (cf. 2 Tim 2:2).

VI. A Man of Compassion

Economic and social problems especially affected the poorer segments of society: these included the high cost of food (Neh 5:2-3),[17] taxes (Neh 5:4),[18] high rates of interest on loans leading to the sale of family members into slavery when the debts could not be paid (Neh 5:5-6).[19] In the Persian period the interest rates rose sharply from 20% under Cyrus and Cambyses to about 40% at the end of the 5th century B.C. as indicated by the banking records of Murashu at Nippur.

As coined money was increasingly taken out of circulation by taxes, inflation became rampant. As M. Dandamayev observes:

Documents from Babylonia show that many inhabitants of this satrapy too had to mortgage their fields and orchards to get silver for the payment of taxes to the king. In many cases they were unable to redeem their property, and became landless hired labourers; sometimes they were compelled to give away their children into slavery.[20]

The acquisition of lands by the Persians and its alienation from production also helped produce a 50% rise in prices.[21]

Under a foreign occupation economic problems were usually aggravated by rapacious governors (cf. Neh 5:15)[22] who took advantage of their powers to extort funds and goods from their subjects. Roman governors, for example, who came to Palestine were quite extortionate. Josephus *War* II.272-73 reports on the procurator Albinus (A.D. 62-64) as follows:

Not only did he, in his official capacity, steal and plunder private property and burden the whole nation with extraordinary taxes, but he accepted ransoms from their relatives on behalf of those who had been imprisoned for robbery by the local councils or by former procurators (cf. Felix, Acts 24:26).

Nehemiah renounced even the rights to which he was entitled (Neh 5:18; cf. 1 Cor 9:1-18). He also denounced the injustices of the day and shamed the wealthy who had taken advantage of their brothers into speechless silence (Neh 5:8). The social and economic reforms which Nehemiah instituted were as far-sighted and far-reaching as those of the great Athenian reformer, Solon (594 B.C.).[23]

The inspiration for Nehemiah's social reforms was his reverence for God (Neh 5:9, 15). Lack of compassion for the material plight of fellow brethren is a blot upon our testimony to nonbelievers (Neh 5:9; cf. James 2:15-16; 1 John 3:17).

VII. A Man Who Triumphed over Opposition

The territory of Judah, which Nehemiah governed, was but a tiny enclave, 30 miles square, which was literally surrounded on all sides by hostile powers.

To the north was Sanballat of Samaria (Neh 2:10, 19; 3:33; 6:1; 13:28). The name is derived from Akkadian *Sin-uballit,* which means "Sin (the moon god) Has Given Life." His epithet the "Horonite," identifies him as coming from either: 1) Hauran east of the Sea of Galilee, 2) Horonaim in Moab, or 3) most probably from either upper or lower Beth-Horon, two key cities 12 miles NW of Jerusalem. We are told that Sanballat was the "governor" of Samaria not in the Scriptures but in an important Elephantine papyrus (Cowley #30:29; ANET, p. 492), a letter which refers to "Delaiah and Shelemiah, the sons of Sanballat the governor of Samaria." It is interesting that Sanballat's sons both bear Yahwistic names.

In 1962 the same Ta'amireh bedouins who discovered the Dead Sea Scrolls found a cave in Wadi ed-Daliyeh, NW of Jericho, which contained fourth-century B.C. Aramaic papyri. Among the names recovered was a Sanballat, probably a descendant of Nehemiah's opponent.[24] The other names confirm the syncretistic nature of the religions of those who lived in the area of Samaria.[25]

To the east was Tobiah of Ammon in Transjordan (Neh 2:19; 4:1; 6:1). *Tobiah* means "Yahweh Is Good"; the name appears in the Murashu documents as *Ṭûbiâma*. He may have possibly been a Judaizing Ammonite but was more probably a Yahwist Jew as indicated not only by his own name but also by that of his son, Jehohanan (Neh 6:18).

Some scholars speculate that Tobiah was descended from an aristocratic family which owned estates in Gilead and was influential in Transjordan and in Jerusalem even as early as the 8th century B.C.[26] B. Mazar has correlated varying lines of evidence to reconstruct the history of the Tobiad family over nine generations.[27]

We learn from Josephus *Antiq.* XII.160 that a later Tobiah was a leader of Jewish hellenizers under Ptolemy II. This is confirmed by the important Zenon Papyri. His descendant Joseph was appointed the chief tax collector for the Asiatic regions under Ptolemy III (fl. 230 B.C.).[28]

The site of ʿArâq el-Emîr "Caverns of the Princes," about 11 miles west of Amman, was the center of the Tobiads' territory. The visible remains of a large building on top of the hill, Qaṣr el-ʿAbd "Castle of the Slave," have been interpreted as a Jewish temple built by the Tobiads. On two halls are inscriptions with the name *Tobiah* in Aramaic characters. The date of the inscriptions is much disputed. Mazar favors the 6th-5th cent. B.C., Naveh the 4th, Cross 4th-3rd, and Lapp, who re-excavated the site in 1961-62, the 3rd-2nd cent.[29]

To the south was Geshem the Arab (Neh 2:19; 4:1; 6:1). In Neh 6:2 the name is given as *gašmû*, which would have been closer to the original Arabic name. The name, which means "bulky" or "stout," is a common North Arabic name, *Jasuma*, found in various Arabic inscriptions including Safaitic, Lihyanite, Thamudic, and Nabataean.

A Lihyanite inscription from Dedan (modern Al-ʿUlā) in NW Arabia reads: "Jašm son of Šahr and ʿAbd, governor of Dedan." This Jašm is identified by Winnett and Albright with the biblical Geshem.[30] In 1947 several silver vessels, some with Aramaic incriptions dating to the late 5th cent. B.C. were discovered at Tell el-Maskhūta near Ismaila by the Suez Canal. One inscription bears the name: "Qaynu the son of Gashmu, the king of Qedar." The son of Geshem (Gashmu) records an offering to the goddess "Han-Ilat."[31]

Biblical and extra-biblical documents indicate that the Arabs became dominant in the Transjordanian area from the Assyrian to the Persian periods (cf. Gen 25:13; Isa 60:7; Jer 49:28-33). Sargon II resettled some Arabs in Samaria in 715 B.C. (ANET, p. 286).[32] Classical sources reveal that the Arabs enjoyed a favored status under the Persians. Cyrus used

Arabs in the army which took Babylon (Xenophon *Cyropaedia* VII.iv.16; v.13). The Arabs assisted Cambyses in his conquest of Egypt in 525 B.C. and were granted exemption from taxes (Herodotus III.88).

It is possible, then, that Geshem was in charge of a powerful north Arabian confederacy of tribes which controlled vast areas from NE Egypt (the LXX of Gen 45:10 reads "the land of Gesem of Arabia" instead of "the land of Goshen") to northern Arabia and southern Palestine. Geshem may have been opposed to Nehemiah's development of an independent kingdom because he feared that it might interfere with his lucrative trade in myrrh and frankincense.[33]

These opponents used every ruse to intimidate Nehemiah. They started first with ridicule. "What kind of wall could they ever build? Even a fox could knock it down!" they jeered (Neh 4:3). They attempted slander (Neh 6:5-7), circulating an open letter accusing Nehemiah of royal pretensions.[34] Hireling prophets gave Nehemiah allegedly inspired but misleading messages (Neh 6:10-14).

To all of these attempts Nehemiah responded with prayer (Neh 4:4), with redoubled efforts (4:6), with vigilance (4:9), with a song (4:10), and with trust in God (4:14). The work to which he was committed was so important that he could not be bothered with their distractions (6:3). As for their accusations he knew they were a pack of lies (6:8). He was able to discern that not every prophet was inspired of God (6:12).

VIII. A Man Who Was Rightly Motivated

Some scholars have suggested that Nehemiah had posted his memoirs in an attempt to vindicate his actions like certain extra-biblical examples that are known to us.[35] But unlike some of these parallels, Nehemiah's primary motive was not to be judged aright by his peers or by posterity.

He was to be sure highly regarded by later generations. Ecclesiasticus 49:13 (c. 180 B.C.) extolled him as follows: "The memory of Nehemiah also is lasting; he raised for us the walls that had fallen, and set up the gates and bars and rebuilt our ruined houses." Josephus *Antiq.* XI.183 speaks of his life and death as follows:

> Then, after performing many other splendid and praiseworthy public services, Nehemiah died at an advanced age. He was a man of kind and just nature and most anxious to serve his countrymen; and he left the walls of Jerusalem as his eternal monument.

The last words of Nehemiah, "Remember me, O my God, for good," (Neh 13:31) recapitulates a theme running through the final chapter (vss. 14, 22, 29). His motive throughout his ministry was to please and to serve his divine Sovereign. His reward would be God's approbation. In this as well as in the other aspects we have discussed Nehemiah has left us an example to follow.

NOTES

1. Much of the materials for this essay is taken from my commentary on "Ezra and Nehemiah," which will appear in volume IV of *The Expositor's Bible Commentary,* and is used here with the kind permission of the editor, Dr. Frank E. Gaebelein, and the publishers, Zondervan Publishing House. Among other expository studies of Nehemiah as an exemplary leader see: A. Redpath, *Victorious Christian Service* (Old Tappan, N.J.: F. H. Revell, 1958); C. J. Barber, *Nehemiah and the Dynamics of Effective Leadership* (Neptune, N.J.: Loizeaux Brothers, 1976); R. H. Seume, *Nehemiah: God's Builder* (Chicago: Moody Press, 1978); D. K. Campbell, *Nehemiah: Man in Charge* (Wheaton: Victor Books, 1979).

2. For the reign of Artaxerxes I, see J. M. Myers, *The World of the Restoration* (Englewood Cliffs, N.J.: Prentice-Hall, 1968), pp. 103 ff.; H. Bengtson, *et al., The Greeks and the Persians* (London: Weidenfeld and Nicolson, 1970), pp. 94 ff., pp. 340 ff.; E. M. Yamauchi, "The Achaemenid Capitals," *Near East Archaeological Society Bulletin,* vol. 8 (1976), *passim; idem,* "The Archaeological Background of Nehemiah," *Bibliotheca Sacra,* vol. 137 (1980), pp. 291-95.

3. See E. Weidner, "Hof- und Harems-Erlasse assyrischer Könige aus dem 2. Jahrtausend v. Chr.," *Archiv für Orientforschung,* vol. 17 (1954-55), pp. 257-93. On the dubious notion that Nehemiah was also a eunuch, see E. M. Yamauchi, "Was Nehemiah the Cupbearer a Eunuch?" *Zeitschrift für die alttestamentliche Wissenschaft,* vol. 92 (1980), pp. 132-42.

4. R. North, "Civil Authority in Ezra," *Studi in onore di Edoardo Volterra* (Milan: Casa Editrice Dott. A. Giuffrè, 1971), vol. VI, p. 397.

5. For recent discoveries of the evidence of the Babylonia attack upon Jerusalem, see S. Singer, "Found in Jerusalem: Remains of the Babylonian Siege," *Biblical Archaeology Review,* vol. 2 (1976), pp. 7-10; Y. Shiloh, "City of David: Excavation 1978," *Biblical Archaeologist,* vol. 42 (1979), pp. 165-73.

6. K. Kenyon, *Jerusalem* (London: Thames and Hudson, 1967), pp. 107-8.

7. Neh 1:1 declares that Nehemiah was in Susa in the month of Chislev in the 20th year of Artaxerxes I. According to a Nisan to Nisan calendar, this regnal year ran from April 13, 445 to April 2, 444; Chislev would be the ninth month from Dec. 5, 445, to Jan. 3, 444. But Neh 2:1 mentions that Nehemiah broached the subject of a mission to Jerusalem in the month of Nisan in the 20th year. Scholars who assume a Nisan to Nisan calendar reason that some scribal error has crept in inasmuch as in a spring to spring year, Nisan precedes rather than follows Chislev. Cf. L. H. Brockington, *Ezra, Nehemiah and Esther* (London: Nelson, 1969), p. 127.

8. N. Glueck, *Hesed in the Bible* (Cincinnati: Hebrew Union College, 1967); K. D. Sakenfeld, *The Meaning of Hesed in the Hebrew Bible* (Missoula: Scholars Press, 1978).

9. "Ezra, Nehemiah and Esther," *The Expositor's Bible,* ed. W. R. Nicoll (London: Hodder & Stoughton, n.d.), vol. XIII, p. 191.

10. Dr. Viggo Olsen, who had to help rebuild houses in war-ravaged Bangladesh in the spring of 1972 derived unexpected inspiration from reading Neh 3. Inspired by principles derived from this chapter, Dr. Olsen was able to supervise the construction of 10,000 houses. V. Olsen and J. Lockerbie, *Daktar* (Chicago: Moody Press, 1973), p. 324.

11. In a remarkable coincidence six centuries later Bar Kochba complained about Tekoans who had failed to cooperate with his orders. Y. Yadin, *Bar Kochba* (New York: Random House, 1971), p. 125.

12. On the general unreliability of Josephus with respect to the Old Testament, see E. M. Yamauchi, "Josephus and the Scriptures," *Fides et Historia,* vol. 13 (1980), pp. 42-51.

13. Kenyon, Jerusalem, p. 111.

14. The contemporaneity of these two leaders has been denied by those who hold that Ezra came after Nehemiah in a "reverse order" in the seventh year of Artaxerxes II (rather than Artaxerxes I). On this issue, see E. M. Yamauchi, "The Reverse Order of Ezra/Nehemiah Reconsidered," *Themelios,* vol. 5 (1980), pp. 7-13.

15. Both in Neh 1:2 and 7:2 Hanani, the shortened form of Hananiah "Yahweh Is Gracious," designates the brother of Nehemiah. Though most translations regard Hanani

and Hananiah as two individuals, some suggest that the second name in 7:2 is explanatory, i.e., "my brother Hanani, namely Hananiah."

16. A man called Hanainah is mentioned in an Aramaic letter offering suggestions from the Persians about the regulation of the Passover at the island of Elephantine in upper Egypt. This is dated to 419 B.C. Cf. A. E. Cowley, *Aramaic Papyri of the Fifth Century B.C.* (Oxford: Clarendon Press, 1923), #21. Some scholars have suggested that this is the same person as Nehemiah's brother. See G. G. Tuland, "Hanani-Hananiah," *Journal of Biblical Literature*, vol. 77 (1958), pp. 157-61.

17. In times of dire need the wealthy usually have enough stored up to feed themselves. It is the poor who suffer because of the huge rise in prices caused by scarcities. See K. S. Gapp, "The Universal Famine under Claudius," *Harvard Theological Review*, vol. 28 (1935), p. 261.

18. The Persian kings collected huge sums in taxes, little of which was ever returned to benefit the provinces. Alexander the Great found at Susa alone about 270 tons of gold and 1200 tons of silver stored as bullion.

19. R. P. Maloney, "Usury in Greek, Roman and Rabbinic Thought," *Traditio*, vol. 27 (1971), pp. 79-109; *idem.* "Usury and Restrictions on Interest-Taking in the Ancient Near East," *Catholic Biblical Quarterly*, vol. 36 (1974), pp. 1-20.

20. "Achaemenid Babylonia," *Ancient Mesopotamia*, ed. I. M. Diakonoff (Moscow: Nauka, 1969), p. 308.

21. W. H. Dubberstein, "Comparative Prices in Later Babylonia," *American Journal of Semitic Languages*, vol. 56 (1939), pp. 20-43.

22. Some scholars had argued that Judah did not have governors before Nehemiah. In 1974 a collection of about 70 bullae (clay seal impressions) and two seals from an unknown proveniance were used by N. Avigad to reconstruct a list of governors prior to Nehemiah. See N. Avigad, *Bullae and Seals from a Post-Exilic Judean Archive* (Jerusalem: Hebrew University, 1976); S. Talmon, "Ezra and Nehemiah," *The Interpreter's Dictionary of the Bible, Supplementary Volume*, ed. K. Crim, *et al.* (Nashville: Abingdon, 1976), pp. 325, 327.

23. Cf. E. M. Yamauchi, "Two Reformers Compared: Solon of Athens and Nehemiah of Jerusalem," *The Bible World: Essays in Honor of Cyrus H. Gordon*, ed. G. Rendsburg, *et al.* (New York: KTAV, 1980), pp. 269-92.

24. F. M. Cross, "The Discovery of the Samaria Papyri," *Biblical Archaeologist*, vol. 26 (1963), pp. 110-20; *idem,* "Aspects of Samaritan and Jewish History in Late Persian and Hellenistic Times," *Harvard Theological Review*, vol. 59 (1966), pp. 201-11; P. W. Lapp, *The Tale of the Tell* (Pittsburgh: Pickwick Press, 1975), ch. 4.

25. Cf. J. McKay, *Religion in Judah under the Assyrians* (London: SCM Press, 1973).

26. B. Obed, "The Historical Background of the Syro-Ephraimite War Reconsidered," *Catholic Biblical Quarterly*, vol. 34 (1972), p. 161.

27. B. Mazar, "The Tobiads," *Israel Exploration Journal*, vol. 7 (1957), pp. 137-45, 229-38.

28. M. Hengel, *Judaism and Hellenism* (Philadelphia: Fortress Press, 1974), I, pp. 49, 267-77.

29. C. C. McCown, "The ʿAraq el-Emir and the Tobiads," *Biblical Archaeologist*, vol. 20 (1957), pp. 63-76; P. W. Lapp, "Soundings at ʿArâq el -Emîr (Jordan)," *Bulletin of the American Schools of Oriental Research*, vol. 165 (1962), pp. 16-34; *idem,* "The Second and Third Campaigns at ʿArâq el-Emîr," *Bulletin of the American Schools of Oriental Research*, vol. 171 (1963); J. Naveh, *The Development of the Aramaic Script* (Jerusalem: Israel Academy of Sciences and Humanities, 1970), pp. 62-64.

30. F. V. Winnett, *A Study of the Lihvanite and Thamudic Inscriptions* (Toronto: University of Toronto, 1937), pp. 50-51; W. F. Albright, "Dedan," *Geschichte und Altes Testament* (Tübingen: J. C. B. Mohr, 1943), pp. 1-12.

31. F. M. Cross, "Geshem the Arabian, Enemy of Nehemiah," *Biblical Archaeologist*, vol. 18 (1955), pp. 46-47; I. Rabinowitz, "Aramaic Inscriptions of the Fifth Century BCE," *Journal of Near Eastern Studies*, vol. 15 (1956), pp. 1-9; W. J. Dumbrell, "The Tell el-Maskhuta Bowls and the 'Kingdom' of Qedar in the Persian Period," *Bulletin of the American Schools of Oriental Research*, vol. 203 (1971), pp. 33-44.

32. B. Obed, *Mass Deportations and Deportees in the Neo-Assyrian Empire* (Wiesbaden: Ludwig Reichert, 1979), pp. 29-31.

33. A. K. Irvine, "The Arabs and Ethiopians," *Peoples of Old Testament Times*, ed. D. J. Wiseman (Oxford: Clarendon Press, 1973), pp. 287-311; J. R. Bartlett, "From Edomites to Nabataeans," *Palestine Exploration Quarterly*, vol. 111 (1979), pp. 53-66.

34. U. Kellerman goes so far as to suggest that Nehemiah came from a Davidic family. See his *Nehemia Quellen, Überlieferung und Geschichte* (Berlin: A. Töpelmann, 1967), pp. 156-69; cf. W. Th. In der Smitten, "Erwägungen zu Nehemias Davidizität," *Journal for the Study of Judaism*, vol. 5 (1974), p. 48. To the question of why this was not made clearer, Kellermann and In der Smitten argue that this fact was concealed for apologetic reasons.

35. Kellermann, Nehemiah, pp. 84-87; M. Smith, *Palestinian Parties and Politics That Shaped the Old Testament* (New York: Columbia University, 1971), p. 126; G. von Rad, "Die Nehemia-Denkschrift," *Zeitschrift für die alttestamentliche Wissenschaft*, vol. 76 (1964), pp. 176-87; R. W. Klein, "Ezra and Nehemiah in Recent Studies," *The Mighty Acts of God*, ed. F. M. Cross, *et al.* (Garden City, N.Y.: Doubleday & Co., 1976), p. 366.

Bibliography

REPRESENTATIVE SELECTIONS FROM THE WRITINGS OF DENNIS F. KINLAW

J. Paul Vincent

As President of Asbury College, Dr. Dennis Kinlaw stirred his faculty with a vision of liberal arts education at its best. For me, he will always remain a priceless model of the Christian scholar—called to his vocation, submitted to the Real, motivated by obedient love. To him, the following bibliography is gratefully dedicated.

Among the many talents which Dennis F. Kinlaw has displayed during his distinguished career is that of writing so that profound truths become plain to all. Dr. Kinlaw's published works convey lofty ideas and penetrating insights in a masterful, inviting way. As demonstrated in his writings, his interests and concerns range from intricate textual analysis to social criticism, from the problems of the scholar to the needs of the layman.

The bibliography which follows contains representative selections from Dr. Kinlaw's published works. These selections fall naturally into four broad categories: Old Testament Studies, Basic Christian Doctrines, Theology and Society, and Christianity and Education.

The reader will also want to watch for Dr. Kinlaw's forthcoming works. For example, he wrote two articles for the new *Beacon Dictionary of Theology*. Also, he contributed a paper entitled "Yahweh and Human Well-Being" to a Duke University Medical School symposium on spiritual diseases; the piece will be published with the proceedings of that symposium.

One who seriously reads the works of Dr. Kinlaw may be assured of an exciting glimpse into the mind and heart of this beloved Christian scholar.

I. Old Testament Studies

"Old Testament Roots of the Wesleyan Message," in *Further Insights Into Holiness: Nineteen Leading Wesleyan Scholars Present Various Phases of Holiness Thinking.* Compiled by Kenneth Geiger. Kansas City, MO: Beacon Hill Press, 1963, pp. 41-53.

This essay emphasizes the fact that all holiness is derivative from God. The Old Testament name of God as "the Holy One of Israel" signifies the overwhelming power and majesty, the ethical purity, and the moral perfection, of God. In spite of man's failure to appropriate God's holiness, the invitation to enter into a New Covenant remains as a bright and shining hope.

A Study of the Personal Names in the Akkadian Texts from Ugarit. Ann Arbor, MI: University Microfilms, 1967. Ph.D. dissertation at Brandeis University.

As a means of gaining access to the life and culture of the Ancient Near East, this doctoral study analyzes the personal names which appear in the Akkadian texts from the city of Ugarit.

"Some Observations on Current Old Testament Studies," *Asbury Seminarian.* 21, no. 2 (1967), pp. 7-13.

A review of the recent scholarship on extra-biblical materials regarding life in the pre-Christian era discloses some mistakes in much biblical scholarship. The prevalent assumption that Israel is ideologically continuous with her environment is increasingly being called into question. In contrast to surrounding religions, Israel's faith was non-mythical, historical, and non-magical. This means that the religion of Israel cannot be explained simply as a variation of the religious patterns of the ancient world. The reason why contemporary scholarship cannot account for the uniqueness of Israel's faith is that it lacks an adequate concept of divine revelation.

"The Book of Ecclesiastes," *The Wesleyan Bible Commentary,* vol II. Grand Rapids, MI: William B. Eerdmans, 1968, pp. 601-36.

The often-neglected spiritual import of this wisdom book is brought out in a way which enriches our overall understanding of the Hebrew-Christian scriptures. The unusual mood of skepticism and pessimism in Ecclesiastes is explained in a helpful way. Various scholarly problems are treated in the course of this article. Bibliography.

"The Song of Solomon," *The Wesleyan Bible Commentary,* vol. II. Grand Rapids, MI: William B. Eerdmans, 1968, pp. 637-59.

This is an enlightening treatment of a frequently misunderstood book of the canon. The presence of very frank descriptions of the intimate love of a maiden and her beloved together with the absence of explicit religious themes make this book an enigma to many. The author carefully puts the Song of Songs in perspective as a legitimate part of Holy Writ. Among the salient points which he makes are that God created romantic and sexual relations to be good, and that we may see something of the relationship between God and the community of faith by reading this Old Testment document. Bibliography.

"Leviticus," *Beacon Bible Commentary,* vol. I. Kansas City, MO: Beacon Hill Press, 1969, pp. 317-95.

Against the more liberal JEDP hypothesis regarding the nature of Leviticus, the author defines a more realistic and conservative interpretation. Dr. Kinlaw uncovers the deeper meaning of this manual given to priests for conducting worship. The overall impact of the book concerns the conditions for atonement for sin and the appropriation of God's holiness. Bibliography.

"What Archaeology Does for Our Faith," *The Herald.* 20 January 1969, pp. 7, 15.

In this brief article, the author contends that current archaeological data—the excavations at the ancient northeastern Mesopotamian town of Nuzu, for example—confirm the Hebrew accounts of their origins. Although archaeological research cannot completely demonstrate the "full inspiration of the biblical text," it can counteract the prevailing skepticism about the reliability of biblical texts. In this way, current research tends to validate the believer's presumption of biblical inspiration and inerrancy.

"Old Testament Ethics," *Baker's Dictionary of Christian Ethics.* Edited by Carl F. H. Henry. Grand Rapids, MI: Baker Book House, 1973, pp. 469-72.

Although the ethical teaching of the Old Testament is in some ways continuous with that of the rest of the ancient world, its central core is discontinuous, unique. The distinctive features of Israel's ethical teaching are to be found in three affirmations: (1) Yahweh's role as Creator, (2) Yahweh's holiness, and (3) Yahweh's election of Israel. Bibliography.

"Putting Demons in Their Place," *Christian Medical Society Journal.* 6, no. 2 (1967), pp. 3-8.

In contrast to its neighbors, Israel explained good and evil in terms of moral realities and not meddling spirits. Even today, fallen man is preoccupied with evil—the sensual, occult, and demonic. Yet the faith of Israel, with its emphasis on God's creation *ex nihilo* and on man's responsibility for his own actions, guarantees a monotheistic perspective. The conclusion is that we should not exaggerate the importance of the demonic.

"The Demythologization of the Demonic in the Old Testament," in *Demon Possession: A Medical, Historical, Anthropological, and Theological Symposium.* Edited by John Warwick Montgomery. Minneapolis, MN: Bethany Fellowship, Inc., 1976, pp. 29-40.

A version of the previous article, this piece stresses the persistent tendency of Old Testament faith to demythologize life. As the author states, "the Old Testament acknowledges the spirit world but seems bent upon minimizing, demythologizing, or marginalizing it." There is no autonomous domain outside of Yahweh or beyond his sovereign control. Evil, then, is explained in terms of man's wrongful use of freedom rather than in terms of demonic agency. Interestingly, the words which in surrounding cultures are names for demonic personalities are in Hebrew merely words for natural phenomena and objects.

"Charles Williams' Concept of Imaging Applied to 'The Song of Songs.' " *Wesleyan Theological Journal.* 16, no. 1 (1981), pp. 85-92.

The author explores the use of the image or symbol in literature with particular attention to what Charles Williams says about the subject. Essentially, the symbol points beyond itself to a greater reality. When one views the Song of Songs in this light, the image of human love may be seen to represent the larger context of God's love for his people. This approach actually de-allegorizes the book, since allegories usually diminish the significance of the obvious realities in favor of the spiritual message.

II. Basic Christian Doctrines

"Sin in Believers: The Biblical Evidence," in *The Word and the Doctrine: Studies in Contemporary Wesleyan-Arminian Theology*. Compiled by Kenneth Geiger. Kansas City, MO: Beacon Hill Press, 1965, pp. 119-125.

This article examines the evidence regarding the presence of sin in Christian believers. Stating that there are only two forces at work in human life, one being fleshly and sinful and the other being the Spirit of God, the author maintains that their relation can be both/and or either/or. In contradistinction to the reformers, Dr. Kinlaw holds, with Wesley, that the former relationship is not acceptable in believers. This position stands, he thinks, even though there are instances of believers in the Bible who sometimes do not act under the complete influence of the Spirit of God.

"The Biblical Basis of the Sanctified Life," in *The Sanctified Life*. Dennis F. Kinlaw, *et al.* Wilmore, KY: The Seminary Press, 1968, pp. 5-8.

The holy life is not an option for the believer, but a biblical command which finds expression whenever God communicates with His people. The holiness of the Christian, however, is derivative, conditional, and partial. The call to holiness is based on God's own holy nature and finds supreme representation in Christ's sacrifice on the cross.

This very same piece was also published in *The Herald* (April 10, 1968), pp. 7-8.

"Authority for the Church in Crisis," *Good News: A Forum for Scriptural Christianity within the United Methodist Church*. October-December 1970, pp.23-27.

The text of this article is condensed from an address given at the Good News Convocation held in Dallas, Texas, in 1970. After outlining the contemporary caricature of authority as an external force imposing upon man an unwanted pattern of life, the author develops an alternative view of the nature of authority. True authority does not connote force, but is a key to the very essence of reality. Submission to the Word of God is the "ideological framework" required for our highest fulfillment and genuine freedom.

This same article was also published in *The Herald* (November 18, 1970), pp. 3, 22-23.

"Campus Roots for Revival," in *One Divine Moment*. Edited by Robert E. Coleman. Old Tappan, NJ: Fleming H. Revell, 1970, pp. 107-11.

This article discusses the role of revivalism in American higher education. Many American college and universities were founded in the aftermath of great revivals. In fact, as the author states, "concern for higher education on this continent was rooted in spiritual revival." The 1970 Asbury Revival can be best interpreted within this perspective.

"When the Oxygen Runs Out," *The Herald*. 10 January 1973, pp. 5, 15.

This article is the first in a series of eight on basic Christian doctrines. The "oxygen" of institutions is some guiding, informing dogma. The fragmentation and pluralism of the contemporary religious scene are the consequences of the loss of a common creed.

The remaining articles in the series follow seriatim below.

"god or God," *The Herald*. 21 February 1973, p. 7.

Without a belief in the biblical God, men tend to project fictive "gods," deifications of themselves. However, men need more than a god who amounts to nothing more than some natural force or even to the universe considered as a whole. Men need the transcendent God of revelation.

"Jesus, the Name High Over All," *The Herald*. 21 March 1973, p. 3.

Beginning with a recollection of the life of Dr. E. Stanley Jones, Dr. Kinlaw describes the biblical principle of "the firstness of Christ." The author treats that part of Christology which implies that the self-abnegating displacement of the rule of the self by Christ is a precondition for a normal Christian life.

"The Unicorn That Came Home," *The Herald.* 4 April 1973, p. 6.
This article is an exposition of the doctrine of creation out of nothing. Since everything that exists, except God, was made by God, it follows that (1) all things are dependent for their existence upon Him, and that (2) all things find their fulfillment in Him.

"The Absolute God," *The Herald.* 13 June 1973, p. 3.
The opening chapters of Genesis present answers to man's ultimate questions. Here man learns that God alone is absolute and that all else is dependent. Although God needs nothing beyond Himself, man can only find contentment and true life through Him. Satan, being a creature and not some cosmic principle, is a threat to us only if we permit him to cut us off from the Absolute God.

"This is My Father's World," *The Herald.* 11 July 1973, p. 3.
Even in our world of uncertainty and disappointment, God reigns. History, in fact, is "the special domain of God's most significant activity." This truth is most vividly demonstrated in the Incarnation, the event in which God subjected Himself to man's lot in the world. Hence, salvation comes in and through history, not outside of history as Buddhism and other escapist religions hold.

"What is Man?" (Part I), *The Herald.* 22 August 1973, pp. 9-10.
In the first installment of a two-part article about Genesis chapters 1-3, the author presents the general crisis of understanding about the nature and destiny of man. Naturalism, humanism, and scientism all fail to satisfy the deepest human needs, since they forfeit the perspective revealed in Genesis 1-3. When man severs himself from his roots in a creative and sovereign deity, then he loses the capacity to be truly human.

"What is Man?" (Part II), *The Herald.* 3 October 1973, pp. 6, 13.
Dr. Kinlaw examines Genesis 1-3 for a biblically informed view of man. The chapters are found to offer clear counsel in four areas: (1) marriage and monogamy, (2) sex roles within the society, (3) the sanctity of work, and (4) worship as fellowship with God. "In the cool of the day" (Gen. 3:8), God sought and found the first couple; there "the real meaning of life was to be consummated."

"The Community of Saints" (Part I), *The Wesleyan Advocate.* 17 December 1979, pp. 10-11.
The text of this article is adapted from the presidential address delivered to the Christian Holiness Association in March of 1979 at

Olivet Nazarene College. Citing Matthew 5:13-16 as his text, Dr. Kinlaw outlines the character of the church as a religio-moral covenant grounded in a relationship with God. The church is a community of mutual respect based on each person's origin, value, and potential. It is a fellowship of love in which Christ dwells.

"The Community of Saints" (Part II), *The Wesleyan Advocate.* 7 January 1980, pp. 13-14.
    The fellowship present in the church is an eternal bond that transcends all of our normal human relationships. The church transcends because of the "extra Person" in its midst. The Spirit of God makes the church a caring community, a prophetic community, and a genuine foretaste of what is to come.

III. Theology and Society
"Theology and Social Action," *Asbury Seminarian.* 68, no. 3 (1968), pp. 3-4.
    This is an editorial upon the occasion of Dr. Martin Luther King's death. The author charges that evangelicalism has too often been unaware of the radical implications for righteousness, justice, and human dignity which a biblical perspective demands. On the other hand, contemporary activists seek the fruits of the gospel while denying the soil in which those fruits must grow—the atoning work of God through His Son. The article concludes with a call to recover the full biblical message at the root of Dr. King's "dream."

"A Biblical View of Homosexuality," in *The Secrets of Our Sexuality: Role Liberation for the Christian.* Edited by Gary R. Collins. Waco, TX: Word Books, 1976, pp. 104-115.
    Dr. Kinlaw bases his analysis on the assumptions that the Scriptures give us the "actual word of God" and that "homosexuality can be dealt with adequately only in relation to the broader teaching of Scripture on sexuality." Emerging out of the creation story is the divine plan for human life—sexual differentiation which makes possible the "union of one male and one female in a mysterious and binding oneness." Furthermore, according to Scripture, homosexuality is a perversion which develops when "the knowledge of the Author of this pattern is lost."

IV. Christianity and Education
"Of Equal Opportunity and Other Bureaucratic Intrusions," *Christianity Today.* 5 November 1976, pp. 16-18.
    This article is the original, unabridged version of the *Good News* article on the same topic. Although independence has characterized American higher education from the outset, in recent years, "non-involvement has changed to intrusion, respect to financial and

regulatory control." In the name of equal opportunity, social justice, consumer protection, and other worthy causes, the government has begun to generate numerous executive orders and bureaucratic regulations. These are increasingly draining the time, energy, and resources of our educational institutions. In fact, government has assumed the role of making pronouncements on matters of deep religious import: marital status, pregnancy, abortion, and human sexuality, among others. One route toward a corrective is the recognition that there is a difference between laws enacted by legislators and derivative regulations penned by "anonymous writers." Many of the rules and regulations we are now under have never been voted upon directly by the people who represent the electorate. A second step would involve the understanding that some areas of human life were intended by the writers of the Constitution to be kept inviolate from governmental intrusion.

"Christian Colleges—Will Bureaucrats Destroy Them?" *Good News: A Forum for Scriptural Christianity within the United Methodist Church.* March-April 1977, pp. 10-15.

This article is a plea for maintenance of the independent colleges in America. The July 1975 HEW redefinition of "federal aid" and the establishment of regulations for Title IX pose serious threats to these institutions. Whereas the family, the church, the press, and the school have traditionally been beyond the sphere of federal regulations, the doctrine of the separation of powers now seems to command little respect. Independent colleges must resist this trend by insisting that they have the right to place before students models of family stability, to differentiate between a pregnancy incurred outside of marriage and one within marriage, to treat abortion as an ethical matter, and to encourage differentiation in sexual roles.

"The Christian Scholar," in *A Celebration of Ministry: Essays in Honor of Frank Bateman Stanger.* Edited by Kenneth Cain Kinghorn. Wilmore, KY: Francis Asbury Publishing Company, 1982, pp. 67-69.

This piece is an analysis of the role of the Christian scholar in the church. The scholar's role is to society as memory is to the individual. He negotiates between the dual impulses present in any society—the demand for change and the effort to protect traditional values. By ascertaining the relationships between facts and ideals, the scholar can assist the decision-makers in their commitment to progress. The Christian scholar, moreover, protects the church from enslavement to the *Zeitgeist* by "perpetual reference to the scriptures in their fullness and constant consideration of the history of the church."